Advance Praise for *Version Control with Subversion*

"Would that all open source projects had documentation this good. If yours doesn't, take this as a model."

—Eric S. Raymond
esr@thyrsus.com

"The authors have approached writing the book much like their authoring of the Subversion software: in an open source way, open from beginning to not only the occasional grammatical fix but also suggestions for wholesale changes; in a thorough way, covering everything someone would need to switch to this from the other popular tools; and in a professional way, taking pride in accuracy and understandability. The result is a book that takes you not only inside the software but inside the minds of the developers themselves. I hope it motivates readers to take the next step and contribute to the Subversion project."

—Brian Behlendorf
brian@collab.net

"I've been using this book as a reference since before it was published, and I've found it accurate, complete, and clear. It is pretty amazing—how many projects have something *this* useful even before making 1.0? It's a pretty solid example of the potential of well-managed free software projects. If you're coming from CVS, Subversion's repository model looks strange at first. Once you've got your head around it, though, CVS will be the one that looks strange. The explanation of these fundamentals is well-done, and the consideration given to people migrating from CVS will ease the trip.

"We designed Subversion's repository model to be as simple as we could and to encourage people to build tools that work on top of it: automated testing, replication, changeset support, and so on. This book should give people the footing they need for that."

—Jim Blandy
Senior software engineer, Red Hat, Inc.

D1469824

Version Control with Subversion

*Ben Collins-Sussman, Brian W. Fitzpatrick
and C. Michael Pilato*

O'REILLY®

Beijing · Cambridge · Farnham · Köln · Paris · Sebastopol · Taipei · Tokyo

Version Control with Subversion

by Ben Collins-Sussman, Brian W. Fitzpatrick, and C. Michael Pilato

Published by O'Reilly Media, Inc., 1005 Gravenstein Highway North, Sebastopol, CA 95472.

O'Reilly Media books may be purchased for educational, business, or sales promotional use.
Online editions are also available for most titles (*safari.oreilly.com*). For more information, contact our
corporate/institutional sales department: (800) 998-9938 or *corporate@oreilly.com*.

Editor:	Tatiana Apandi Diaz
Production Editor:	Reg Aubry
Cover Designer:	Ellie Volckhausen
Interior Designer:	Melanie Wang

Printing History:

June 2004:	First Edition.

 This book uses RepKover™, a durable and flexible lay-flat binding.

ISBN: 0-596-00448-6
[C]

Table of Contents

Foreword

A bad Frequently Asked Questions (FAQ) sheet is one that is composed not of the questions people actually asked, but of the questions the FAQ's author *wished* people had asked. Perhaps you've seen the type before:

> Q: How can I use Glorbosoft XYZ to maximize team productivity?

> A: Many of our customers want to know how they can maximize productivity through our patented office groupware innovations. The answer is simple: first, click on the File menu, scroll down to Increase Productivity, then...

The problem with such FAQs is that they are not, in a literal sense, FAQs at all. No one ever called the tech support line and asked, How can we maximize productivity?. Rather, people asked highly specific questions, like, How can we change the calendaring system to send reminders two days in advance instead of one? and so on. But it's a lot easier to make up imaginary Frequently Asked Questions than it is to discover the real ones. Compiling a true FAQ sheet requires a sustained, organized effort: over the lifetime of the software, incoming questions must be tracked, responses monitored, and all gathered into a coherent, searchable whole that reflects the collective experience of users in the wild. It calls for the patient, observant attitude of a field naturalist. No grand hypothesizing, no visionary pronouncements here—open eyes and accurate note-taking are what's needed most.

What I love about this book is that it grew out of just such a process, and shows it on every page. It is the direct result of the authors' encounters with users. It began with Ben Collins-Sussman's observation that people were asking the same basic questions over and over on the Subversion mailing lists: What are the standard workflows to use with Subversion? Do branches and tags work the same way as in other version control systems? How can I find out who made a particular change?

Frustrated at seeing the same questions day after day, Ben worked intensely over a month in the summer of 2002 to write *The Subversion Handbook*, a 60-page manual that covered all the basics of using Subversion. The manual made no pretense of being complete, but it was distributed with Subversion and got users over that initial hump in the learning curve. When O'Reilly decided to publish a full-length Subversion book, the path of least resistance was obvious: just expand the Subversion handbook.

The three coauthors of the new book were thus presented with an unusual opportunity. Officially, their task was to write a book top-down, starting from a table of contents and an initial draft. But they also had access to a steady stream—indeed, an uncontrollable geyser—of bottom-up source material. Subversion was already in the hands of thousands of early adopters, and those users were giving tons of feedback, not only about Subversion, but about its existing documentation.

During the entire time they wrote this book, Ben, Mike, and Brian haunted the Subversion mailing lists and chat rooms incessantly, carefully noting the problems users were having in real-life situations. Monitoring such feedback is part of their job descriptions at CollabNet anyway, and it gave them a huge advantage when they set out to document Subversion. The book they produced is grounded firmly in the bedrock of experience, not in the shifting sands of wishful thinking; and it combines the best aspects of user manual and FAQ sheet. This duality might not be noticeable on a first reading. Taken in order, front to back, the book is simply a straightforward description of a piece of software. There's the overview, the obligatory guided tour, the chapter on administrative configuration, some advanced topics, and, of course, a command reference and troubleshooting guide. Only when you come back to it later, seeking the solution to some specific problem, does its authenticity shine out: the telling details that can only result from encounters with the unexpected, the examples honed from genuine use cases, and most of all the sensitivity to the user's needs and the user's point of view.

Of course, no one can promise that this book will answer every question you have about Subversion. Sometimes, the precision with which it anticipates your questions will seem eerily telepathic; yet, occasionally, you will stumble into a hole in the community's knowledge, and come away empty-handed. When this happens, the best thing you can do is email *users@subversion.tigris.org* and present your problem. The authors are still there, still watching, and they include not just the three listed on the cover, but many others who contributed corrections and original material. From the community's point of view, solving your problem is merely a pleasant side effect of a much larger project—namely, slowly adjusting this book, and ultimately Subversion itself, to more closely match the way people actually use it. They are eager to hear from you not merely because they can help you, but because you can help them. With Subversion, as with all active free software projects, *you are not alone.*

Let this book be your first companion.

—Karl Fogel, Chicago, 14 March, 2004

Preface

If C gives you enough rope to hang yourself,
think of Subversion as a sort of rope storage facility.
—Brian W. Fitzpatrick

In the world of open-source software, the Concurrent Versions System (CVS) has long been the tool of choice for version control. And rightly so. CVS itself is free software, and its non-restrictive modus operandi and support for networked operation—which allow dozens of geographically dispersed programmers to share their work—fit the collaborative nature of the open-source world very well. CVS and its semi-chaotic development model have become cornerstones of open-source culture.

But like many tools, CVS is starting to show its age. Subversion is a relatively new version control system designed to be the successor to CVS. The designers set out to win the hearts of CVS users in two ways: by creating an open-source system with a design (and look and feel) similar to CVS, and by attempting to fix most of CVS's noticeable flaws. While the result isn't necessarily the next great evolution in version control design, Subversion *is* very powerful, very usable, and very flexible.

This book is written to document the version 1.0 series of the Subversion version control system. We have made every attempt to be thorough in our coverage. However, Subversion has a thriving and energetic development community, so there are already a number of features and improvements planned for future versions of Subversion that may change some of the commands and specific notes in this book.

Audience

This book is written for computer-literate folk who want to use Subversion to manage their data. While Subversion runs on a number of different operating systems, its primary user interface is command-line based. It is that command-line tool (svn) which is discussed and used in this book. For consistency, the examples in this book assume the reader is using a Unix-like operating system, and is relatively comfortable with Unix and command-line interfaces.

That said, the svn program also runs on non-Unix platforms, such as Microsoft Windows. With a few minor exceptions, such as the use of backward slashes (\) instead of forward slashes (/) for path separators, the input to and output from this tool when run on Windows are identical to its Unix counterpart. However, Windows users may find more success by running the examples inside the Cygwin Unix emulation environment.

We assume our readers are programmers or sysadmins who need to track changes to source code. This is the most common use for Subversion, and therefore it is the scenario underlying all of the book's examples. But Subversion can be used to manage changes to any sort of information: images, music, databases, documentation, and so on. To Subversion, all data is just data.

While this book is written with the assumption that the reader has never used version control, we've also tried to make it easy for users of CVS to make a painless leap into Subversion. Special sidebars may discuss CVS from time to time, and a special appendix summarizes most of the differences between CVS and Subversion.

How to Read this Book

This book aims to be useful to people of widely different backgrounds—from people with no previous experience in version control to experienced sysadmins. Depending on your own background, certain chapters may be more or less important to you. The following can be considered a recommended reading list for various types of readers:

Experienced sysadmins
> The assumption here is that you've probably used CVS before, and are dying to get a Subversion server up and running ASAP. Chapters 5 and 6 will show you how to create your first repository and make it available over the network. After that's done, Chapter 3 and Appendix A are the fastest routes to learning the Subversion client while drawing on your CVS experience.

New users
> Your administrator has probably set up Subversion already, and you need to learn how to use the client. If you've never used a version control system (like CVS), then Chapters 2 and 3 are a vital introduction. If you're already an old hand at CVS, Chapter 3 and Appendix A are the best place to start.

Advanced users
> Whether you're a user or administrator, eventually your project will grow larger. You're going to want to learn how to do more advanced things with Subversion, such as how to use branches and perform merges (Chapter 4), how to use Subversion's property support, how to configure runtime options (Chapter 7), and

other things. Chapters 4 and 7 aren't vital at first, but be sure to read them once you're comfortable with the basics.

Developers

Presumably, you're already familiar with Subversion, and now want to either extend it or build new software on top of its many APIs. Chapter 8 is just for you.

The book ends with reference material—Chapter 9 is a reference guide for all Subversion commands, and the appendices cover a number of useful topics. These are the chapters you're mostly likely to come back to after you've finished the book.

Conventions Used in This Book

This section covers the various conventions used in this book.

Typographic Conventions

`Constant width`
    Used for commands, command output, and switches

`Constant width italic`
    Used for replaceable items in code and text

Italic
    Used for file and directory names

Icons

This icon designates a note or helpful tip relating to the surrounding text.

This icon designates a warning relating to the surrounding text.

Note that the source code examples are just that—examples. While they will compile with the proper compiler incantations, they are intended to illustrate the problem at hand, not necessarily serve as examples of good programming style.

Organization of This Book

The chapters that follow and their contents are summarized here:

Chapter 1, *Introduction*
> Covers the history of Subversion, as well as its features, architecture, components, and install methods. Also includes a quick-start guide.

Chapter 2, *Basic Concepts*
> Explains the basics of version control and different versioning models, along with Subversion's repository, working copies, and revisions.

Chapter 3, *Guided Tour*
> Walks you through a day in the life of a Subversion user. It demonstrates how to use Subversion to obtain, modify, and commit data.

Chapter 4, *Branching and Merging*
> Discusses branches, merges, and tagging, including best practices for branching and merging, common use-cases, how to undo changes, and how to easily swing from one branch to the next.

Chapter 5, *Repository Administration*
> Describes the basics of the Subversion repository, how to create, configure, and maintain a repository, and the tools you can use to do all of this.

Chapter 6, *Server Configuration*
> Explains how to configure your Subversion server and the three ways to access your repository: HTTP, the svn protocol, and local access. It also covers the details of authentication, authorization and anonymous access.

Chapter 7, *Advanced Topics*
> Explores the Subversion client configuration files, file and directory properties, how to ignore files in your working copy, how to include external trees in your working copy, and lastly, how to handle vendor branches.

Chapter 8, *Developer Information*
> Describes the internals of Subversion, the Subversion filesystem, and the working copy administrative areas from a programmer's point of view. Demonstrates how to use the public APIs to write a program that uses Subversion, and most importantly, how to contribute to the development of Subversion.

Chapter 9, *Subversion Complete Reference*
> Explains in great detail every subcommand of svn, svnadmin, and svnlook with plenty of examples for the whole family!

Appendix A, *Subversion for CVS Users*
> Covers the similarities and differences between Subversion and CVS, with numerous suggestions on how to break all the bad habits you picked up from years of using CVS. Included are descriptions of Subversion revision numbers, versioned directories, offline operations, update vs. status, branches, tags, metadata, conflict resolution, and authentication.

Appendix B, *Troubleshooting*
    Addresses common problems and difficulties using and building Subversion.

Appendix C, *WebDAV and Autoversioning*
    Describes the details of WebDAV and DeltaV, and how you can configure your Subversion repository to be mounted read/write as a DAV share.

Appendix D, *Third-Party Tools*
    Discusses tools that support or use Subversion, including alternative client programs, repository browser tools, and so on.

Appendix E, *Creative Commons Attribution License*
    Lists the Creative Commons Attribution 2.0 legal code.

This Book is Free

This book started out as bits of documentation written by Subversion project developers, which were then coalesced into a single work and rewritten. As such, it has always had the same free, open-source license as Subversion itself. In fact, the book was written in the public eye, as a part of Subversion. This means two things:

- You can always find the latest version of this book in Subversion's own source tree.

- You can distribute and make changes to this book however you wish—it's under a free license. Of course, rather than distribute your own private version of this book, we'd much rather you send feedback and patches to the Subversion developer community. See "Contributing to Subversion" in Chapter 8" to learn about joining this community.

A relatively recent online version of this book can be found at *http://svnbook.red-bean.com*.

Comments and Questions

Please address comments and questions concerning this book to the publisher:

    O'Reilly Media, Inc.
    1005 Gravenstein Highway North
    Sebastopol, CA 95472
    (800) 998-9938 (in the United States or Canada)
    (707) 829-0515 (international or local)
    (707) 829-0104 (fax)

O'Reilly maintains a web page for this book, that lists errata, examples, and any additional information. You can access this page at:

    http://www.oreilly.com/catalog/postfix/

To comment or ask technical questions about this book, send email to:

bookquestions@oreilly.com

For more information about O'Reilly books, conferences, Resource Centers, and the O'Reilly Network, see O'Reilly's web site at:

http://www.oreilly.com/

Acknowledgments

This book would not be possible (nor very useful) if Subversion did not exist. For that, the authors would like to thank Brian Behlendorf and CollabNet for the vision to fund such a risky and ambitious new Open Source project; Jim Blandy for the original Subversion name and design—we love you, Jim; and Karl Fogel* for being such a good friend and a great community leader, in that order.

Thanks to O'Reilly and our editors, Linda Mui and Tatiana Diaz, for their patience and support.

Finally, we thank the countless people who contributed to this book with informal reviews, suggestions, and fixes. While this is undoubtedly not a complete list, this book would be incomplete and incorrect without the help of: Jani Averbach, Ryan Barrett, Francois Beausoleil, Jennifer Bevan, Matt Blais, Zack Brown, Martin Buchholz, Brane Cibej, John R. Daily, Peter Davis, Olivier Davy, Robert P. J. Day, Mo DeJong, Brian Denny, Joe Drew, Nick Duffek, Ben Elliston, Justin Erenkrantz, Shlomi Fish, Julian Foad, Chris Foote, Martin Furter, Dave Gilbert, Eric Gillespie, Matthew Gregan, Art Haas, Greg Hudson, Alexis Huxley, Jens B. Jorgensen, Tez Kamihira, David Kimdon, Mark Benedetto King, Andreas J. Koenig, Nuutti Kotivuori, Matt Kraai, Scott Lamb, Vincent Lefevre, Morten Ludvigsen, Paul Lussier, Bruce A. Mah, Philip Martin, Feliciano Matias, Patrick Mayweg, Gareth McCaughan, Jon Middleton, Tim Moloney, Mats Nilsson, Joe Orton, Amy Lyn Pilato, Kevin Pilch-Bisson, Dmitriy Popkov, Michael Price, Mark Proctor, Steffen Prohaska, Daniel Rall, Tobias Ringstrom, Garrett Rooney, Joel Rosdahl, Christian Sauer, Larry Shatzer, Russell Steicke, Sander Striker, Erik Sjoelund, Johan Sundstroem, John Szakmeister, Mason Thomas, Eric Wadsworth, Colin Watson, Alex Waugh, Chad Whitacre, Josef Wolf, Blair Zajac, and the entire Subversion community.

---

* Oh, and thanks, Karl, for being too overworked to write this book yourself.

From Ben Collins-Sussman

Thanks to my wife Frances, who, for many months, got to hear, "But honey, I'm still working on the book," rather than the usual, "But honey, I'm still doing email." I don't know where she gets all that patience! She's my perfect counterbalance.

Thanks to my extended family for their sincere encouragement, despite having no actual interest in the subject. (You know, the ones who say, "Ooh, you're writing a book?"—and then when you tell them it's a computer book, sort of glaze over.)

Thanks to all my close friends, who make me a rich, rich man. Don't look at me that way—you know who you are.

From Brian W. Fitzpatrick

Huge thanks to my wife Marie for being incredibly understanding, supportive, and, most of all, patient. Thank you to my brother Eric who first introduced me to Unix programming way back when. Thanks to my Mom and Grandmother for all their support, not to mention enduring a Christmas holiday where I came home and promptly buried my head in my laptop to work on the book.

To Mike and Ben: it was a pleasure working with you on the book. Heck, it's a pleasure working with you at work!

To everyone in the Subversion community and the Apache Software Foundation, thanks for having me. Not a day goes by where I don't learn something from at least one of you.

Lastly, thanks to my grandfather, who always told me that freedom equals responsibility. I couldn't agree more.

From C. Michael Pilato

Special thanks to my wife Amy, for her love and patient support, for putting up with late nights, and for even reviewing entire sections of this book—you always go the extra mile, and do so with incredible grace. Gavin, when you're old enough to read, I hope you're as proud of your Daddy as he is of you. Mom and Dad (and the rest of the family), thanks for your constant support and enthusiasm.

Hats off to Shep Kendall, through whom the world of computers was first opened to me; Ben Collins-Sussman, my tour guide through the open-source world; Karl Fogel—you *are* my *.emacs*; Greg Stein, for oozing practical programming know-how; Brian Fitzpatrick, for sharing this writing experience with me. To the many folks from whom I am constantly picking up new knowledge—keep dropping it!

Finally, to the One who perfectly demonstrates creative excellence—thank you.

## CHAPTER 1

Introduction

Version control is the art of managing changes to information. It has long been a critical tool for programmers, who typically spend their time making small changes to software and then undoing those changes the next day. But the usefulness of version control software extends far beyond the bounds of the software development world. Anywhere you can find people using computers to manage information that changes often, there is room for version control. And that's where Subversion comes into play.

This chapter contains a high-level introduction to Subversion: what it is; what it does; how to get it.

What Is Subversion?

Subversion is a free/open-source version control system. That is, Subversion manages files and directories over time. A tree of files is placed into a central *repository*. The repository is much like an ordinary file server, except that it remembers every change ever made to the files and directories. This lets you recover older versions of data, or examine the history of how your data changed. In this regard, many people think of a version control system as a sort of time machine.

Subversion can access its repository across networks, which allows it to be used by people on different computers. At some level, the ability for various people to modify and manage the same set of data from their respective locations fosters collaboration. Progress can occur more quickly without a single conduit through which all modifications must occur. And because the work is versioned, you need not fear that quality is the trade-off for losing that conduit—if some incorrect change is made to the data, just undo that change.

Some version control systems are also software configuration management (SCM) systems. These systems are specifically tailored to manage trees of source code, and have many features that are specific to software development—such as natively understanding programming languages, or supplying tools for building software. Subversion, however, is not one of these systems. It is a general system that can be used to manage *any* collection of files. For you, those files might be source code—for others, anything from grocery shopping lists to digital video mixdowns and beyond.

Subversion's History

In early 2000, CollabNet, Inc. (*http://www.collab.net*) began seeking developers to write a replacement for CVS. CollabNet offers a collaboration software suite called SourceCast, of which one component is version control. Although SourceCast used CVS as its initial version control system, CVS's limitations were obvious from the beginning, and CollabNet knew it would eventually have to find something better. Unfortunately, CVS had become the de facto standard in the open source world largely because there *wasn't* anything better, at least not under a free license. So CollabNet determined to write a new version control system from scratch, retaining the basic ideas of CVS, but without the bugs and misfeatures.

In February 2000, they contacted Karl Fogel, the author of *Open Source Development with CVS* (Coriolis, 1999), and asked if he'd like to work on this new project. Coincidentally, at the time Karl was already discussing a design for a new version control system with his friend Jim Blandy. In 1995, the two had started Cyclic Software, a company providing CVS support contracts, and although they later sold the business, they still used CVS every day at their jobs. Their frustration with CVS had led Jim to think carefully about better ways to manage versioned data, and he'd already come up with not only the name Subversion, but also with the basic design of the Subversion repository. When CollabNet called, Karl immediately agreed to work on the project, and Jim got his employer, RedHat Software, to essentially donate him to the project for an indefinite period of time. CollabNet hired Karl and Ben Collins-Sussman, and detailed design work began in May. With the help of some well-placed prods from Brian Behlendorf and Jason Robbins of CollabNet, and Greg Stein (at the time an independent developer active in the WebDAV/DeltaV specification process), Subversion quickly attracted a community of active developers. It turned out that many people had had the same frustrating experiences with CVS, and welcomed the chance to finally do something about it.

The original design team settled on some simple goals. They didn't want to break new ground in version control methodology; they just wanted to fix CVS. They decided that Subversion would match CVS's features, and preserve the same development model, but not duplicate CVS's most obvious flaws. And although it did not need to be a drop-in replacement for CVS, it should be similar enough that any CVS user could make the switch with little effort.

After fourteen months of coding, Subversion became self-hosting on August 31, 2001. That is, Subversion developers stopped using CVS to manage Subversion's own source code, and started using Subversion instead.

While CollabNet started the project, and still funds a large chunk of the work (it pays the salaries of a few full-time Subversion developers), Subversion is run like most open-source projects, governed by a loose, transparent set of rules that encourage meritocracy. CollabNet's copyright license is fully compliant with the Debian Free Software Guidelines. In other words, anyone is free to download, modify, and redistribute Subversion as he pleases; no permission from CollabNet or anyone else is required.

Subversion's Features

When discussing the features that Subversion brings to the version control table, it is often helpful to speak of them in terms of how they improve upon CVS's design. If you're not familiar with CVS, you may not understand all of these features. And if you're not familiar with version control at all, your eyes may glaze over unless you first read Chapter 2, in which we provide a gentle introduction to version control in general.

Subversion provides:

Directory versioning
> CVS only tracks the history of individual files, but Subversion implements a virtual versioned filesystem that tracks changes to whole directory trees over time. Files *and* directories are versioned.

True version history
> Since CVS is limited to file versioning, operations such as copies and renames—which might happen to files, but which are really changes to the contents of some containing directory—aren't supported in CVS. Additionally, in CVS you cannot replace a versioned file with some new thing of the same name without the new item inheriting the history of the old—perhaps completely unrelated—file. With Subversion, you can add, delete, copy, and rename both files and directories. And every newly added file begins a with a fresh clean history all its own.

Atomic commits
> A collection of modifications either goes into the repository completely, or not at all. This allows developers to construct and commit changes as logical chunks, and prevents problems that can occur when only a portion of a set of changes is successfully sent to the repository.

Versioned metadata

Each file and directory has a set of properties—keys and their values— associated with it. You can create and store any arbitrary key/value pairs you wish. Properties are versioned over time, just like file contents.

Choice of network layers

Subversion has an abstracted notion of repository access, making it easy for people to implement new network mechanisms. Subversion can plug into the Apache HTTP Server as an extension module. This gives Subversion a big advantage in stability and interoperability, and instant access to existing features provided by that server—authentication, authorization, wire compression, and so on. A more lightweight, standalone Subversion server process is also available. This server speaks a custom protocol which can be easily tunneled over SSH.

Consistent data handling

Subversion expresses file differences using a binary differencing algorithm, which works identically on both text (human-readable) and binary (human-unreadable) files. Both types of files are stored equally compressed in the repository, and differences are transmitted in both directions across the network.

Efficient branching and tagging

The cost of branching and tagging need not be proportional to the project size. Subversion creates branches and tags by simply copying the project, using a mechanism similar to a hard-link. Thus these operations take only a very small, constant amount of time.

Hackability

Subversion has no historical baggage; it is implemented as a collection of shared C libraries with well-defined APIs. This makes Subversion extremely maintainable and usable by other applications and languages.

Subversion's Architecture

On one end is a Subversion repository that holds all of your versioned data. On the other end is your Subversion client program, which manages local reflections of portions of that versioned data (called working copies). Between these extremes are multiple routes through various Repository Access (RA) layers. Some of these routes go across computer networks and through network servers which then access the repository. Others bypass the network altogether and access the repository directly.

Figure 1-1 illustrates what one might call a mile-high view of Subversion's design.

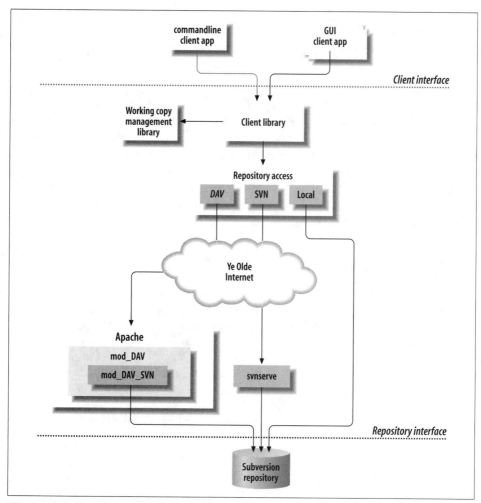

Figure 1-1. Subversion's architecture

Installing Subversion

Subversion is built on a portability layer called APR (the Apache Portable Runtime library). This means Subversion should work on any operating system that the Apache httpd server runs on: Windows, Linux, all flavors of BSD, Mac OS X, Netware, and others.

The easiest way to get Subversion is to download a binary package built for your operating system. Subversion's web site (*http://subversion.tigris.org*) often has these packages available for download, posted by volunteers. The site usually contains graphical installer packages for users of Microsoft operating systems. If you run a Unix-like operating system, you can use your system's native package distribution system (RPMs, DEBs, the ports tree, etc.) to get Subversion.

Alternatively, you can build Subversion directly from source code. From the Subversion website, download the latest source-code release. After unpacking it, follow the instructions in the *INSTALL* file to build it. Note that a released source package contains everything you need to build a command-line client capable of talking to a remote repository (in particular, the apr, apr-util, and neon libraries). But optional portions of Subversion have many other dependencies, such as Berkeley DB and possibly Apache httpd. If you want to do a complete build, make sure you have all of the packages documented in the *INSTALL* file. If you plan to work on Subversion itself, you can use your client program to grab the latest, bleeding-edge source code. This is documented in "Get the Source Code" in Chapter 8."

Subversion's Components

Subversion, once installed, has a number of different pieces. The following is a quick overview of what you get. Don't be alarmed if the brief descriptions leave you scratching your head—there are *plenty* more pages in this book devoted to alleviating that confusion.

svn
> The command-line client program

svnversion
> A program for reporting the state (in terms of revisions of the items present) of a working copy

svnlook
> A tool for inspecting a Subversion repository

svnadmin
> A tool for creating, tweaking or repairing a Subversion repository

svndumpfilter
> A program for filtering Subversion repository dumpfile format streams

mod_dav_svn
> A plug-in module for the Apache HTTP Server, used to make your repository available to others over a network

svnserve
> A custom standalone server program, runnable as a daemon process or invokable by SSH; another way to make your repository available to others over a network

Assuming you have Subversion installed correctly, you should be ready to start. The next two chapters walk you through the use of svn, Subversion's command-line client program.

A Quick Start

Some people have trouble absorbing a new technology by reading the sort of top-down approach provided by this book. This section is a very short introduction to Subversion, and is designed to give bottom-up learners a fighting chance. If you're one of those folks who prefers to learn by experimentation, the following demonstration will get you up and running. Along the way, we give links to the relevant chapters of this book.

If you're new to the entire concept of version control or to the copy-modify-merge model used by both CVS and Subversion, then you should read Chapter 2 before going any further.

 The following example assumes that you have svn, the Subversion commandline client, and svnadmin, the administrative tool, ready to go. It also assumes that your svn client has been compiled against Berkeley DB. To verify this, run svn --version and make sure the ra_local module is available. Without this module, the client cannot access file:// URLs.

Subversion stores all versioned data in a central repository. To begin, create a new repository:

```
$ svnadmin create /path/to/repos
$ ls /path/to/repos
conf/  dav/  db/  format  hooks/  locks/  README.txt
```

This command creates a new directory /path/to/repos which contains a Subversion repository. Make sure that this directory lives on a local disk, *not* a network share. This new directory mainly contains a collection of Berkeley DB database files. You won't see your versioned files if you peek inside. For more information about repository creation and maintenance, see Chapter 5.

Next, create a tree of files and directories to import into the repository. For reasons that will be clear later on (see Chapter 4), your structure should contain three top-level directories named *branches*, *tags*, and *trunk*:

```
/tmp/project/branches/
/tmp/project/tags/
/tmp/project/trunk/
            foo.c
            bar.c
            Makefile
            …
```

Once you have a tree of data ready to go, import the data into the repository with the svn import command ("svn import" in Chapter 3):

```
$ svn import /tmp/project file:///path/to/repos -m "initial import"
Adding        /tmp/project/branches
```

```
Adding        /tmp/project/tags
Adding        /tmp/project/trunk
Adding        /tmp/project/trunk/foo.c
Adding        /tmp/project/trunk/bar.c
Adding        /tmp/project/trunk/Makefile
…
Committed revision 1.
$
```

Now the repository contains your tree of data. At this point, you create a working copy of the *trunk* directory. This is where your actual work will happen:

```
$ svn checkout file://path/to/repos/trunk project
A  project/foo.c
A  project/bar.c
A  project/Makefile
…
Checked out revision 1.
```

Now you have a personal copy of part of the repository in a new directory named *project*. You can edit the files in your working copy and then commit those changes back into the repository:

- Enter your working copy and edit a file's contents.
- Run svn diff to see unified diff output of your changes.
- Run svn commit to commit the new version of your file to the repository.
- Run svn update to bring your working copy up-to-date with the repository.

For a full tour of all the things you can do with your working copy, read Chaper 3.

At this point, you have the option of making your repository available to others over a network. See Chapter 6 to learn about the different sorts of server processes available and how to configure them.

## CHAPTER 2

Basic Concepts

This chapter is a short, casual introduction to Subversion. If you're new to version control, this chapter is definitely for you. We begin with a discussion of general version control concepts, work our way into the specific ideas behind Subversion, and show some simple examples of Subversion in use.

Even though the examples in this chapter show people sharing collections of program source code, keep in mind that Subversion can manage any sort of file collection—it's not limited to helping computer programmers.

The Repository

Subversion is a centralized system for sharing information. At its core is a repository, which is a central store of data. The repository stores information in the form of a *filesystem tree*—a typical hierarchy of files and directories. Any number of *clients* connect to the repository, and then read or write to these files. By writing data, a client makes the information available to others; by reading data, the client receives information from others. Figure 2-1 illustrates this. Why is this interesting? So far,

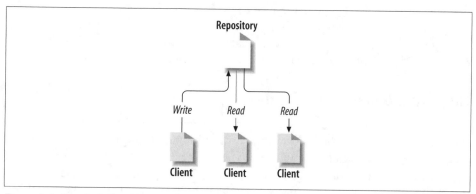

Figure 2-1. A typical client/server system

this sounds like the definition of a typical file server. And, indeed, the repository *is* a kind of file server, although it's not your usual breed. What makes the Subversion repository special is that *it remembers every change* ever written to it: every change to every file, and even changes to the directory tree itself, such as the addition, deletion, and rearrangement of files and directories.

When a client reads data from the repository, it normally sees only the latest version of the filesystem tree. But the client also has the ability to view *previous* states of the filesystem. For example, a client can ask historical questions like, What did this directory contain last Wednesday? or Who was the last person to change this file, and what changes did they make? These are the sorts of questions that are at the heart of any *version control system*: systems that are designed to record and track changes to data over time.

Versioning Models

The core mission of a version control system is to enable collaborative editing and sharing of data. However, different systems use different strategies to achieve this.

The Problem of File Sharing

All version control systems have to solve the same fundamental problem: how will the system allow users to share information, but prevent them from accidentally stepping on each other's feet? It's all too easy for users to accidentally overwrite each other's changes in the repository.

Consider the scenario shown in Figure 2-2. Suppose we have two co-workers, Harry and Sally. They each decide to edit the same repository file at the same time. If Harry saves his changes to the repository first, then it's possible that (a few moments later) Sally could accidentally overwrite them with her own new version of the file. While Harry's version of the file won't be lost forever (because the system remembers every change), any changes Harry made *won't* be present in Sally's newer version of the file, because she never saw Harry's changes to begin with. Harry's work is still effectively lost—or at least missing from the latest version of the file—and probably by accident. This is definitely a situation we want to avoid!

The Lock-Modify-Unlock Solution

Many version control systems use a *lock-modify-unlock* model to address this problem. In such a system, the repository allows only one person to change a file at a time. First Harry must lock the file before he can begin making changes to it. Locking a file is a lot like borrowing a book from the library; if Harry has locked a file, then Sally cannot make any changes to it. If she tries to lock the file, the repository will deny the request. All she can do is read the file, and wait for Harry to finish his

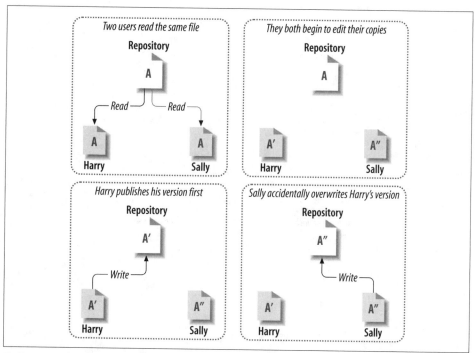

Figure 2-2. The problem to avoid

changes and release his lock. After Harry unlocks the file, his turn is over, and now Sally can take her turn by locking and editing. Figure 2-3 demonstrates this simple solution.

The problem with the lock-modify-unlock model is that it's a bit restrictive, and often becomes a roadblock for users:

Locking may cause administrative problems.
Sometimes Harry locks a file and then forget about it. Meanwhile, because Sally is still waiting to edit the file, her hands are tied. And then Harry goes on vacation. Now Sally has to get an administrator to release Harry's lock. The situation ends up causing a lot of unnecessary delay and wasted time.

Locking may cause unnecessary serialization.
What if Harry is editing the beginning of a text file, and Sally simply wants to edit the end of the same file? These changes don't overlap at all. They could easily edit the file simultaneously, and no great harm would come, assuming the changes were properly merged together. There's no need for them to take turns in this situation.

Locking may create a false sense of security.
Pretend that Harry locks and edits file A, while Sally simultaneously locks and edits file B. But suppose that A and B depend on one another, and the changes

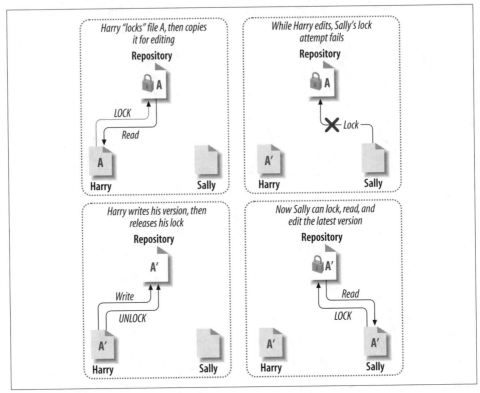

Figure 2-3. The lock-modify-unlock solution

made to each are semantically incompatible. Suddenly A and B don't work together anymore. The locking system was powerless to prevent the problem—yet it somehow provided a false sense of security. It's easy for Harry and Sally to imagine that by locking files, each is beginning a safe, insulated task, and thus inhibits them from discussing their incompatible changes early on.

The Copy-Modify-Merge Solution

Subversion, CVS, and other version control systems use a *copy-modify-merge* model as an alternative to locking. In this model, each user's client contacts the project repository and creates a personal *working copy*—a local reflection of the repository's files and directories. Users then work in parallel, modifying their private copies. Finally, the private copies are merged together into a new, final version. The version control system often assists with the merging, but ultimately a human being is responsible for making it happen correctly.

Here's an example. Say that Harry and Sally each create working copies of the same project, copied from the repository. They work concurrently, and make changes to the same file A within their copies. Sally saves her changes to the repository first.

When Harry attempts to save his changes later, the repository informs him that his file A is *out-of-date*. In other words, that file A in the repository has somehow changed since he last copied it. So Harry asks his client to *merge* any new changes from the repository into his working copy of file A. Chances are that Sally's changes don't overlap with his own; so once he has both sets of changes integrated, he saves his working copy back to the repository. Figures 2-4 and 2-5 show this process.

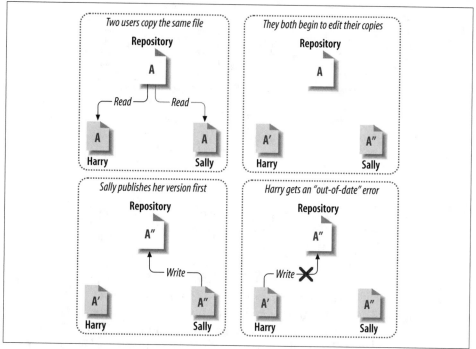

Figure 2-4. The copy-modify-merge solution

But what if Sally's changes *do* overlap with Harry's changes? What then? This situation is called a *conflict*, and it's usually not much of a problem. When Harry asks his client to merge the latest repository changes into his working copy, his copy of file A is somehow flagged as being in a state of conflict: he'll be able to see both sets of conflicting changes, and manually choose between them. Note that software can't automatically resolve conflicts; only humans are capable of understanding and making the necessary intelligent choices. Once Harry has manually resolved the overlapping changes—perhaps after a discussion with Sally—he can safely save the merged file back to the repository.

The copy-modify-merge model may sound a bit chaotic, but in practice, it runs extremely smoothly. Users can work in parallel, never waiting for one another. When they work on the same files, it turns out that most of their concurrent changes don't overlap at all; conflicts are infrequent. And the amount of time it takes to resolve conflicts is far less than the time lost by a locking system.

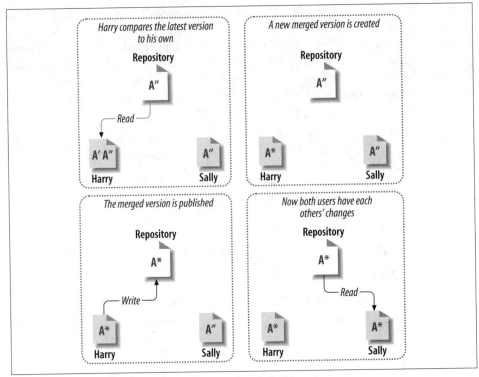

Figure 2-5. The copy-modify-merge solution (continued)

In the end, it all comes down to one critical factor: user communication. When users communicate poorly, both syntactic and semantic conflicts increase. No system can force users to communicate perfectly, and no system can detect semantic conflicts. So there's no point in being lulled into a false promise that a locking system will somehow prevent conflicts; in practice, locking seems to inhibit productivity more than anything else.

Subversion in Action

It's time to move from the abstract to the concrete. In this section, we'll show real examples of Subversion being used.

Working Copies

You've already read about working copies; now we'll demonstrate how the Subversion client creates and uses them.

A Subversion working copy is an ordinary directory tree on your local system, containing a collection of files. You can edit these files however you wish, and if they're source code files, you can compile your program from them in the usual way. Your working copy is your own private work area: Subversion will never incorporate other people's changes, nor make your own changes available to others, until you explicitly tell it to do so.

After you've made some changes to the files in your working copy and verified that they work properly, Subversion provides you with commands to publish your changes to the other people working with you on your project (by writing to the repository). If other people publish their own changes, Subversion provides you with commands to merge those changes into your working directory (by reading from the repository).

A working copy also contains some extra files, created and maintained by Subversion, to help it carry out these commands. In particular, each directory in your working copy contains a subdirectory named *.svn*, also known as the working copy *administrative directory*. The files in each administrative directory help Subversion recognize which files contain unpublished changes, and which files are out-of-date with respect to others' work.

A typical Subversion repository often holds the files (or source code) for several projects; usually, each project is a subdirectory in the repository's filesystem tree. In this arrangement, a user's working copy will usually correspond to a particular sub-tree of the repository.

For example, suppose you have a repository that contains two software projects, *paint* and *calc*. Each project lives in its own top-level directory, as shown in Figure 2-6.

To get a working copy, you must *check out* some subtree of the repository. (The term check out may sound like it has something to do with locking or reserving resources, but it doesn't; it simply creates a private copy of the project for you.) For example, if you check out */calc*, you will get a working copy like this:

```
$ svn checkout http://svn.example.com/repos/calc
A  calc
A  calc/Makefile
A  calc/integer.c
A  calc/button.c

$ ls -a calc
Makefile  integer.c  button.c  .svn/
```

The list of letter A's indicates that Subversion is adding a number of items to your working copy. You now have a personal copy of the repository's */calc* directory, with one additional entry—*.svn*—that holds the extra information needed by Subversion, as mentioned earlier.

Suppose you make changes to *button.c*. Since the *.svn* directory remembers the file's modification date and original contents, Subversion can tell that you've changed the file. However, Subversion does not make your changes public until you explicitly tell it to do so. The act of publishing your changes is more commonly known as *committing* (or *checking in*) changes to the repository.

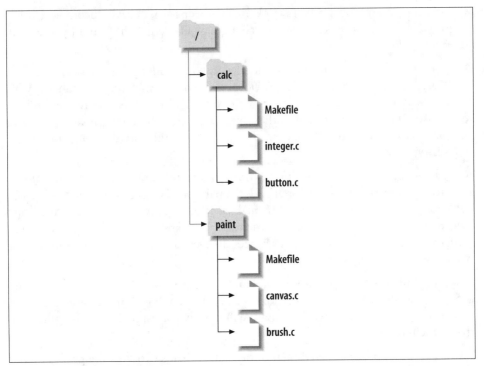

Figure 2-6. The repository's filesystem

To publish your changes to others, you can use Subversion's commit command:

```
$ svn commit button.c
Sending        button.c
Transmitting file data .
Committed revision 57.
```

Now your changes to *button.c* have been committed to the repository; if another user checks out a working copy of */calc*, they will see your changes in the latest version of the file.

Suppose you have a collaborator, Sally, who checked out a working copy of */calc* at the same time you did. When you commit your change to *button.c*, Sally's working copy is left unchanged; Subversion only modifies working copies at the user's request.

To bring her project up to date, Sally can ask Subversion to *update* her working copy, by using the Subversion update command. This incorporates your changes into her working copy, as well as any others that have been committed since she checked it out.

```
$ pwd
/home/sally/calc
```

Repository URLs

Subversion repositories can be accessed through many different methods—on local disk, or through various network protocols. A repository location, however, is always a URL. Table 2-1 describes how different URL schemas map to the available access methods.

For the most part, Subversion's URLs use the standard syntax, allowing for server names and port numbers to be specified as part of the URL. Remember that the `file:` access method is valid only for locations on the same server as the client—in fact, in accordance with convention, the server name portion of the URL needs to be either absent or `localhost`:

```
$ svn checkout file:///path/to/repos
...
$ svn checkout file://localhost/path/to/repos
...
```

Also, users of the `file:` scheme on Windows platforms need to use an unofficially standard syntax for accessing repositories that are on the same machine, but on a different drive than the client's current working drive. Either of the two following URL path syntaxes will work where `X` is the drive on which the repository resides:

```
C:\> svn checkout file:///X:/path/to/repos
...
C:\> svn checkout "file:///X|/path/to/repos"
...
```

In the second syntax, you need to quote the URL so that the vertical bar character is not interpreted as a pipe.

Note that a URL uses ordinary slashes even though the native (non-URL) form of a path on Windows uses backslashes.

Table 2-1. Repository access URLs

Schema	Access Method
`file:///`	direct repository access (on local disk)
`http://`	access via WebDAV protocol to Subversion-aware Apache server
`https://`	same as `http://`, but with SSL encryption.
`svn://`	access via custom protocol to an `svnserve` server
`svn+ssh://`	same as `svn://`, but through an SSH tunnel.

```
$ ls -a
.svn/ Makefile integer.c button.c

$ svn update
U button.c
```

The output from the svn update command indicates that Subversion updated the contents of *button.c*. Note that Sally didn't need to specify which files to update; Subversion uses the information in the *.svn* directory, and further information in the repository, to decide which files need to be brought up to date.

Revisions

An svn commit operation can publish changes to any number of files and directories as a single atomic transaction. In your working copy, you can change files' contents; create, delete, rename and copy files and directories; and then commit the complete set of changes as a unit.

In the repository, each commit is treated as an atomic transaction: either all the commit's changes take place, or none of them take place. Subversion tries to retain this atomicity in the face of program crashes, system crashes, network problems, and other users' actions.

Each time the repository accepts a commit, this creates a new state of the filesystem tree, called a *revision*. Each revision is assigned a unique natural number, one greater than the number of the previous revision. The initial revision of a freshly created repository is numbered 0, and consists of nothing but an empty root directory.

Figure 2-7 illustrates a nice way to visualize the repository. Imagine an array of revision numbers, starting at 0, stretching from left to right. Each revision number has a filesystem tree hanging below it, and each tree is a snapshot of the way the repository looked after each commit.

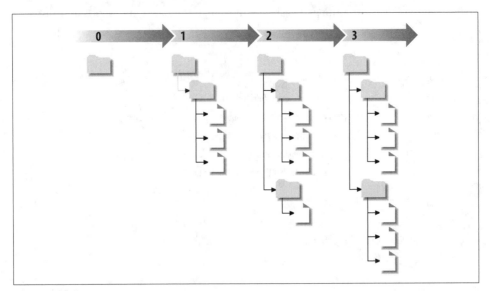

Figure 2-7. The repository

Global Revision Numbers

Unlike those of many other version control systems, Subversion's revision numbers apply to *entire trees*, not individual files. Each revision number selects an entire tree, a particular state of the repository after some committed change. Another way to think about it is that revision N represents the state of the repository filesystem after the Nth commit. When a Subversion user talks about revision 5 of *foo.c*, they really mean *foo.c* as it appears in revision 5. Notice that in general, revisions N and M of a file do *not* necessarily differ! Because CVS uses per-file revision numbers, CVS users might want to see Appendix A for more details.

It's important to note that working copies do not always correspond to any single revision in the repository; they may contain files from several different revisions. For example, suppose you check out a working copy from a repository whose most recent revision is 4:

```
calc/Makefile:4
    integer.c:4
    button.c:4
```

At the moment, this working directory corresponds exactly to revision 4 in the repository. However, suppose you make a change to *button.c*, and commit that change. Assuming no other commits have taken place, your commit will create revision 5 of the repository, and your working copy now looks like this:

```
calc/Makefile:4
    integer.c:4
    button.c:5
```

Suppose that, at this point, Sally commits a change to *integer.c*, creating revision 6. If you use svn update to bring your working copy up to date, then it looks like this:

```
calc/Makefile:6
    integer.c:6
    button.c:6
```

Sally's changes to *integer.c* appears in your working copy, and your change is still present in *button.c*. In this example, the text of *Makefile* is identical in revisions 4, 5, and 6, but Subversion marks your working copy of *Makefile* with revision 6 to indicate that it is still current. Thus, after you do a clean update at the top of your working copy, it generally corresponds to exactly one revision in the repository.

How Working Copies Track the Repository

For each file in a working directory, Subversion records two essential pieces of information in the *.svn/* administrative area:

- what revision your working file is based on (this is called the file's *working revision*)
- a timestamp recording when the local copy was last updated by the repository.

Given this information, by talking to the repository, Subversion can tell which of the following four states a working file is in:

Unchanged, and current
> The file is unchanged in the working directory, and no changes to that file have been committed to the repository since its working revision. A svn commit of the file will do nothing, and an svn update of the file will do nothing.

Locally changed, and current
> The file has been changed in the working directory, and no changes to that file have been committed to the repository since its base revision. There are local changes that have not been committed to the repository; thus an svn commit of the file will succeed in publishing your changes, and an svn update of the file will do nothing.

Unchanged, and out-of-date
> The file has not been changed in the working directory, but it has been changed in the repository. The file should eventually be updated, to make it current with the public revision. An svn commit of the file will do nothing, and an svn update of the file will fold the latest changes into your working copy.

Locally changed, and out-of-date
> The file has been changed both in the working directory, and in the repository. An svn commit of the file will fail with an out-of-date error. The file should be updated first; an svn update command will attempt to merge the public changes with the local changes. If Subversion can't complete the merge in a plausible way automatically, it leaves it to the user to resolve the conflict.

This may sound like a lot to keep track of, but the svn status command will show you the state of any item in your working copy. For more information on that command, see "svn status" in Chapter 3."

The Limitations of Mixed Revisions

As a general principle, Subversion tries to be as flexible as possible. One special kind of flexibility is the ability to have a working copy containing mixed revision numbers.

At first, it may not be entirely clear why this sort of flexibility is considered a feature, and not a liability. After completing a commit to the repository, the freshly committed files and directories are at a more recent working revision than the rest of the working copy. It looks like a bit of a mess. As demonstrated earlier, the working copy can always be brought to a single working revision by running svn update. Why would someone *deliberately* want a mixture of working revisions?

Assuming your project is sufficiently complex, you'll discover that it's sometimes nice to forcibly backdate portions of your working copy to an earlier revision; you'll learn how to do that in Chapter 3. Perhaps you'd like to test an earlier version of a submodule, contained in a subdirectory, or perhaps you'd like to examine a number of previous versions of a file in the context of the latest tree.

However you make use of mixed revisions in your working copy, there are limitations to this flexibility.

First, you cannot commit the deletion of a file or directory which isn't fully up-to-date. If a newer version of the item exists in the repository, your attempt to delete will be rejected, to prevent you from accidentally destroying changes you've not yet seen.

Second, you cannot commit a metadata change to a directory unless it's fully up-to-date. You'll learn about attaching properties to items in Chapter 6. A directory's working revision defines a specific set of entries and properties, and thus committing a property change to an out-of-date directory may destroy properties you've not yet seen.

Summary

We covered a number of fundamental Subversion concepts in this chapter:

- We introduced the notions of the central repository, the client working copy, and the array of repository revision trees.
- We gave some simple examples of how two collaborators can use Subversion to publish and receive changes from one another, using the copy-modify-merge model.
- We talked a bit about the way Subversion tracks and manages information in a working copy.

At this point, you should have a good idea of how Subversion works in the most general sense. Armed with this knowledge, you should now be ready to jump into the next chapter, which is a detailed tour of Subversion's commands and features.

## CHAPTER 3

Guided Tour

Now we go into the details of using Subversion. By the time you reach the end of this chapter, you will be able to perform almost all the tasks you need to use Subversion in a normal day's work. You'll start with an initial checkout of your code, and walk through making changes and examining those changes. You'll also see how to bring changes made by others into your working copy, examine them, and work through any conflicts that might arise.

Note that this chapter is not meant to be an exhaustive list of all Subversion's commands—rather, it's a conversational introduction to the most common Subversion tasks you'll encounter. This chapter assumes that you've read and understood Chapter 2 and are familiar with the general model of Subversion. For a complete reference of all commands, see Chapter 9.

Help!

Before reading on, here is the most important command you'll need when using Subversion: svn help. The Subversion command-line client is self-documenting—at any time, a quick svn help <subcommand> will describe the syntax, switches, and behavior of the subcommand.

Import

You use svn import to import a new project into a Subversion repository. While this is most likely the very first thing you will do when you set up your Subversion server, it's not something that happens very often. For a detailed description of import, see "svn import" later in this chapter.

Revisions: Numbers, Keywords, and Dates, Oh My!

Before we continue, you should know a bit about how to identify a particular revision in your repository. As you learned in "Revisions" in Chapter 2," a revision is a snapshot of the repository at a particular moment in time. As you continue to commit and grow your repository, you need a mechanism for identifying these snapshots.

You specify these revisions by using the `--revision` (`-r`) switch plus the revision you want (`svn --revision REV`), or you can specify a range by separating two revisions with a colon (`svn --revision REV1:REV2`). Subversion lets you refer to these revisions by number, keyword, or date.

Revision Numbers

When you create a new Subversion repository, it begins its life at revision zero and each successive commit increases the revision number by one. After your commit completes, the Subversion client informs you of the new revision number:

```
$ svn commit --message "Corrected number of cheese slices."
Sending        sandwich.txt
Transmitting file data .
Committed revision 3.
```

If at any point in the future you want to refer to that revision (we'll show how and why you might want to do that later in this chapter), you can refer to it as 3.

Revision Keywords

The Subversion client understands a number of *revision keywords*. These keywords can be used instead of integer arguments to the `--revision` switch, and are resolved into specific revision numbers by Subversion:

> Each directory in your working copy contains an administrative subdirectory called *.svn*. For every file in a directory, Subversion keeps a copy of each file in the administrative area. This copy is an unmodified (no keyword expansion, no end-of-line translation, no nothing) copy of the file as it existed in the last revision (called the BASE revision) that you updated it to in your working copy. We refer to this file as the *pristine copy* or *text-base* version of your file, and it's always an exact byte-for-byte copy of the file as it exists in the repository.

HEAD
    The latest revision in the repository.

BASE
    The pristine revision of an item in a working copy.

COMMITTED
> The last revision in which an item changed before (or at) BASE.

PREV
> The revision just *before* the last revision in which an item changed. (Technically, COMMITTED - 1.)

Here are some examples of revision keywords in action. Don't worry if the commands don't make sense yet; we explain these commands as we go through the chapter:

```
$ svn diff --revision PREV:COMMITTED foo.c
# shows the last change committed to foo.c

$ svn log --revision HEAD
# shows log message for the latest repository commit

$ svn diff --revision HEAD
# compares your working file (with local mods) to the latest version
# in the repository.

$ svn diff --revision BASE:HEAD foo.c
# compares your "pristine" foo.c (no local mods) with the
# latest version in the repository

$ svn log --revision BASE:HEAD
# shows all commit logs since you last updated

$ svn update --revision PREV foo.c
# rewinds the last change on foo.c.
# (foo.c's working revision is decreased.)
```

These keywords allow you to perform many common (and helpful) operations without having to look up specific revision numbers or remember the exact revision of your working copy.

Revision Dates

Anywhere that you specify a revision number or revision keyword, you can also specify a date by specifying the date inside curly braces { }. You can even access a range of changes in the repository using both dates and revisions together!

Here are examples of the date formats that Subversion accepts. Remember to use quotes around any date that contains spaces.

```
$ svn checkout --revision {2002-02-17}
$ svn checkout --revision {15:30}
$ svn checkout --revision {15:30:00.200000}
$ svn checkout --revision {"2002-02-17 15:30"}
$ svn checkout --revision {"2002-02-17 15:30 +0230"}
$ svn checkout --revision {2002-02-17T15:30}
$ svn checkout --revision {2002-02-17T15:30Z}
```

```
$ svn checkout --revision {2002-02-17T15:30-04:00}
$ svn checkout --revision {20020217T1530}
$ svn checkout --revision {20020217T1530Z}
$ svn checkout --revision {20020217T1530-0500}
...
```

When you specify a date as a revision, Subversion finds the most recent revision of the repository as of that date:

```
$ svn log --revision {2002-11-28}
------------------------------------------------------------------------
r12 | ira | 2002-11-27 12:31:51 -0600 (Wed, 27 Nov 2002) | 6 lines
...
```

Is Subversion a Day Early?

If you specify a single date as a revision without specifying a time of day (for example 2002-11-27), you may think that Subversion should give you the last revision that took place on the 27th of November. Instead, you'll get back a revision from the 26th, or even earlier. Remember that Subversion will find the *most recent revision of the repository* as of the date you give. If you give a date without a timestamp, like 2002-11-27, Subversion assumes a time of 00:00:00, so looking for the most recent revision won't return anything on the day of the 27th.

If you want to include the 27th in your search, you can either specify the 27th with the time ({"2002-11-27 23:59"}), or just specify the next day ({2002-11-28}).

You can also use a range of dates. Subversion will find all revisions between both dates, inclusive:

```
$ svn log --revision {2002-11-20}:{2002-11-29}
...
```

As we pointed out, you can also mix dates and revisions:

```
$ svn log --revision {2002-11-20}:4040
```

Users should be aware of a subtlety that can become quite a stumbling block when dealing with dates in Subversion. Since the timestamp of a revision is stored as a property of the revision—an unversioned, modifiable property—revision timestamps can be changed to represent complete falsifications of true chronology, or even removed altogether. This will wreak havoc on the internal date-to-revision conversion that Subversion performs.

Initial Checkout

Most of the time, you start using a Subversion repository by doing a *checkout* of your project. Checking out a repository creates a copy of it on your local machine. This copy contains the HEAD (latest revision) of the Subversion repository that you specify on the command line:

```
$ svn checkout http://svn.collab.net/repos/svn/trunk
A  trunk/subversion.dsw
A  trunk/svn_check.dsp
A  trunk/COMMITTERS
A  trunk/configure.in
A  trunk/IDEAS
...
Checked out revision 2499.
```

Repository Layout

If you're wondering what trunk is all about in the above URL, it's part of the way we recommend you lay out your Subversion repository, a topic we'll talk about a lot more in Chapter 4.

Although the previous example checks out the trunk directory, you can just as easily check out any deep subdirectory of a repository by specifying the subdirectory in the checkout URL:

```
$ svn checkout http://svn.collab.net/repos/svn/trunk/doc/book/tools
A  tools/readme-dblite.html
A  tools/fo-stylesheet.xsl
A  tools/svnbook.el
A  tools/dtd
A  tools/dtd/dblite.dtd
...
Checked out revision 3678.
```

Since Subversion uses a copy-modify-merge model instead of lock-modify-unlock (see Chapter 2), you're already able to start making changes to the files and directories in your working copy. Your working copy is just like any other collection of files and directories on your system. You can edit and change them, move them around, you can even delete the entire working copy and forget about it.

 While your working copy is just like any other collection of files and directories on your system, you need to let Subversion know if you're going to be rearranging anything inside of your working copy. If you want to copy or move an item in a working copy, you should use svn copy or svn move instead of the copy and move commands provided by your operating system. We'll talk more about svn copy and svn move later in this chapter.

Unless you're ready to commit a new file or directory, or changes to existing ones, there's no need to further notify the Subversion server that you've done anything.

Every directory in a working copy contains an administrative area, a subdirectory named *.svn*. Usually, directory listing commands won't show this subdirectory, but it is nevertheless an important directory. Whatever you do, don't delete or change anything in the administrative area! Subversion depends on it to manage your working copy.

While you can certainly check out a working copy with the URL of the repository as the only argument, you can also specify a directory after your repository URL. This places your working copy into a new directory that you name. For example:

```
$ svn checkout http://svn.collab.net/repos/svn/trunk subv
A  subv/subversion.dsw
A  subv/svn_check.dsp
A  subv/COMMITTERS
A  subv/configure.in
A  subv/IDEAS
...
Checked out revision 2499.
```

That will place your working copy in a directory named subv instead of a directory named trunk, as we did previously.

Basic Work Cycle

Subversion has numerous features, options, bells, and whistles, but on a day-to-day basis, odds are that you will only use a few of them. In this section we run through the most common things that you might find yourself doing with Subversion in the course of a day's work.

The typical work cycle looks like this:

- Update your working copy
  - svn update
- Make changes
  - svn add
  - svn delete
  - svn copy
  - svn move
- Examine your changes
  - svn status
  - svn diff
  - svn revert

- Merge others' changes
  - `svn merge`
  - `svn resolved`
- Commit your changes
  - `svn commit`

Update Your Working Copy

When working on a project with a team, you may want to update your working copy to receive any changes made since your last update by other developers on the project. Use svn update to bring your working copy in sync with the latest revision in the repository.

```
$ svn update
U  foo.c
U  bar.c
Updated to revision 2.
```

In this case, someone else checked in modifications to both *foo.c* and *bar.c* since the last time you updated, and Subversion has updated your working copy to include those changes.

Let's examine the output of svn update a bit more. When the server sends changes to your working copy, a letter code is displayed next to each item to let you know what actions Subversion performed to bring your working copy up-to-date:

U foo

> File *foo* was Updated (received changes from the server).

A foo

> File or directory *foo* was Added to your working copy.

D foo

> File or directory *foo* was Deleted from your working copy.

R foo

> File or directory *foo* was Replaced in your working copy; that is, *foo* was deleted, and a new item with the same name was added. While they may have the same name, the repository considers them to be distinct objects with distinct histories.

G foo

> File *foo* received new changes from the repository, but your local copy of the file had your modifications. The changes did not intersect, however, so Subversion has merGed the repository's changes into the file without a problem.

C foo

> File *foo* received Conflicting changes from the server. The changes from the server directly overlap your own changes to the file. No need to panic, though. This overlap needs to be resolved by a human (you); we discuss this situation later in this chapter.

Make Changes to Your Working Copy

Now you can get to work and make changes in your working copy. It's usually most convenient to decide on a particular change (or set of changes) to make, such as writing a new feature, fixing a bug, etc. The Subversion commands that you use here are svn add, svn delete, svn copy, and svn move. However, if you are merely editing a file (or files) that is already in Subversion, you may not need to use any of these commands until you commit. Changes you can make to your working copy:

File changes

> This is the simplest sort of change. You don't need to tell Subversion that you intend to change a file; just make your changes. Subversion will be able to automatically detect which files have been changed.

Tree changes

> You can ask Subversion to mark files and directories for scheduled removal, addition, copying, or moving. While these changes may take place immediately in your working copy, no additions or removals happen in the repository until you commit them.

To make file changes, use your text editor, word processor, graphics program, or whatever tool you would normally use. Subversion handles binary files just as easily as it handles text files—and just as efficiently, too.

Here is an overview of the four Subversion subcommands that you use most often to make tree changes (we'll cover svn import and svn mkdir later).

svn add foo

> Schedule *foo* to be added to the repository. When you next commit, *foo* becomes a child of its parent directory. Note that if *foo* is a directory, everything underneath *foo* will be scheduled for addition. If you only want to schedule *foo* itself, pass the --non-recursive (-N) switch.

svn delete foo

> Schedule *foo* to be deleted from the repository. If *foo* is a file, it is immediately deleted from your working copy. If *foo* is a directory, it is not deleted, but Subversion schedules it for deletion. When you commit your changes, *foo* will be removed from your working copy and the repository.

> Of course, nothing is ever totally deleted from the repository—just from the HEAD of the repository. You can get back anything you delete by checking out (or updating your working copy of) a revision earlier than the one in which you deleted it.

svn copy foo bar

> Create a new item *bar* as a duplicate of *foo*. *bar* is automatically scheduled for addition. When *bar* is added to the repository on the next commit, its copy history is recorded (as having originally come from *foo*). svn copy does not create intermediate directories.

```
svn move foo bar
```
This command is exactly the same as running `svn copy foo bar`; `svn delete foo`. That is, *bar* is scheduled for addition as a copy of *foo*, and *foo* is scheduled for removal. `svn move` does not create intermediate directories.

Changing the Repository Without a Working Copy

Earlier in this chapter, we said that you have to commit any changes that you make in order for the repository to reflect these changes. That's not entirely true—there *are* some use-cases that immediately commit tree changes to the repository. This only happens when a subcommand is operating directly on a URL, rather than on a working-copy path. In particular, specific uses of `svn mkdir`, `svn copy`, `svn move`, and `svn delete` can work with URLs.

URL operations behave in this manner because commands that operate on a working copy can use the working copy as a sort of staging area to set up your changes before committing them to the repository. Commands that operate on URLs don't have this luxury, so when you operate directly on a URL, any of the previously mentioned actions represent an immediate commit.

Examine Your Changes

Once you've finished making changes, you need to commit them to the repository, but before you do so, it's usually a good idea to take a look at exactly what you've changed. By examining your changes before you commit, you can make a more accurate log message. You may also discover that you've inadvertently changed a file, and this gives you a chance to revert those changes before committing. Additionally, this is a good opportunity to review and scrutinize changes before publishing them. You can see exactly what changes you've made by using `svn status`, `svn diff`, and `svn revert`. You will usually use the first two commands to find out what files have changed in your working copy, and then perhaps the third to revert some (or all) of those changes.

Subversion has been optimized to help you with this task, and is able to do many things without communicating with the repository. In particular, your working copy contains a secret cached pristine copy of each version controlled file within the *.svn* area. Because of this, Subversion can quickly show you how your working files have changed, or even allow you to undo your changes without contacting the repository.

svn status

You'll probably use the `svn status` command more than any other Subversion command.

If you run svn status at the top of your working copy with no arguments, it will detect all file and tree changes you've made. This example is designed to show all the different status codes that svn status can return. (Note that the text following # in the following example is not actually printed by svn status.)

```
$ svn status
L     abc.c              # svn has a lock in its .svn directory for abc.c
M     bar.c              # the content in bar.c has local modifications
M     baz.c              # baz.c has property but no content modifications
?     foo.o              # svn doesn't manage foo.o
!     some_dir           # svn manages this, but it's either missing or incomplete
~     qux                # versioned as dir, but is file, or vice versa
A  +  moved_dir          # added with history of where it came from
M  +  moved_dir/README   # added with history and has local modifications
D     stuff/fish.c       # this file is scheduled for deletion
A     stuff/loot/bloo.h  # this file is scheduled for addition
C     stuff/loot/lump.c  # this file has conflicts from an update
S     stuff/squawk       # this file or dir has been switched to a branch
...
```

In this output format svn status prints five columns of characters, followed by several whitespace characters, followed by a file or directory name. The first column tells the status of a file or directory and/or its contents. The codes printed here are as follows:

A file_or_dir

The file or directory *file_or_dir* has been scheduled for addition into the repository.

C file

file_or_dir is in a state of conflict. That is, changes received from the server during an update overlap with local changes that you have in your working copy. You must resolve this conflict before committing your changes to the repository.

D file_or_dir

> The file or directory *file_or_dir* has been scheduled for deletion from the repository.

M file

> The contents of file *file* have been modified.

X dir

> The directory *dir* is unversioned, but is related to a Subversion externals definition. To find out more about externals definitions, see "Externals Definitions" in Chapter 7."

? file_or_dir

> The file or directory *file_or_dir* is not under version control. You can silence the question marks by either passing the --quiet (-q) switch to svn status, or by setting the svn:ignore property on the parent directory. For more information on ignored files, see "svn:ignore."

! file_or_dir

> The file or directory *file_or_dir* is under version control but is missing or somehow incomplete. The item can be missing if it's removed using a non-Subversion command. In the case of a directory, it can be incomplete if you happened to interrupt a checkout or update. A quick svn update will refetch the file or directory from the repository, or svn revert file will restore a missing file.

~ file_or_dir

> The file or directory *file_or_dir* is in the repository as one kind of object, but what's actually in your working copy is some other kind. For example, Subversion might have a file in the repository, but you removed the file and created a directory in its place, without using the svn delete or svn add commands.

The second column tells the status of a file or directory's properties (see "Properties" in Chapter 7" for more information on properties). If an M appears in the second column, then the properties have been modified, otherwise a whitespace will be printed.

The third column only shows whitespace or an L, which means that Subversion has locked the item in the *.svn* working area. You see an L if you run svn status in a directory where an svn commit is in progress—perhaps when you are editing the log message. If Subversion is not running, then presumably Subversion was interrupted and the lock needs to be cleaned up by running svn cleanup (more about that later in this chapter).

The fourth column only shows a + or whitespace, which means that the file or directory is scheduled to be added or modified with additional attached history. This typically happens when you svn move or svn copy a file or directory. If you see A +, this means the item is scheduled for addition-with-history. It could be a file or the root of a copied directory. + means the item is part of a subtree scheduled for addition-with-history, i.e., some parent was copied, and it's just coming along for the ride. M +

means the item is part of a subtree scheduled for addition-with-history, and it has local modifications. When you commit, first the parent is added-with-history (copied), which means this file automatically exists in the copy. Then the local modifications are uploaded into the copy.

The fifth column only shows an S or whitespace. This signifies that the file or directory has been switched from the path of the rest of the working copy (using svn switch) to a branch.

If you pass a specific path to svn status, it gives you information about that item alone:

```
$ svn status stuff/fish.c
D       stuff/fish.c
```

svn status also has a --verbose (-v) switch, which will show you the status of every item in your working copy, even if it has not been changed:

```
$ svn status --verbose
M       44      23      sally   README
        44      30      sally   INSTALL
M       44      20      harry   bar.c
        44      18      ira     stuff
        44      35      harry   stuff/trout.c
D       44      19      ira     stuff/fish.c
        44      21      sally   stuff/things
A       0       ?       ?       stuff/things/bloo.h
        44      36      harry   stuff/things/gloo.c
```

This is the long form output of svn status. The first column remains the same, but the second column shows the working revision of the item. The third and fourth columns show the revision in which the item last changed, and who changed it.

None of the previously mentioned invocations to svn status contact the repository; they work only locally by comparing the metadata in the .svn directory with the working copy. Finally, there is the --show-updates (-u) switch, which contacts the repository and adds information about things that are out-of-date:

```
$ svn status --show-updates --verbose
M       *       44      23      sally   README
M               44      20      harry   bar.c
        *       44      35      harry   stuff/trout.c
D               44      19      ira     stuff/fish.c
A               0       ?       ?       stuff/things/bloo.h
Status against revision:    46
```

Notice the two asterisks: if you were to run svn update at this point, you would receive changes to *README* and *trout.c*. This tells you some very useful information—you'll need to update and get the server changes on *README* before you commit, or the repository will reject your commit for being out-of-date. (More on this subject later.)

svn diff

Another way to examine your changes is with the svn diff command. You can find out *exactly* how you've modified things by running svn diff with no arguments, which prints out file changes in unified diff format:[*]

```
$ svn diff
Index: bar.c
===============================================================
===
--- bar.c       (revision 3)
+++ bar.c       (working copy)
@@ -1,7 +1,12 @@
+#include <sys/types.h>
+#include <sys/stat.h>
+#include <unistd.h>
+
+#include <stdio.h>

 int main(void) {
-  printf("Sixty-four slices of American Cheese...\n");
+  printf("Sixty-five slices of American Cheese...\n");
 return 0;
 }

Index: README
===============================================================
===
--- README      (revision 3)
+++ README      (working copy)
@@ -193,3 +193,4 @@
+Note to self:  pick up laundry.

Index: stuff/fish.c
===============================================================
===
--- stuff/fish.c        (revision 1)
+++ stuff/fish.c        (working copy)
-Welcome to the file known as 'fish'.
-Information on fish will be here soon.

Index: stuff/things/bloo.h
===============================================================
===
--- stuff/things/bloo.h         (revision 8)
+++ stuff/things/bloo.h         (working copy)
+Here is a new file to describe
+things about bloo.
```

----

[*] Subversion uses its internal diff engine, which produces unified diff format, by default. If you want diff output in a different format, specify an external diff program using --diff-cmd and pass any flags you'd like to it using the --extensions switch. For example, to see local differences in file *foo.c* in context output format while ignoring whitespace changes, you might run svn diff --diff-cmd /usr/bin/diff --extensions '-bc' foo.c.

The svn diff command produces this output by comparing your working files against the cached pristine copies within the *.svn* area. Files scheduled for addition are displayed as all added-text, and files scheduled for deletion are displayed as all deleted text.

Output is displayed in *unified diff format*. That is, removed lines are prefaced with a - and added lines are prefaced with a +. the svn diff command also prints filename and offset information useful to the patch program, so you can generate patches by redirecting the diff output to a file:

```
$ svn diff > patchfile
```

For example, you could email the patchfile to another developer for review or testing prior to commit.

svn revert

Now suppose you see the previous diff output, and realize that your changes to *README* are a mistake; perhaps you accidentally typed that text into the wrong file in your editor.

This is a perfect opportunity to use svn revert.

```
$ svn revert README
Reverted 'README'
```

Subversion reverts the file to its pre-modified state by overwriting it with the cached pristine copy from the *.svn* area. But also note that svn revert can undo *any* scheduled operations—for example, you might decide that you don't want to add a new file after all:

```
$ svn status foo
?       foo

$ svn add foo
A       foo

$ svn revert foo
Reverted 'foo'

$ svn status foo
?       foo
```

 svn revert *ITEM* has exactly the same effect as deleting *ITEM* from your working copy and then running svn update -r BASE *ITEM*. However, if you're reverting a file, svn revert has one very noticeable difference—it doesn't have to communicate with the repository to restore your file.

Or perhaps you mistakenly removed a file from version control:

```
$ svn status README
        README
```

```
$ svn delete README
D           README

$ svn revert README
Reverted 'README'

$ svn status README
        README
```

Resolve Conflicts (Merging Others' Changes)

We've already seen how svn status -u can predict conflicts. Suppose you run svn update and some interesting things occur:

```
$ svn update
U  INSTALL
G  README
C  bar.c
Updated to revision 46.
```

The U and G codes are no cause for concern; those files cleanly absorbed changes from the repository. The files marked with U contained no local changes but were Updated with changes from the repository. The G stands for merGed, which means that the file had local changes to begin with, but the changes coming from the repository didn't overlap in any way.

But the C stands for conflict. This means that the changes from the server overlapped with your own, and now you have to manually choose between them.

Whenever a conflict occurs, three things occur to assist you in noticing and resolving that conflict:

- Subversion prints a C during the update, and remembers that the file is in a state of conflict.

- Subversion places *conflict markers*—special strings of text which delimit the sides of the conflict—into the file to visibly demonstrate the overlapping areas.

- For every conflicted file, Subversion places three extra files in your working copy:

filename.mine
> This is your file as it existed in your working copy before you updated your working copy—that is, without conflict markers. This file has your latest changes in it and nothing else.

filename.rOLDREV
> This is the file that was the BASE revision before you updated your working copy. That is, the file that you checked out before you made your latest edits.

---

filename.rNEWREV

> This is the file that your Subversion client just received from the server when you updated your working copy. This file corresponds to the HEAD revision of the repository.

> Here OLDREV is the revision number of the file in your *.svn* directory and NEWREV is the revision number of the repository HEAD.

For example, Sally makes changes to the file *sandwich.txt* in the repository. Harry has just changed the file in his working copy and checked it in. Sally updates her working copy before checking in and she gets a conflict:

```
$ svn update
C  sandwich.txt
Updated to revision 2.
$ ls -1
sandwich.txt
sandwich.txt.mine
sandwich.txt.r1
sandwich.txt.r2
```

At this point, Subversion will *not* allow you to commit the file *sandwich.txt* until the three temporary files are removed.

```
$ svn commit --message "Add a few more things"
svn: Commit failed (details follow):
svn: Aborting commit: '/home/sally/svn-work/sandwich.txt' remains in conflict
```

If you get a conflict, you need to do one of three things:

- Merge the conflicted text by hand (by examining and editing the conflict markers within the file).
- Copy one of the temporary files on top of your working file.
- Run svn revert <filename> to throw away all of your local changes.

Once you've resolved the conflict, you need to let Subversion know by running svn resolved. This removes the three temporary files and Subversion no longer considers the file to be in a state of conflict.[*]

```
$ svn resolved sandwich.txt
Resolved conflicted state of 'sandwich.txt'
```

Merging conflicts by hand

Merging conflicts by hand can be quite intimidating the first time you attempt it, but with a little practice, it can become as easy as falling off a bike.

---

[*] You can always remove the temporary files yourself, but would you really want to do that when Subversion can do it for you?

Here's an example. Due to a miscommunication, you and Sally, your collaborator, both edit the file sandwich.txt at the same time. Sally commits her changes, and when you go to update your working copy, you get a conflict and are going to have to edit *sandwich.txt* to resolve the conflicts. First, let's take a look at the file:

```
$ cat sandwich.txt
Top piece of bread
Mayonnaise
Lettuce
Tomato
Provolone
<<<<<<< .mine
Salami
Mortadella
Prosciutto
=======
Sauerkraut
Grilled Chicken
>>>>>>> .r2
Creole Mustard
Bottom piece of bread
```

The strings of less-than signs, equal signs, and greater-than signs are conflict markers, and are not part of the actual data in conflict. You generally want to ensure that those are removed from the file before your next commit. The text between the first two sets of markers is composed of the changes you made in the conflicting area:

```
<<<<<<< .mine
Salami
Mortadella
Prosciutto
=======
```

The text between the second and third sets of conflict markers is the text from Sally's commit:

```
=======
Sauerkraut
Grilled Chicken
>>>>>>> .r2
```

Usually you won't want to just delete the conflict markers and Sally's changes—she's going to be awfully surprised when the sandwich arrives and it's not what she wanted. So this is where you pick up the phone or walk across the office and explain to Sally that you can't get sauerkraut from an Italian deli.* Once you've agreed on the changes you will check in, edit your file and remove the conflict markers.

```
Top piece of bread
Mayonnaise
Lettuce
```

---

* And if you ask them for it, they may very well ride you out of town on a rail.

```
Tomato
Provolone
Salami
Mortadella
Prosciutto
Creole Mustard
Bottom piece of bread
```

Now run svn resolved, and you're ready to commit your changes:

```
$ svn resolved sandwich.txt
$ svn commit -m "Go ahead and use my sandwich, discarding Sally's edits."
```

Remember, if you ever get confused while editing the conflicted file, you can always consult the three files that Subversion creates for you in your working copy—including your file as it was before you updated. You can even use a third-party interactive merging tool to examine those three files.

Copying a file onto your working file

If you get a conflict and decide that you want to throw out your changes, you can merely copy one of the temporary files created by Subversion over the file in your working copy:

```
$ svn update
C  sandwich.txt
Updated to revision 2.
$ ls sandwich.*
sandwich.txt  sandwich.txt.mine  sandwich.txt.r2  sandwich.txt.r1
$ cp sandwich.txt.r2 sandwich.txt
$ svn resolved sandwich.txt
```

Punting: Using svn revert

If you get a conflict, and upon examination decide that you want to throw out your changes and start your edits again, just revert your changes:

```
$ svn revert sandwich.txt
Reverted 'sandwich.txt'
$ ls sandwich.*
sandwich.txt
```

Note that when you revert a conflicted file, you don't have to run svn resolved.

Now you're ready to check in your changes. Note that svn resolved, unlike most of the other commands we've dealt with in this chapter, requires an argument. In any case, you want to be careful and only run svn resolved when you're certain that you've fixed the conflict in your file—once the temporary files are removed, Subversion will let you commit the file even if it still contains conflict markers.

Commit Your Changes

Finally! Your edits are finished, you've merged all changes from the server, and you're ready to commit your changes to the repository.

The svn commit command sends all of your changes to the repository. When you commit a change, you need to supply a *log message*, describing your change. Your log message will be attached to the new revision you create. If your log message is brief, you may wish to supply it on the command line using the --message (or -m) option:

```
$ svn commit --message "Corrected number of cheese slices."
Sending        sandwich.txt
Transmitting file data .
Committed revision 3.
```

However, if you've been composing your log message as you work, you may want to tell Subversion to get the message from a file by passing the filename with the --file switch:

```
$ svn commit --file logmsg
Sending        sandwich
Transmitting file data .
Committed revision 4.
```

If you fail to specify either the --message or --file switch, then Subversion will automatically launch your favorite editor (as defined in the environment variable $EDITOR) for composing a log message.

 If you're in your editor writing a commit message and decide that you want to cancel your commit, you can just quit your editor without saving changes. If you've already saved your commit message, simply delete the text and save again.

```
$ svn commit
Waiting for Emacs...Done
Log message unchanged or not specified
a)bort, c)ontinue, e)dit
a
$
```

The repository doesn't know or care if your changes make any sense as a whole; it only checks to make sure that nobody else has changed any of the same files that you did when you weren't looking. If somebody *has* done that, the entire commit will fail with a message informing you that one or more of your files is out-of-date:

```
$ svn commit --message "Add another rule"
Sending        rules.txt
svn: Commit failed (details follow):
svn: Out of date: 'rules.txt' in transaction 'g'
```

At this point, you need to run svn update, deal with any merges or conflicts that result, and attempt your commit again.

That covers the basic work cycle for using Subversion. There are many other features in Subversion that you can use to manage your repository and working copy, but you can get by quite easily using only the commands that we've discussed so far in this chapter.

Examining History

As we mentioned earlier, the repository is like a time machine. It keeps a record of every change ever committed, and allows you to explore this history by examining previous versions of files and directories, as well as the metadata that accompanies them. With a single Subversion command, you can check out the repository (or restore an existing working copy) exactly as it was at any date or revision number in the past. However, sometimes you just want to "peer into" the past instead of "going into" the past.

There are several commands that can provide you with historical data from the repository:

svn log
> Shows you broad information: log messages attached to revisions, and which paths changed in each revision.

svn diff
> Shows you the specific details of how a file changed over time.

svn cat
> Used to retrieve any file as it existed in a particular revision number and display it on your screen.

svn list
> Displays the files in a directory for any given revision.

svn log

To find out information about the history of a file or directory, use the svn log command. svn log will provide you with a record of who made changes to a file or directory, at what revision it changed, the time and date of that revision, and, if it was provided, the log message that accompanied the commit.

```
$ svn log
------------------------------------------------------------------------
r3 | sally | Mon, 15 Jul 2002 18:03:46 -0500 | 1 line

Added include lines and corrected # of cheese slices.
```

```
-----------------------------------------------------------------
r2 | harry | Mon, 15 Jul 2002 17:47:57 -0500 | 1 line

Added main( ) methods.
-----------------------------------------------------------------
r1 | sally | Mon, 15 Jul 2002 17:40:08 -0500 | 1 line

Initial import
-----------------------------------------------------------------
```

Note that the log messages are printed in *reverse chronological order* by default. If you wish to see a different range of revisions in a particular order, or just a single revision, use the --revision (-r) switch:

```
$ svn log --revision 5:19    # shows logs 5 through 19 in chronological order

$ svn log -r 19:5            # shows logs 5 through 19 in reverse order

$ svn log -r 8              # shows log for revision 8
```

You can also examine the log history of a single file or directory. For example:

```
$ svn log foo.c
...
$ svn log http://foo.com/svn/trunk/code/foo.c
...
```

These display log messages *only* for those revisions in which the working file (or URL) changed.

If you want even more information about a file or directory, svn log also takes a --verbose (-v) switch. Because Subversion allows you to move and copy files and directories, it is important to be able to track path changes in the filesystem, so in verbose mode, svn log will include a list of changed paths in a revision in its output:

```
$ svn log -r 8 -v
-----------------------------------------------------------------
r8 | sally | 2002-07-14 08:15:29 -0500 | 1 line
Changed paths:
U /trunk/code/foo.c
U /trunk/code/bar.h
A /trunk/code/doc/README

Frozzled the sub-space winch.

-----------------------------------------------------------------
```

svn diff

We've already seen svn diff before—it displays file differences in unified diff format, and it was used to show the local modifications made to our working copy before committing to the repository.

In fact, it turns out that there are *three* distinct uses of svn diff:

- Examine local changes
- Compare your working copy to the repository
- Compare repository to repository

Examining local changes

As we've seen, invoking svn diff with no switches will compare your working files to the cached pristine copies in the *.svn* area:

```
$ svn diff
Index: rules.txt
===================================================================
--- rules.txt       (revision 3)
+++ rules.txt       (working copy)
@@ -1,4 +1,5 @@
 Be kind to others
 Freedom = Responsibility
 Everything in moderation
-Chew with your mouth open
+Chew with your mouth closed
+Listen when others are speaking
$
```

Comparing working copy to repository

If a single --revision (-r) number is passed, then your working copy is compared to the specified revision in the repository.

```
$ svn diff --revision 3 rules.txt
Index: rules.txt
================================================================
===
--- rules.txt        (revision 3)
+++ rules.txt        (working copy)
@@ -1,4 +1,5 @@
 Be kind to others
 Freedom = Responsibility
 Everything in moderation
-Chew with your mouth open
+Chew with your mouth closed
+Listen when others are speaking
$
```

Comparing repository to repository

If two revision numbers, separated by a colon, are passed via --revision (-r), then
the two revisions are directly compared.

```
$ svn diff --revision 2:3 rules.txt
Index: rules.txt
================================================================
===
--- rules.txt        (revision 2)
+++ rules.txt        (revision 3)
@@ -1,4 +1,4 @@
 Be kind to others
-Freedom = Chocolate Ice Cream
+Freedom = Responsibility
 Everything in moderation
 Chew with your mouth closed
$
```

Not only can you use svn diff to compare files in your working copy to the repository, but if you supply a URL argument, you can examine the differences between
items in the repository without even having a working copy. This is especially useful
if you wish to inspect changes in a file when you don't have a working copy on your
local machine:

```
$ svn diff --revision 4:5 http://svn.red-bean.com/repos/example/trunk/text/rules.txt
...
$
```

svn cat

If you want to examine an earlier version of a file and not necessarily the differences
between two files, you can use svn cat:

```
$ svn cat --revision 2 rules.txt
Be kind to others
Freedom = Chocolate Ice Cream
```

```
Everything in moderation
Chew with your mouth closed
$
```

You can also redirect the output directly into a file:

```
$ svn cat --revision 2 rules.txt > rules.txt.v2
$
```

You're probably wondering why we don't just use svn update --revision to update the file to the older revision. There are a few reasons why we might prefer to use svn cat.

First, you may want to see the differences between two revisions of a file using an external diff program (perhaps a graphical one, or perhaps your file is in such a format that the output of unified diff is nonsensical). In this case, you'll need to grab a copy of the old revision, redirect it to a file, and pass both that and the file in your working copy to your external diff program.

Sometimes it's easier to look at an older version of a file in its entirety as opposed to only the differences between it and another revision.

svn list

The svn list command shows you what files are in a repository directory without actually downloading the files to your local machine:

```
$ svn list http://svn.collab.net/repos/svn
README
branches/
clients/
tags/
trunk/
```

If you want a more detailed listing, pass the --verbose (-v) flag to get output like this:

```
$ svn list --verbose http://svn.collab.net/repos/svn
    2755 harry        1331 Jul 28 02:07 README
    2773 sally             Jul 29 15:07 branches/
    2769 sally             Jul 29 12:07 clients/
    2698 harry             Jul 24 18:07 tags/
    2785 sally             Jul 29 19:07 trunk/
```

The columns tell you the revision at which the file or directory was last modified, the user who modified it, the size (if it is a file), the date it was last modified, and the item's name.

A Final Word on History

In addition to all of the previous commands, you can use svn update and svn checkout with the --revision switch to take an entire working copy back in time. (See? We told you that Subversion was a time machine.)

```
$ svn checkout --revision 1729 # Checks out a new working copy at r1729
...
$ svn update --revision 1729 # Updates an existing working copy to r1729
...
```

Other Useful Commands

While not as frequently used as the commands previously discussed in this chapter, you occasionally need the following commands.

svn cleanup

When Subversion modifies your working copy (or any information within .*svn*), it tries to do so as safely as possible. Before changing anything, it writes its intentions to a log file, executes the commands in the log file, then removes the log file (this is similar in design to a journaled filesystem). If a Subversion operation is interrupted (if the process is killed, or if the machine crashes, for example), the log files remain on disk. By re-executing the log files, Subversion can complete the previously started operation, and your working copy can get itself back into a consistent state.

And this is exactly what svn cleanup does: it searches your working copy and runs any leftover logs, removing locks in the process. If Subversion ever tells you that some part of your working copy is locked, then this is the command that you should run. Also, svn status will display an L next to locked items:

```
$ svn status
  L      somedir
M        somedir/foo.c

$ svn cleanup
$ svn status
M        somedir/foo.c
```

svn import

The svn import command is a quick way to copy an unversioned tree of files into a repository, creating intermediate directories as necessary.

```
$ svnadmin create /usr/local/svn/newrepos
$ svn import mytree file:///usr/local/svn/newrepos/some/project
Adding         mytree/foo.c
Adding         mytree/bar.c
Adding         mytree/subdir
Adding         mytree/subdir/quux.h

Committed revision 1.
```

The previous example copied the contents of directory *mytree* under the directory *some/project* in the repository:

```
$ svn ls file:///usr/local/svn/newrepos/some/project
bar.c
foo.c
subdir/
```

Summary

At this point, we've covered most of the Subversion client commands. Notable exceptions are those dealing with branching and merging (see Chapter 4) and properties (see "Properties" in Chapter 7"). However, you may want to take a moment to skim through Chapter 9 to get an idea of all the many different commands that Subversion has—and how you can use them to make your work easier.

Branching and Merging

Branching, tagging, and merging are concepts common to almost all version control systems. If you're not familiar with these ideas, we provide a good introduction in this chapter. If you are familiar with them, then hopefully you'll find it interesting to see how Subversion implements these ideas.

Branching is a fundamental part of version control. If you're going to allow Subversion to manage your data, this is a feature you'll eventually come to depend on. This chapter assumes that you're already familiar with Subversion's basic concepts (Chapter 2).

What's a Branch?

Suppose it's your job to maintain a document for a division in your company, a handbook of some sort. One day a different division asks you for the same handbook, but with a few parts "tweaked" for them, since they do things slightly differently.

What do you do in this situation? You do the obvious thing: you make a second copy of your document, and begin maintaining the two copies separately. As each department asks you to make small changes, you incorporate them into one copy or the other.

You often want to make the same change to both copies. For example, if you discover a typo in the first copy, it's very likely that the same typo exists in the second copy. The two documents are almost the same, after all; they only differ in small, specific ways.

This is the basic concept of a *branch*—namely, a line of development that exists independently of another line, yet still shares a common history if you look far enough back in time. A branch always begins life as a copy of something, and moves on from there, generating its own history (see Figure 4-1).

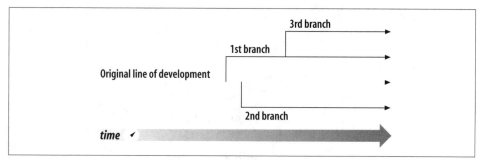

Figure 4-1. Branches of development

Subversion has commands to help you maintain parallel branches of your files and directories. It allows you to create branches by copying your data, and remembers that the copies are related to one another. It also helps you duplicate changes from one branch to another. Finally, it can make portions of your working copy reflect different branches, so that you can mix and match different lines of development in your daily work.

Using Branches

At this point, you should understand how each commit creates an entire new filesystem tree (called a revision) in the repository. If not, go back and read about revisions in "Revisions" in Chapter 2.

For this chapter, we'll go back to the same example from Chapter 2. Remember that you and your collaborator, Sally, are sharing a repository that contains two projects, *paint* and *calc*. Notice, however, that in Figure 4-2 each project directory now contains subdirectories named *trunk* and *branches*. The reason for this will soon become clear.

As before, assume that Sally and you both have working copies of the calc project. Specifically, you each have a working copy of */calc/trunk*. All the files for the project are in this subdirectory rather than in */calc* itself, because your team has decided that */calc/trunk* is where the main line of development is going to take place.

Let's say that you've been given the task of performing a radical reorganization of the project. It will take a long time to write, and will affect all the files in the project. The problem here is that you don't want to interfere with Sally, who is in the process of fixing small bugs here and there. She's depending on the fact that the latest version of the project (in */calc/trunk*) is always usable. If you start committing your changes bit by bit, you'll surely break things for Sally.

One strategy is to crawl into a hole: you and Sally can stop sharing information for a week or two. That is, start gutting and reorganizing all the files in your working copy, but don't commit or update until you're completely finished with the task.

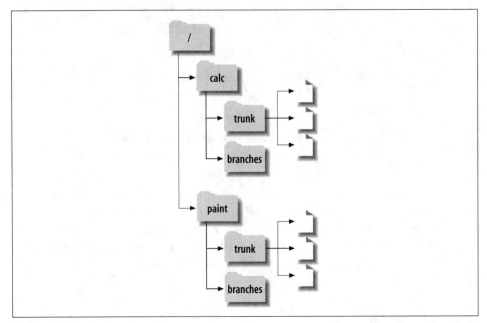

Figure 4-2. Starting repository layout

There are a number of problems with this, though. First, it's not very safe. Most people like to save their work to the repository frequently, should something bad accidentally happen to their working copy. Second, it's not very flexible. If you do your work on different computers (perhaps you have a working copy of */calc/trunk* on two different machines), you'll need to manually copy your changes back and forth, or just do all the work on a single computer. By that same token, it's difficult to share your changes in progress with anyone else. A common software development best practice is to allow your peers to review your work as you go. If nobody sees your intermediate commits, you lose potential feedback. Finally, when you're finished with all your changes, you might find it very difficult to remerge your final work with the rest of the company's main body of code. Sally (or others) may have made many other changes in the repository that are difficult to incorporate into your working copy—especially if you run svn update after weeks of isolation.

The better solution is to create your own branch, or line of development, in the repository. This allows you to save your half-broken work frequently without interfering with others, yet you can still selectively share information with your collaborators. You'll see exactly how this works later on.

Creating a Branch

Creating a branch is very simple—you make a copy of the project in the repository using the svn copy command. Subversion is not only able to copy single files, but whole directories as well. In this case, you want to make a copy of the */calc/trunk* directory. Where should the new copy live? Wherever you wish—it's a matter of project policy. Let's say that your team has a policy of creating branches in the */calc/ branches* area of the repository, and you want to name your branch my-calc-branch. You'll want to create a new directory, */calc/branches/my-calc-branch*, which begins its life as a copy of */calc/trunk*.

There are two different ways to make a copy. We'll demonstrate the messy way first, just to make the concept clear. To begin, check out a working copy of the project's root directory, */calc*:

```
$ svn checkout http://svn.example.com/repos/calc bigwc
A  bigwc/trunk/
A  bigwc/trunk/Makefile
A  bigwc/trunk/integer.c
A  bigwc/trunk/button.c
A  bigwc/branches/
Checked out revision 340.
```

Making a copy is now simply a matter of passing two working-copy paths to the svn copy command:

```
$ cd bigwc
$ svn copy trunk/ branches/my-calc-branch
$ svn status
A  +   branches/my-calc-branch
```

In this case, the svn copy command recursively copies the *trunk/* working directory to a new working directory, *branches/my-calc-branch*. As you can see from the svn status command, the new directory is now scheduled for addition to the repository. But also notice the + sign next to the letter A. This indicates that the scheduled addition is a *copy* of something, not something new. When you commit your changes, Subversion will create */calc/branches/my-calc-branch* in the repository by copying */calc/trunk*, rather than resending all of the working copy data over the network:

```
$ svn commit -m "Creating a private branch of /calc/trunk."
Adding         branches/my-calc-branch
Committed revision 341.
```

What follows is the easier method of creating a branch, which we should have told you in the first place: svn copy is able to operate directly on two URLs.

```
$ svn copy http://svn.example.com/repos/calc/trunk \
           http://svn.example.com/repos/calc/branches/my-calc-branch \
      -m "Creating a private branch of /calc/trunk."

Committed revision 341.
```

There's really no difference between these two methods. Both procedures create a new directory in revision 341, and the new directory is a copy of /calc/trunk. This is shown in Figure 4-3. Notice that the second method, however, performs an *immediate* commit. (Subversion does not support cross-repository copying. When using URLs with svn copy or svn move, you can only copy items within the same repository.) It's an easier procedure, because it doesn't require you to check out a large mirror of the repository. In fact, this technique doesn't even require you to have a working copy at all.

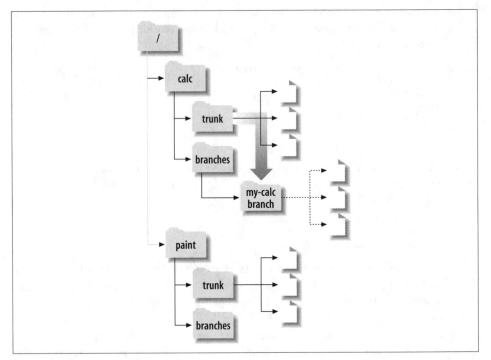

Figure 4-3. Repository with new copy

Working with Your Branch

Now that you've created a branch of the project, you can check out a new working copy to start using it:

```
$ svn checkout http://svn.example.com/repos/calc/branches/my-calc-branch
A  my-calc-branch/Makefile
A  my-calc-branch/integer.c
A  my-calc-branch/button.c
Checked out revision 341.
```

There's nothing special about this working copy; it simply mirrors a different directory in the repository. When you commit changes, however, Sally won't ever see them when she updates. Her working copy is of */calc/trunk*. (Be sure to read "Switching a Working Copy" later in this chapter: the svn switch command is an alternate way of creating a working copy of a branch.)

Cheap Copies

Subversion's repository has a special design. When you copy a directory, you don't need to worry about the repository growing huge—Subversion doesn't actually duplicate any data. Instead, it creates a new directory entry that points to an *existing* tree. If you're a Unix user, this is the same concept as a hard link. From there, the copy is said to be lazy. That is, if you commit a change to one file within the copied directory, then only that file changes—the rest of the files continue to exist as links to the original files in the original directory.

This is why you'll often hear Subversion users talk about cheap copies. It doesn't matter how large the directory is—it takes a very tiny, constant amount of time to make a copy of it. In fact, this feature is the basis of how commits work in Subversion: each revision is a cheap copy of the previous revision, with a few items lazily changed within. (To read more about this, visit Subversion's website and read about the bubble-up method in Subversion's design documents.)

Of course, these internal mechanics of copying and sharing data are hidden from the user, who simply sees copies of trees. The main point here is that copies are cheap, both in time and space. Make branches as often as you want.

Let's pretend that a week goes by, and the following commits happen:

- You make a change to */calc/branches/my-calc-branch/button.c*, which creates revision 342

- You make a change to */calc/branches/my-calc-branch/integer.c*, which creates revision 343

- Sally makes a change to */calc/trunk/integer.c*, which creates revision 344

Figure 4-4 shows that there are now two independent lines of development happening on *integer.c.*:

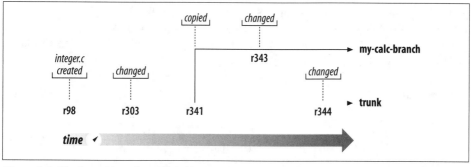

Figure 4-4. The branching of one file's history

Things get interesting when you look at the history of changes made to your copy of *integer.c*:

```
$ pwd
/home/user/my-calc-branch

$ svn log --verbose integer.c
------------------------------------------------------------------------
r343 | user | 2002-11-07 15:27:56 -0600 (Thu, 07 Nov 2002) | 2 lines
Changed paths:
    M /calc/branches/my-calc-branch/integer.c

* integer.c:  frozzled the wazjub.

------------------------------------------------------------------------
r341 | user | 2002-11-03 15:27:56 -0600 (Thu, 07 Nov 2002) | 2 lines
Changed paths:
    A /calc/branches/my-calc-branch (from /calc/trunk:340)

Creating a private branch of /calc/trunk.

------------------------------------------------------------------------
r303 | sally | 2002-10-29 21:14:35 -0600 (Tue, 29 Oct 2002) | 2 lines
Changed paths:
    M /calc/trunk/integer.c

* integer.c:  changed a docstring.

------------------------------------------------------------------------
r98 | sally | 2002-02-22 15:35:29 -0600 (Fri, 22 Feb 2002) | 2 lines
Changed paths:
    M /calc/trunk/integer.c

* integer.c:  adding this file to the project.

------------------------------------------------------------------------
```

Notice that Subversion is tracing the history of your branch's *integer.c* all the way back through time, even traversing the point where it was copied. It shows the creation of the branch as an event in the history, because *integer.c* was implicitly copied when all of */calc/trunk/* was copied. Observe what happens when Sally runs the same command on her copy of the file:

```
$ pwd
/home/sally/calc

$ svn log --verbose integer.c
------------------------------------------------------------------------
r344 | sally | 2002-11-07 15:27:56 -0600 (Thu, 07 Nov 2002) | 2 lines
Changed paths:
    M /calc/trunk/integer.c

* integer.c:  fix a bunch of spelling errors.
```

```
-----------------------------------------------------------------------
r303 | sally | 2002-10-29 21:14:35 -0600 (Tue, 29 Oct 2002) | 2 lines
Changed paths:
   M /calc/trunk/integer.c

* integer.c:  changed a docstring.

-----------------------------------------------------------------------
r98 | sally | 2002-02-22 15:35:29 -0600 (Fri, 22 Feb 2002) | 2 lines
Changed paths:
   M /calc/trunk/integer.c

* integer.c:  adding this file to the project.

-----------------------------------------------------------------------
```

Sally sees her own revision 344 change, but not the change you made in revision 343. As far as Subversion is concerned, these two commits affected different files in different repository locations. However, Subversion *does* show that the two files share a common history. Before the branch-copy was made in revision 341, they used to be the same file. That's why you and Sally both see the changes made in revisions 303 and 98.

The Key Concepts Behind Branches

The two important lessons that you should remember from this section are as follows.

1. Unlike many other version control systems, Subversion's branches exist as *normal filesystem directories* in the repository, not in an extra dimension. These directories just happen to carry some extra historical information.

2. Subversion has no internal concept of a branch—only copies. When you copy a directory, the resulting directory is only a branch because *you* attach that meaning to it. You may think of the directory differently, or treat it differently, but to Subversion it's just an ordinary directory that happens to have been created by copying.

Copying Changes Between Branches

Now you and Sally are working on parallel branches of the project: you're working on a private branch, and Sally is working on the *trunk*, or main line of development.

For projects that have a large number of contributors, it's common for most people to have working copies of the trunk. Whenever someone needs to make a long-running change that is likely to disrupt the trunk, a standard procedure is to create a private branch and commit changes there until all the work is complete.

So, the good news is that you and Sally aren't interfering with each other. The bad news is that it's very easy to drift *too* far apart. Remember that one of the problems with the crawl-in-a-hole strategy is that by the time you're finished with your branch, it may be near impossible to merge your changes back into the trunk without a huge number of conflicts.

Instead, you and Sally might continue to share changes as you work. It's up to you to decide which changes are worth sharing; Subversion gives you the ability to selectively copy changes between branches. And when you're completely finished with your branch, your entire set of branch changes can be copied back into the trunk.

Copying Specific Changes

In the previous section, we mentioned that both you and Sally made changes to *integer.c* on different branches. If you look at Sally's log message for revision 344, you can see that she fixed some spelling errors. No doubt, your copy of the same file still has the same spelling errors. It's likely that your future changes to this file will be affecting the same areas that have the spelling errors, so you're in for some potential conflicts when you merge your branch someday. It's better, then, to receive Sally's change now, *before* you start working too heavily in the same places.

It's time to use the svn merge command. This command, it turns out, is a very close cousin to the svn diff command (which you read about in Chapter 3). Both commands are able to compare any two objects in the repository and describe the differences. For example, you can ask svn diff to show you the exact change made by Sally in revision 344:

```
$ svn diff -r 343:344 http://svn.example.com/repos/calc/trunk

Index: integer.c
================================================================
===
--- integer.c       (revision 343)
+++ integer.c       (revision 344)
@@ -147,7 +147,7 @@
    case 6:  sprintf(info->operating_system, "HPFS (OS/2 or NT)"); break;
    case 7:  sprintf(info->operating_system, "Macintosh"); break;
    case 8:  sprintf(info->operating_system, "Z-System"); break;
-    case 9:  sprintf(info->operating_system, "CPM"); break;
+    case 9:  sprintf(info->operating_system, "CP/M"); break;
    case 10: sprintf(info->operating_system, "TOPS-20"); break;
    case 11: sprintf(info->operating_system, "NTFS (Windows NT)"); break;
    case 12: sprintf(info->operating_system, "QDOS"); break;
@@ -164,7 +164,7 @@
    low = (unsigned short) read_byte(gzfile);  /* read LSB */
    high = (unsigned short) read_byte(gzfile); /* read MSB */
    high = high << 8;  /* interpret MSB correctly */
-    total = low + high; /* add them togethe for correct total */
+    total = low + high; /* add them together for correct total */

    info->extra_header = (unsigned char *) my_malloc(total);
    fread(info->extra_header, total, 1, gzfile);
```

```
@@ -241,7 +241,7 @@
     Store the offset with ftell() ! */

   if ((info->data_offset = ftell(gzfile))== -1) {
-    printf("error: ftell() retturned -1.\n");
+    printf("error: ftell() returned -1.\n");
     exit(1);
   }

@@ -249,7 +249,7 @@
   printf("I believe start of compressed data is %u\n", info->data_offset);
   #endif

-  /* Set postion eight bytes from the end of the file. */
+  /* Set position eight bytes from the end of the file. */

   if (fseek(gzfile, -8, SEEK_END)) {
     printf("error: fseek() returned non-zero\n");
```

The svn merge is almost exactly the same. Instead of printing the differences to your terminal, however, it applies them directly to your working copy as *local modifications*:

```
$ svn merge -r 343:344 http://svn.example.com/repos/calc/trunk
U   integer.c

$ svn status
M   integer.c
```

The output of svn merge shows that your copy of *integer.c* was patched. It now contains Sally's change—the change has been copied from the trunk to your working copy of your private branch, and now exists as a local modification. At this point, it's up to you to review the local modification and make sure it works correctly.

In another scenario, it's possible that things may not have gone so well, and that *integer.c* may have entered a conflicted state. You might need to resolve the conflict using standard procedures (see Chapter 3), or if you decide that the merge was a bad idea altogether, simply give up and svn revert the local change.

But assuming that you've reviewed the merged change, you can svn commit the change as usual. At that point, the change has been merged into your repository branch. In version control terminology, this act of copying changes between branches is commonly called *porting* changes.

When you commit the local modification, make sure your log message mentions that you're porting a specific change from one branch to another. For example:

```
$ svn commit -m "integer.c: ported r344 (spelling fixes) from trunk."
Sending        integer.c
Transmitting file data .
Committed revision 360.
```

As you'll see in the next sections, this is a very important best practice to follow.

Why Not Use Patches Instead?

A question may be on your mind, especially if you're a Unix user: why bother to use svn merge at all? Why not simply use the operating system's patch command to accomplish the same job? For example:

```
$ svn diff -r 343:344 http://svn.example.com/repos/calc/trunk > patchfile
$ patch -p0 < patchfile
Patching file integer.c using Plan A...
Hunk #1 succeeded at 147.
Hunk #2 succeeded at 164.
Hunk #3 succeeded at 241.
Hunk #4 succeeded at 249.
done
```

In this particular case, yes, there really is no difference. But svn merge has special abilities that surpass the patch program. The file format used by patch is quite limited; it's only able to tweak file contents. There's no way to represent changes to *trees*, such as the addition, removal, or renaming of files and directories. If Sally's change had, for instance, added a new directory, the output of svn diff wouldn't have mentioned it at all. svn diff only outputs the limited patch-format, so there are some ideas it simply can't express.[a] The svn merge command, however, can express tree changes by directly applying them to your working copy.

a. *In the future, the Subversion project plans to use (or invent) an expanded patch format that describes tree-changes.*

A word of warning: while svn diff and svn merge are very similar in concept, they do have different syntax in many cases. Be sure to read about them in Chapter 8 for details, or ask svn help. For example, svn merge requires a working-copy path as a target, i.e., a place where it should apply the tree-changes. If the target isn't specified, it assumes you are trying to perform one of the following common operations:

1. You want to merge directory changes into your current working directory.
2. You want to merge the changes in a specific file into a file by the same name that exists in your current working directory.

If you are merging a directory and haven't specified a target path, svn merge assumes the first case and tries to apply the changes into your current directory. If you are merging a file, and that file (or a file by the same name) exists in your current working directory, svn merge assumes the second case and tries to apply the changes to a local file with the same name.

If you want changes applied somewhere else, you need to say so explicitly. For example, if you're sitting in the parent directory of your working copy, you have to specify the target directory to receive the changes:

```
$ svn merge -r 343:344 http://svn.example.com/repos/calc/trunk my-calc-branch
U   my-calc-branch/integer.c
```

Best Practices for Merging

Merging changes sounds simple enough, but in practice it can become a headache. The problem is that if you repeatedly merge changes from one branch to another, you might accidentally merge the same change *twice*. When this happens, sometimes things will work fine. When patching a file, Subversion typically notices if the file already has the change, and does nothing. But if the already existing change has been modified in any way, you'll get a conflict.

Ideally, your version control system should prevent the double application of changes to a branch. It should automatically remember which changes a branch has already received, and be able to list them for you. It should use this information to help automate merges as much as possible.

Unfortunately, Subversion is not such a system. Like CVS, Subversion 1.0 does not yet record any information about merge operations. When you commit local modifications, the repository has no idea whether those changes came from running svn merge, or from just hand-editing the files.

Tracking merges manually

What does this mean to you, the user? It means that until the day Subversion grows this feature, you'll have to track merge information yourself. The best place to do this is in the commit log-message. As demonstrated in the earlier example, it's recommended that your log-message mention a specific revision number (or range of revisions) that are being merged into your branch. Later on, you can run svn log to review which changes your branch already contains. This lets you carefully construct a subsequent svn merge command that won't be redundant with previously ported changes.

In the next section, we show some examples of this merge tracking technique in action.

Previewing merges

Because merging only results in local modifications, it's not usually a high-risk operation. If you get the merge wrong the first time, simply svn revert the changes and try again.

It's possible, however, that your working copy might already have local modifications. The changes applied by a merge will be mixed with your preexisting ones, and running svn revert is no longer an option. The two sets of changes may be impossible to separate.

In cases such as this, people take comfort in being able to predict or examine merges before they happen. One simple way to do that is to run svn diff with the same arguments you plan to pass to svn merge, as we already showed in our first example of merging. Another method of previewing is to pass the --dry-run option to the merge command:

```
$ svn merge --dry-run -r 343:344 http://svn.example.com/repos/calc/trunk
U  integer.c

$ svn status
#  nothing printed, working copy is still unchanged.
```

The --dry-run option doesn't actually apply any local changes to the working copy. It only shows status codes that would be printed in a real merge. It's useful for getting a high-level preview of the potential merge, for those times when running svn diff gives too much detail.

Noticing or Ignoring Ancestry

When conversing with a Subversion developer, you might very likely hear reference to the term *ancestry*. This word is used to describe the relationship between two objects in a repository: if they're related to each other, than one object is said to be an ancestor of the other.

For example, suppose you commit revision 100, which includes a change to a file *foo.c*. Then *foo.c@99* is an ancestor of *foo.c@100*. On the other hand, suppose you commit the deletion of *foo.c* in revision 101, and then add a new file by the same name in revision 102. In this case, *foo.c@99* and *foo.c@102* may appear to be related (they have the same path), but in fact are completely different objects in the repository. They share no history or ancestry.

The reason for bringing this up is to point out an important difference between svn diff and svn merge. The former command ignores ancestry, while the latter command is quite sensitive to it. For example, if you asked svn diff to compare revisions 99 and 102 of *foo.c*, you would see line-based diffs; the diff command is blindly comparing two paths. But if you asked svn merge to compare the same two objects, it would notice that they're unrelated and first attempt to delete the old file, then add the new file; you would see a D foo.c followed by a A foo.c.

Most merges involve comparing trees that are ancestrally related to one another, and therefore svn merge defaults to this behavior. Occasionally, however, you may want the merge command to compare two unrelated trees. For example, you may have imported two source-code trees representing different vendor releases of a software project (see "Vendor Branches" in Chapter 7). If you asked svn merge to compare the two trees, you'd see the entire first tree being deleted, followed by an add of the entire second tree!

In these situations, you'll want svn merge to do a path-based comparison only, ignoring any relations between files and directories. Add the --ignore-ancestry option to your merge command, and it will behave just like svn diff. (And conversely, the --notice-ancestry option will cause svn diff to behave like the merge command.)

Common Use-Cases for Merging

There are many different uses for svn merge, and this section describes the most common scenarios.

Merging a Whole Branch to Another

To complete our running example, we'll move forward in time. Suppose several days have passed, and many changes have happened on both the trunk and your private branch. Suppose that you've finished working on your private branch; the feature or bug fix is finally complete, and now you want to merge all of your branch changes back into the trunk for others to enjoy.

So how do we use svn merge in this scenario? Remember that this command compares two trees, and applies the differences to a working copy. So to receive the changes, you need to have a working copy of the trunk. We'll assume that either you still have your original one lying around (fully updated), or that you recently checked out a fresh working copy of */calc/trunk*.

But which two trees should be compared? At first glance, the answer may seem obvious: just compare the latest trunk tree with your latest branch tree. But beware—this assumption is *wrong*, and has burned many a new user! Since svn merge operates like svn diff, comparing the latest trunk and branch trees will *not* merely describe the set of changes you made to your branch. Such a comparison shows too many changes: it would not only show the addition of your branch changes, but also the *removal* of trunk changes that never happened on your branch.

To express only the changes that happened on your branch, you need to compare the initial state of your branch to its final state. Using svn log on your branch, you can see that your branch was created in revision 341. And the final state of your branch is simply a matter of using the HEAD revision. That means you want to compare revisions 341 and HEAD of your branch directory, and apply those differences to a working copy of the trunk.

A nice way of finding the revision in which a branch was created (the "base" of the branch) is to use the -stop-on-copy option to svn log. The log subcommand normally shows every change ever made to the branch, including tracing back through the copy which created the branch—so, normally, you'll see history from the trunk as well. The -stop-on-copy halts log output as soon as svn log detects that its target was copied or renamed.

So in our continuing example:

```
$ svn log --verbose --stop-on-copy
       http://svn.example.com/repos/calc/branches/my-calc-
branch

...

------------------------------------------------------------
-----------

r341 | user | 2002-11-03 15:27:56 -0600 (Thu, 07 Nov 2002) |
2 lines
Changed paths:
  A /calc/branches/my-calc-branch (from /calc/trunk:340)
$
```

As expected, the final revision printed by this command is the revision in which *my-calc-branch* was created by copying.

Here's the final merging procedure, then:

```
$ cd calc/trunk
$ svn update
At revision 405.

$ svn merge -r 341:HEAD http://svn.example.com/repos/calc/branches/my-calc-branch
U    integer.c
U    button.c
U    Makefile

$ svn status
M    integer.c
M    button.c
M    Makefile

# ...examine the diffs, compile, test, etc...

$ svn commit -m "Merged my-calc-branch changes r341:405 into the trunk."
Sending        integer.c
Sending        button.c
Sending        Makefile
Transmitting file data ...
Committed revision 406.
```

Again, notice that the commit log message very specifically mentions the range of changes that was merged into the trunk. Always remember to do this, because it's critical information you'll need later on.

For example, suppose you decide to keep working on your branch for another week, in order to complete an enhancement to your original feature or bug fix. The repository's HEAD revision is now 480, and you're ready to do another merge from your private branch to the trunk. But as discussed earlier in this chapter, "Best Practices for Merging," you don't want to merge the changes you've already merged before; you only want to merge everything new on your branch since the last time you merged. The trick is to figure out what's new.

The first step is to run svn log on the trunk, and look for a log message about the last time you merged from the branch:

```
$ cd calc/trunk
$ svn log
...
------------------------------------------------------------------------
r406 | user | 2004-02-08 11:17:26 -0600 (Sun, 08 Feb 2004) | 1 line

Merged my-calc-branch changes r341:405 into the trunk.
------------------------------------------------------------------------
...
```

Aha! Since all branch changes that happened between revisions 341 and 405 were previously merged to the trunk as revision 406, you now know that you want to merge only the branch changes after that—revisions 406 through HEAD.

```
$ cd calc/trunk
$ svn update
At revision 480.
# We notice that HEAD is currently 480, so we use it to do the merge:
$ svn merge -r 406:480 http://svn.example.com/repos/calc/branches/my-calc-branch
U integer.c
U button.c
U Makefile

$ svn commit -m "Merged my-calc-branch changes r406:480 into the trunk."
Sending        integer.c
Sending        button.c
Sending        Makefile
Transmitting file data ...
Committed revision 481.
```

Now the trunk contains the complete second wave of changes made to the branch. At this point, you can either delete your branch (we discuss this later on), or continue working on your branch and repeat this procedure for subsequent merges.

Undoing Changes

Another common use for svn merge is to roll back a change that has already been committed. Suppose you're working away happily on a working copy of */calc/trunk*, and you discover that the change made way back in revision 303, which changed *integer.c*, is completely wrong. It never should have been committed. You can use svn merge to undo the change in your working copy, and then commit the local modification to the repository. All you need to do is to specify a *reverse* difference:

```
$ svn merge -r 303:302 http://svn.example.com/repos/calc/trunk
U  integer.c

$ svn status
M  integer.c

$ svn diff
...
# verify that the change is removed
...

$ svn commit -m "Undoing change committed in r303."
Sending        integer.c
Transmitting file data .
Committed revision 350.
```

One way to think about a repository revision is as a specific group of changes (some version control systems call these *changesets*). By using the -r switch, you can ask svn merge to apply a changeset, or whole range of changesets, to your working copy. In our case of undoing a change, we're asking svn merge to apply changeset 303 to our working copy *backwards*.

Keep in mind that rolling back a change like this is just like any other svn merge operation, so you should use svn status and svn diff to confirm that your work is in the state you want it to be in, and then use svn commit to send the final version to the repository. After committing, this particular changeset is no longer reflected in the HEAD revision.

Again, you may be thinking: well, that really didn't undo the commit, did it? The change still exists in revision 303. If somebody checks out a version of the *calc* project between revisions 303 and 349, they'll still see the bad change, right?

Yes, that's true. When we talk about removing a change, we're really talking about removing it from HEAD. The original change still exists in the repository's history. For most situations, this is good enough. Most people are only interested in tracking the HEAD of a project anyway. There are special cases, however, where you really might want to destroy all evidence of the commit. (Perhaps somebody accidentally committed a confidential document.) This isn't so easy, it turns out, because Subversion was deliberately designed to never lose information. Revisions are immutable trees which build upon one another. Removing a revision from history would cause a domino effect, creating chaos in all subsequent revisions and possibly invalidating all working copies.[*]

Resurrecting Deleted Items

The great thing about version control systems is that information is never lost. Even when you delete a file or directory, it may be gone from the HEAD revision, but the object still exists in earlier revisions. One of the most common questions new users ask is, how do I get my old file or directory back?

The first step is to define exactly which item you're trying to resurrect. Here's a useful metaphor: you can think of every object in the repository as existing in a sort of two-dimensional coordinate system. The first coordinate is a particular revision tree, and the second coordinate is a path within that tree. So every version of your file or directory can be defined by a specific coordinate pair.

Subversion has no *Attic* directory as CVS does,[†] so you need to use svn log to discover the exact coordinate pair you wish to resurrect. A good strategy is to run svn log --verbose in a directory which used to contain your deleted item. The --verbose option shows a list of all changed items in each revision; all you need to do is find the revision in which you deleted the file or directory. You can do this visually, or by using another tool to examine the log output (via grep, or perhaps via an incremental search in an editor.)

```
$ cd parent-dir
$ svn log --verbose
...
------------------------------------------------------------------------
r808 | joe | 2003-12-26 14:29:40 -0600 (Fri, 26 Dec 2003) | 3 lines
Changed paths:
   D /calc/trunk/real.c
   M /calc/trunk/integer.c

Added fast fourier transform functions to integer.c.
Removed real.c because code now in double.c.
...
```

In the example, we're assuming that you're looking for a deleted file *real.c*. By looking through the logs of a parent directory, you've spotted that this file was deleted in revision 808. Therefore, the last version of the file to exist was in the revision right before that. Conclusion: you want to resurrect the path */calc/trunk/real.c* from revision 807.

---

[*] The Subversion project has plans, however, to someday implement an svnadmin obliterate command that would accomplish the task of permanently deleting information. In the meantime, see "svndumpfilter" for a possible workaround.

[†] Because CVS doesn't version trees, it creates an *Attic* area within each repository directory as a way of remembering deleted files.

That was the hard part—the research. Now that you know what you want to restore, you have two different choices.

One option is to use svn merge to apply revision 808 in reverse. (We've already discussed how to undo changes; see "Undoing Changes" earlier in this chapter.) This would have the effect of re-adding *real.c* as a local modification. The file would be scheduled for addition, and after a commit, the file would again exist in HEAD.

In this particular example, however, this is probably not the best strategy. Reverse-applying revision 808 would not only schedule *real.c* for addition, but the log message indicates that it would also undo certain changes to *integer.c*, which you don't want. Certainly, you could reverse-merge revision 808 and then svn revert the local modifications to *integer.c*, but this technique doesn't scale well. What if there were 90 files changed in revision 808?

A second, more targeted strategy is not to use svn merge at all, but rather the svn copy command. Simply copy the exact revision and path coordinate pair from the repository to your working copy:

```
$ svn copy --revision 807 \
           http://svn.example.com/repos/calc/trunk/real.c ./real.c

$ svn status
A  +   real.c

$ svn commit -m "Resurrected real.c from revision 807, /calc/trunk/real.c."
Adding         real.c
Transmitting file data .
Committed revision 1390.
```

The plus sign in the status output indicates that the item isn't merely scheduled for addition, but scheduled for addition with history. Subversion remembers where it was copied from. In the future, running svn log on this file will traverse back through the file's resurrection and through all the history it had prior to revision 807. In other words, this new *real.c* isn't really new; it's a direct descendant of the original, deleted file.

Although our example shows us resurrecting a file, note that these same techniques work just as well for resurrecting deleted directories.

Switching a Working Copy

The svn switch command transforms an existing working copy into a different branch. While this command isn't strictly necessary for working with branches, it provides a nice shortcut to users. In an earlier example, after creating your private branch, you checked out a fresh working copy of the new repository directory. Instead, you can simply ask Subversion to change your working copy of */calc/trunk* to mirror the new branch location:

```
$ cd calc

$ svn info | grep URL
URL: http://svn.example.com/repos/calc/trunk

$ svn switch http://svn.example.com/repos/calc/branches/my-calc-branch
U    integer.c
U    button.c
U    Makefile
Updated to revision 341.

$ svn info | grep URL
URL: http://svn.example.com/repos/calc/branches/my-calc-branch
```

After switching to the branch, your working copy is no different than what you would get from doing a fresh checkout of the directory. And it's usually more efficient to use this command, because often branches only differ by a small degree. The server sends only the minimal set of changes necessary to make your working copy reflect the branch directory.

The svn switch command also takes a --revision (-r) option, so you need not always move your working copy to the tip of the branch.

Of course, most projects are more complicated than our *calc* example, containing multiple subdirectories. Subversion users often follow a specific algorithm when using branches:

1. Copy the project's entire trunk to a new branch directory.
2. Switch only part of the trunk's working copy to mirror the branch.

In other words, if users know that the branch-work only needs to happen on a specific subdirectory, they use svn switch to move only that subdirectory to the branch. (Sometimes users will switch just a single working file to the branch!) That way, they can continue to receive normal trunk updates to most of their working copy, but the switched portions will remain immune (unless someone commits a change to their branch). This feature adds a whole new dimension to the concept of a mixed working copy—not only can working copies contain a mixture of working revisions, but a mixture of repository locations as well.

If your working copy contains a number of switched subtrees from different repository locations, it continues to function as normal. When you update, you'll receive patches to each subtree as appropriate. When you commit, your local changes will still be applied as a single, atomic change to the repository.

Note that while it's OK for your working copy to reflect a mixture of repository locations, these locations must all be within the *same* repository. Subversion repositories aren't yet able to communicate with one another; that's a feature planned beyond Subversion 1.0.*

Switches and Updates

Have you noticed that the output of svn switch and svn update look the same? The switch command is actually a superset of the update command.

When you run svn update, you're asking the repository to compare two trees. The repository does so, and then sends a description of the differences back to the client. The only difference between svn switch and svn update is that the update command always compares two identical paths.

That is, if your working copy is a mirror of */calc/trunk*, then svn update will automatically compare your working copy of */calc/trunk* to */calc/trunk* in the HEAD revision. If you're switching your working copy to a branch, then svn switch will compare your working copy of */calc/trunk* to some *other* branch-directory in the HEAD revision.

In other words, an update moves your working copy through time. A switch moves your working copy through time *and* space.

Because svn switch is essentially a variant of svn update, it shares the same behaviors; any local modifications in your working copy are preserved when new data arrives from the repository. This allows you to perform all sorts of clever tricks.

For example, suppose you have a working copy of */calc/trunk* and make a number of changes to it. Then you suddenly realize that you meant to make the changes to a branch instead. No problem! When you svn switch your working copy to the branch, the local changes will remain. You can then test and commit them to the branch.

Tags

Another common version control concept is a *tag*. A tag is just a snapshot of a project in time. In Subversion, this idea already seems to be everywhere. Each repository revision is exactly that—a snapshot of the filesystem after each commit.

However, people often want to give more human-friendly names to tags, like release-1.0. And they want to make snapshots of smaller subdirectories of the filesystem. After all, it's not so easy to remember that release-1.0 of a piece of software is a particular subdirectory of revision 4822.

---

* You *can*, however, use svn switch with the --relocate switch if the URL of your server changes and you don't want to abandon an existing working copy. See the svn switch section in Chapter 9 for more information and an example.

Creating a Simple Tag

Once again, svn copy comes to the rescue. If you want to create a snapshot of */calc/ trunk* exactly as it looks in the HEAD revision, then make a copy of it:

```
$ svn copy http://svn.example.com/repos/calc/trunk \
           http://svn.example.com/repos/calc/tags/release-1.0 \
      -m "Tagging the 1.0 release of the 'calc' project."

Committed revision 351.
```

This example assumes that a */calc/tags* directory already exists. After the copy completes, the new *release-1.0* directory is forever a snapshot of how the project looked in the HEAD revision at the time you made the copy. Of course you might want to be more precise about exactly which revision you copy, in case somebody else may have committed changes to the project when you weren't looking. So if you know that revision 350 of */calc/trunk* is exactly the snapshot you want, you can specify it by passing -r 350 to the svn copy command.

But wait a moment: isn't this tag creation procedure the same procedure we used to create a branch? Yes, in fact, it is. In Subversion, there's no difference between a tag and a branch. Both are just ordinary directories that are created by copying. Just as with branches, the only reason a copied directory is a tag is because *humans* have decided to treat it that way: as long as nobody ever commits to the directory, it forever remains a snapshot. If people start committing to it, it becomes a branch.

If you are administering a repository, there are two approaches you can take to managing tags. The first approach is hands-off: as a matter of project policy, decide where your tags will live, and make sure all users know how to treat the directories they copy in there. (That is, make sure they know not to commit to them.) The second approach is more paranoid: you can use one of the access-control scripts provided with Subversion to prevent anyone from doing anything but creating new copies in the tags area (See Chapter 6.) The paranoid approach, however, isn't usually necessary. If a user accidentally commits a change to a tag directory, you can simply undo the change as discussed in the previous section. This is version control, after all.

Creating a Complex Tag

Sometimes you may want your snapshot to be more complicated than a single directory at a single revision.

For example, pretend your project is much larger than our *calc* example: suppose it contains a number of subdirectories and many more files. In the course of your work, you may decide that you need to create a working copy that is designed to have specific features and bug fixes. You can accomplish this by selectively backdating files or directories to particular revisions (using svn update -r liberally), or by switching files and directories to particular branches (making use of svn switch). When you're done, your working copy is a hodgepodge of repository locations from different revisions. But after testing, you know it's the precise combination of data you need.

Time to make a snapshot. Copying one URL to another won't work here. In this case, you want to make a snapshot of your exact working copy arrangement and store it in the repository. Luckily, svn copy actually has four different uses (which you can read about in Chapter 9), including the ability to copy a working-copy tree to the repository:

```
$ ls
./   ../   my-working-copy/

$ svn copy my-working-copy http://svn.example.com/repos/calc/tags/mytag

Committed revision 352.
```

Now there is a new directory in the repository, */calc/tags/mytag*, which is an exact snapshot of your working copy—mixed revisions, URLs, and all.

Other users have found interesting uses for this feature. Sometimes there are situations where you have a bunch of local changes made to your working copy, and you'd like a collaborator to see them. Instead of running svn diff and sending a patchfile (which won't capture tree changes), you can instead use svn copy to upload your working copy to a private area of the repository. Your collaborator can then either check out a verbatim copy of your working copy, or use svn merge to receive your exact changes.

Branch Maintenance

You may have noticed by now that Subversion is extremely flexible. Because it implements branches and tags with the same underlying mechanism (directory copies), and because branches and tags appear in normal filesystem space, many people find Subversion intimidating. It's almost *too* flexible. In this section, we'll offer some suggestions for arranging and managing your data over time.

Repository Layout

There are some standard, recommended ways to organize a repository. Most people create a *trunk* directory to hold the main line of development, a *branches* directory to contain branch copies, and a *tags* directory to contain tag copies. If a repository holds only one project, then often people create these top-level directories:

```
/trunk
/branches
/tags
```

If a repository contains multiple projects, admins typically index their layout by project (see "Choosing a Repository Layout" in Chapter 5 to read more about project roots):

```
/paint/trunk
/paint/branches
/paint/tags
/calc/trunk
/calc/branches
/calc/tags
```

Of course, you're free to ignore these common layouts. You can create any sort of variation, whatever works best for you or your team. Remember that whatever you choose, it's not a permanent commitment. You can reorganize your repository at any time. Because branches and tags are ordinary directories, the svn move command can move or rename them however you wish. Switching from one layout to another is just a matter of issuing a series of server-side moves; if you don't like the way things are organized in the repository, just juggle the directories around.

Remember, though, that while moving directories may be easy to do, you need to be considerate of your users as well. Your juggling can be disorienting to users with existing working copies. If a user has a working copy of a particular repository directory, your svn move operation might remove the path from the latest revision. When the user next runs svn update, they'll be told that their working copy represents a path that no longer exists, and the user will be forced to svn switch to the new location.

Data Lifetimes

Another nice feature of Subversion's model is that branches and tags can have finite lifetimes, just like any other versioned item. For example, suppose you eventually finish all your work on your personal branch of the *calc* project. After merging all of your changes back into */calc/trunk*, there's no need for your private branch directory to stick around anymore:

```
$ svn delete http://svn.example.com/repos/calc/branches/my-calc-branch \
      -m "Removing obsolete branch of calc project."

Committed revision 375.
```

And now your branch is gone. Of course it's not really gone: the directory is simply missing from the HEAD revision, no longer distracting anyone. If you use svn checkout, svn switch, or svn list to examine an earlier revision, you'll still be able to see your old branch.

If browsing your deleted directory isn't enough, you can always bring it back. Resurrecting data is very easy in Subversion. If there's a deleted directory (or file) that you'd like to bring back into HEAD, simply use svn copy -r to copy it from the old revision:

```
$ svn copy -r 374 http://svn.example.com/repos/calc/branches/my-calc-branch \
                http://svn.example.com/repos/calc/branches/my-calc-branch

Committed revision 376.
```

In our example, your personal branch had a relatively short lifetime: you may have created it to fix a bug or implement a new feature. When your task is done, so is the branch. In software development, though, it's also common to have two main branches running side-by-side for very long periods. For example, suppose it's time to release a stable *calc* project to the public, and you know it's going to take a couple of months to shake bugs out of the software. You don't want people to add new features to the project, but you don't want to tell all developers to stop programming either. So instead, you create a stable branch of the software that won't change much:

```
$ svn copy http://svn.example.com/repos/calc/trunk \
        http://svn.example.com/repos/calc/branches/stable-1.0 \
        -m "Creating stable branch of calc project."

Committed revision 377.
```

And now developers are free to continue adding cutting-edge (or experimental) features to */calc/trunk*, and you can declare a project policy that only bug fixes are to be committed to */calc/branches/stable-1.0*. That is, as people continue to work on the trunk, a human selectively ports bug fixes over to the stable branch. Even after the stable branch has shipped, you'll probably continue to maintain the branch for a long time—that is, as long as you continue to support that release for customers.

Summary

We covered a lot of ground in this chapter. We discussed the concepts of tags and branches, and demonstrated how Subversion implements these concepts by copying directories with the svn copy command. We showed how to use svn merge to copy changes from one branch to another, or for rolling back bad changes. We went over the use of svn switch to create mixed-location working copies. And we talked about how one might manage the organization and lifetimes of branches in a repository.

Remember the Subversion mantra: branches and tags are cheap—use them liberally!

## CHAPTER 5

Repository Administration

The Subversion repository is the central storehouse of versioned data for any number of projects. As such, it becomes an obvious candidate for all the love and attention an administrator can offer. While the repository is generally a low-maintenance item, it is important to understand how to properly configure and care for it, so that potential problems are avoided and actual problems are safely resolved.

In this chapter, we discuss how to create and configure a Subversion repository, and how to expose that repository for network accessibility. We also talk about repository maintenance, including the use of the `svnlook` and `svnadmin` tools (which are provided with Subversion). We address some common questions and mistakes, and give some suggestions on how to arrange the data in the repository.

If you plan to access a Subversion repository only in the role of a user whose data is under version control (that is, via a Subversion client), you can skip this chapter altogether. However, if you are, or wish to become, a Subversion repository administrator,* you should definitely pay attention to this chapter.

Repository Basics

Before jumping into the broader topic of repository administration, let's further define what a repository is. How does it look? How does it feel? Does it take its tea hot or iced, or sweetened and with lemon? As an administrator, you'll be expected to understand the composition of a repository both from a logical perspective—dealing with how data is represented inside the repository--and from a physical nuts-and-bolts perspective—how a repository looks and acts with respect to non-Subversion tools. The following section covers some of these basic concepts at a very high level.

---

* This may sound really prestigious and lofty, but we're just talking about anyone who is interested in that mysterious realm beyond the working copy where everyone's data hangs out.

Understanding Transactions and Revisions

Conceptually speaking, a Subversion repository is a sequence of directory trees. Each tree is a snapshot of how the files and directories versioned in your repository looked at some point in time. These snapshots are created as a result of client operations, and are called revisions.

Every revision begins life as a transaction tree. When doing a commit, a client builds a Subversion transaction that mirrors their local changes (plus any additional changes that might have been made to the repository since the beginning of the client's commit process), and then instructs the repository to store that tree as the next snapshot in the sequence. If the commit succeeds, the transaction is effectively promoted into a new revision tree, and is assigned a new revision number. If the commit fails for some reason, the transaction is destroyed and the client is informed of the failure.

Updates work in a similar way. The client builds a temporary transaction tree that mirrors the state of the working copy. The repository then compares that transaction tree with the revision tree at the requested revision (usually the most recent, or youngest tree), and sends back information that informs the client about what changes are needed to transform their working copy into a replica of that revision tree. After the update completes, the temporary transaction is deleted.

The use of transaction trees is the only way to make permanent changes to a repository's versioned filesystem. However, it's important to understand that the lifetime of a transaction is completely flexible. In the case of updates, transactions are temporary trees that are immediately destroyed. In the case of commits, transactions are transformed into permanent revisions (or removed if the commit fails). In the case of an error or bug, it's possible that a transaction can be accidentally left lying around in the repository (not really affecting anything, but still taking up space).

In theory, someday whole workflow applications might revolve around more fine-grained control of transaction lifetime. It is feasible to imagine a system whereby each transaction slated to become a revision is left in stasis well after the client finishes describing its changes to repository. This would enable each new commit to be reviewed by someone else, perhaps a manager or engineering QA team, who can choose to promote the transaction into a revision, or abort it.

Unversioned Properties

Transactions and revisions in the Subversion repository can have properties attached to them. These properties are generic key-to-value mappings, and are generally used to store information about the tree to which they are attached. The names and values of these properties are stored in the repository's filesystem, along with the rest of your tree data.

Revision and transaction properties are useful for associating information with a tree that is not strictly related to the files and directories in that tree—the kind of information that isn't managed by client working copies. For example, when a new commit transaction is created in the repository, Subversion adds a property to that transaction named svn:date—a datestamp representing the time that the transaction was created. By the time the commit process is finished, and the transaction is promoted to a permanent revision, the tree has also been given a property to store the username of the revision's author (svn:author) and a property to store the log message attached to that revision (svn:log).

Revision and transaction properties are *unversioned properties*—as they are modified, their previous values are permanently discarded. Also, while revision trees themselves are immutable, the properties attached to those trees are not. You can add, remove, and modify revision properties at any time in the future. If you commit a new revision and later realize that you had some misinformation or spelling error in your log message, you can simply replace the value of the svn:log property with a new, corrected log message.

Berkeley DB

The data housed within Subversion repositories actually lives inside a database, specifically a Berkeley DB Data Store. When the initial design phase of Subversion was in progress, the developers decided to use Berkeley DB for a variety of reasons, including its open-source license, transaction support, reliability, performance, API simplicity, thread-safety, support for cursors, and so on.

Berkeley DB provides real transaction support—perhaps its most powerful feature. Multiple processes accessing your Subversion repositories don't have to worry about accidentally clobbering each other's data. The isolation provided by the transaction system is such that for any given operation, the Subversion repository code sees a static view of the database—not a database that is constantly changing at the hand of some other process—and can make decisions based on that view. If the decision made happens to conflict with what another process is doing, the entire operation is rolled back as if it never happened, and Subversion gracefully retries the operation against a new, updated (and yet still static) view of the database.

Another great feature of Berkeley DB is *hot backups*—the ability to back up the database environment without taking it offline. We'll discuss how to back up your repository in "Repository Backup," later in this chapter, but the benefits of being able to make fully functional copies of your repositories without any downtime should be obvious.

Berkeley DB is also a very reliable database system. Subversion uses Berkeley DB's logging facilities, which means that the database first writes to on-disk logfiles a description of any modifications it is about to make, and then makes the modification itself. This is to ensure that if anything goes wrong, the database system can back up to a previous *checkpoint*—a location in the logfiles known not to be corrupt—and replay transactions until the data is restored to a usable state. See "Managing Disk Space" later in this chapter for more about Berkeley DB logfiles.

But every rose has its thorn, and so we must note some known limitations of Berkeley DB. First, Berkeley DB environments are not portable. You cannot simply copy a Subversion repository that was created on a Unix system onto a Windows system and expect it to work. While much of the Berkeley DB database format is architecture independent, there are other aspects of the environment that are not. Secondly, Subversion uses Berkeley DB in a way that will not operate on Windows 95/98 systems—if you need to house a repository on a Windows machine, stick with Windows 2000 or Windows XP. Finally, you should never keep a Subversion repository on a network share. While Berkeley DB promises to behave correctly on network shares that meet a particular set of specifications, almost no known shares actually meet all those specifications.

Repository Creation and Configuration

Creating a Subversion repository is an incredibly simple task. The svnadmin utility, provided with Subversion, has a subcommand for doing just that. To create a new repository, run:

```
$ svnadmin create path/to/repos
```

This creates a new repository in the directory *path/to/repos*. This new repository begins life at revision 0, which is defined to consist of nothing but the top-level root (/) filesystem directory. Initially, revision 0 also has a single revision property, svn: date, set to the time at which the repository was created.

Do not create your repository on a network share—it *cannot* exist on a remote filesystem such as NFS, AFS, or Windows SMB. Berkeley DB requires that the underlying filesystem implement strict POSIX locking semantics, and, more importantly, the ability to map files directly into process memory. Almost no network filesystems provide these features. If you attempt to use Berkeley DB on a network share, the results are unpredictable—you may see mysterious errors right away, or it may be months before you discover that your repository database is subtly corrupted.

If you need multiple computers to access the repository, you should set up a server process (such as Apache or svnserve), store the repository on a local filesystem that the server can access, and make the repository available over a network. Chapter 6 covers this process in detail.

You may have noticed that the path argument to svnadmin was just a regular filesystem path and not a URL like the svn client program uses when referring to repositories. Both svnadmin and svnlook are considered server-side utilities—they are used on the machine where the repository resides to examine or modify aspects of the repository, and are in fact unable to perform tasks across a network. A common mistake made by Subversion newcomers is trying to pass URLs (even local file: ones) to these two programs.

After you've run the svnadmin create command, you have a shiny new Subversion repository in its own directory. Let's take a peek at what is actually created inside that subdirectory:

```
$ ls repos
conf/  dav/  db/  format  hooks/  locks/  README.txt
```

With the exception of the *README.txt* and *format* files, the repository directory is a collection of subdirectories. As in other areas of the Subversion design, modularity is given high regard, and hierarchical organization is preferred to cluttered chaos. Here is a brief description of all of the items you see in your new repository directory:

conf
A directory containing repository configuration files

dav
A directory provided to Apache and mod_dav_svn for their private housekeeping data

db
The main Berkeley DB environment, full of DB tables that comprise the data store for Subversion's filesystem (where all of your versioned data resides)

format
A file whose contents are a single integer value that dictates the version number of the repository layout

hooks
A directory full of hook script templates (and hook scripts themselves, once you've installed some)

locks
A directory for Subversion's repository locking data, used for tracking accessors to the repository

README.txt
A file which merely informs its readers that they are looking at a Subversion repository

In general, you shouldn't tamper with your repository by hand. The svnadmin tool should be sufficient for any changes necessary to your repository, or you can look to third-party tools (such as Berkeley DB's tool suite) for tweaking relevant subsections of the repository. Some exceptions exist, though, and we'll cover those here.

Hook Scripts

A *hook* is a program triggered by some repository event, such as the creation of a new revision or the modification of an unversioned property. Each hook is handed enough information to tell what that event is, what target(s) it's operating on, and the username of the person who triggered the event. Depending on the hook's output or return status, the hook program may continue the action, stop it, or suspend it in some way.

The *hooks* subdirectory is, by default, filled with templates for various repository hooks:

```
$ ls repos/hooks/
post-commit.tmpl         pre-revprop-change.tmpl
post-revprop-change.tmpl start-commit.tmpl
pre-commit.tmpl
```

There is one template for each hook that the Subversion repository implements, and by examining the contents of those template scripts, you can see what triggers each such script to run and what data is passed to that script. Also present in many of these templates are examples of how one might use that script, in conjunction with other Subversion-supplied programs, to perform common useful tasks. To actually install a working hook, you need only place some executable program or script into the *repos/hooks* directory which can be executed as the name (like start-commit or post-commit) of the hook.

On Unix platforms, this means supplying a script or program (which could be a shell script, a Python program, a compiled C binary, or any number of other things) named exactly like the name of the hook. Of course, the template files are present for more than just informational purposes—the easiest way to install a hook on Unix platforms is to simply copy the appropriate template file to a new file that lacks the *.tmpl* extension, customize the hook's contents, and ensure that the script is executable. Windows, however, uses file extensions to determine whether or not a program is executable, so you would need to supply a program whose base name is the name of the hook, and whose extension is one of the special extensions recognized by Windows for executable programs, such as *.exe* or *.com* for programs, and *.bat* for batch files.

Currently there are five hooks implemented by the Subversion repository:

start-commit
> This is run before the commit transaction is even created. It is typically used to decide if the user has commit privileges at all. The repository passes two arguments to this program: the path to the repository and the username which is attempting the commit. If the program returns a non-zero exit value, the commit is stopped before the transaction is even created.

pre-commit

This is run when the transaction is complete, but before it is committed. Typically, this hook is used to protect against commits that are disallowed due to content or location (for example, your site might require that all commits to a certain branch include a ticket number from the bug tracker, or that the incoming log message is non-empty). The repository passes two arguments to this program: the path to the repository, and the name of the transaction being committed. If the program returns a non-zero exit value, the commit is aborted and the transaction is removed.

The Subversion distribution includes some access control scripts (located in the *tools/hook-scripts* directory of the Subversion source tree) that can be called from pre-commit to implement fine-grained access control. At this time, this is the only method by which administrators can implement finer-grained access control beyond what Apache's *httpd.conf* offers. In a future version of Subversion, we plan to implement access control lists (ACLs) directly in the filesystem.

post-commit

This is run after the transaction is committed, and a new revision is created. Most people use this hook to send out descriptive emails about the commit or to make a backup of the repository. The repository passes two arguments to this program: the path to the repository, and the new revision number that was created. The exit code of the program is ignored.

The Subversion distribution includes a commit-email.pl script (located in the *tools/hook-scripts/* directory of the Subversion source tree) that can be used to send email with (and/or append to a log file) a description of a given commit. This mail contains a list of the paths that were changed, the log message attached to the commit, the author and date of the commit, as well as a GNU diff-style display of the changes made to the various versioned files as part of the commit.

Another useful tool provided by Subversion is the hot-backup.py script (located in the *tools/backup/* directory of the Subversion source tree). This script performs hot backups of your Subversion repository (a feature supported by the Berkeley DB database back-end), and can be used to make a per-commit snapshot of your repository for archival or emergency recovery purposes.

pre-revprop-change

Because Subversion's revision properties are not versioned, making modifications to such a property (for example, the svn:log commit message property) will overwrite the previous value of that property forever. Since data can be potentially lost here, Subversion supplies this hook (and its counterpart, *post-revprop-change*) so that repository administrators can keep records of changes to these items using some external means if they so desire. As a precaution against losing unversioned property data, Subversion clients will not be allowed to remotely modify revision properties at all unless this hook is implemented for your repository.

This hook runs just before such a modification is made to the repository. The repository passes four arguments to this hook: the path to the repository, the revision on which the to-be-modified property exists, the authenticated username of the person making the change, and the name of the property itself.

post-revprop-change

As mentioned earlier, this hook is the counterpart of the *pre-revprop-change* hook. In fact, for the sake of paranoia this script will not run unless the *pre-revprop-change* hook exists. When both of these hooks are present, the *post-revprop-change* hook runs just after a revision property has been changed, and is typically used to send an email containing the new value of the changed property. The repository passes four arguments to this hook: the path to the repository, the revision on which the property exists, the authenticated username of the person making the change, and the name of the property itself.

The Subversion distribution includes a `propchange-email.pl` script (located in the *tools/hook-scripts/* directory of the Subversion source tree) that can be used to send email with (and/or append to a log file) the details of a revision property change. This mail contains the revision and name of the changed property, the user who made the change, and the new property value.

Subversion will attempt to execute hooks as the same user who owns the process which is accessing the Subversion repository. In most cases, the repository is being accessed via Apache HTTP server and mod_dav_svn, so this user is the same user that Apache runs as. The hooks themselves will need to be configured with OS-level permissions that allow that user to execute them. Also, this means that any file or programs (including the Subversion repository itself) accessed directly or indirectly by the hook will be accessed as the same user. In other words, be alert to potential permission-related problems that could prevent the hook from performing the tasks you've written it to perform.

Berkeley DB Configuration

A Berkeley DB environment is an encapsulation of one or more databases, log files, region files and configuration files. The Berkeley DB environment has its own set of default configuration values for things like the number of locks allowed to be taken out at any given time, or the maximum size of the journaling log files, etc. Subversion's filesystem code additionally chooses default values for some of the Berkeley DB configuration options. However, sometimes your particular repository, with its unique collection of data and access patterns, might require a different set of configuration option values.

The folks at SleepyCat (the producers of Berkeley DB) understand that different databases have different requirements, and so they have provided a mechanism for overriding at runtime many of the configuration values for the Berkeley DB environment. Berkeley checks for the presence of a file named *DB_CONFIG* in each environment directory, and parses the options found in that file for use with that particular Berkeley environment.

The Berkeley configuration file for your repository is located in the *db* environment directory, at *repos/db/DB_CONFIG*. Subversion itself creates this file when it creates the rest of the repository. The file initially contains some default options, as well as pointers to the Berkeley DB online documentation so you can read about what those options do. Of course, you are free to add any of the supported Berkeley DB options to your *DB_CONFIG* file. Just be aware that while Subversion never attempts to read or interpret the contents of the file, and makes no use of the option settings in it, you'll want to avoid any configuration changes that may cause Berkeley DB to behave in a fashion that is unexpected by the rest of the Subversion code. Also, changes made to *DB_CONFIG* won't take effect until you recover the database environment (using svnadmin recover).

Repository Maintenance

Maintaining a Subversion repository can be a daunting task, mostly due to the complexities inherent in systems that have a database backend. Doing the task well is all about knowing the tools—what they are, when to use them, and how to use them. This section will introduce you to the repository administration tools provided by Subversion, and how to wield them to accomplish tasks such as repository migrations, upgrades, backups and cleanups.

An Administrator's Toolkit

Subversion provides a handful of utilities useful for creating, inspecting, modifying, and repairing your repository. Let's look more closely at each of those tools. Afterward, we'll briefly examine some of the utilities included in the Berkeley DB distribution that provide functionality specific to your repository's database backend that otherwise are not provided by Subversion's own tools.

svnlook

svnlook is a tool provided by Subversion for examining the various revisions and transactions in a repository. No part of this program attempts to change the repository—it's a read-only tool. svnlook is typically used by the repository hooks for reporting the changes that are about to be committed (in the case of the pre-commit hook) or that were just committed (in the case of the post-commit hook) to the repository. A repository administrator may use this tool for diagnostic purposes.

svnlook has a straightforward syntax:

```
$ svnlook help
general usage: svnlook SUBCOMMAND REPOS_PATH [ARGS & OPTIONS ...]
Note: any subcommand which takes the '--revision' and '--transaction'
      options will, if invoked without one of those options, act on
      the repository's youngest revision.
Type "svnlook help <subcommand>" for help on a specific subcommand.
...
```

Nearly every one of svnlook's subcommands can operate on either a revision or a transaction tree, printing information about the tree itself, or how it differs from the previous revision of the repository. You use the --revision and --transaction options to specify which revision or transaction, respectively, to examine. Note that while revision numbers appear as natural numbers, transaction names are alphanumeric strings. Keep in mind that the filesystem only allows browsing of uncommitted transactions (transactions that have not resulted in a new revision). Most repositories will have no such transactions, because transactions are usually either committed (which disqualifies them from viewing) or aborted and removed.

In the absence of both the --revision and --transaction options, svnlook will examine the youngest (or HEAD) revision in the repository. So the following two commands do exactly the same thing when 19 is the youngest revision in the repository located at */path/to/repos*:

```
$ svnlook info /path/to/repos
$ svnlook info /path/to/repos --revision 19
```

The only exception to these rules about subcommands is the svnlook youngest subcommand, which takes no options, and simply prints out the HEAD revision number.

```
$ svnlook youngest /path/to/repos
19
```

Output from svnlook is designed to be both human- and machine-parsable. Take as an example the output of the info subcommand:

```
$ svnlook info path/to/repos
sally
2002-11-04 09:29:13 -0600 (Mon, 04 Nov 2002)
27
Added the usual
Greek tree.
```

The output of the info subcommand is defined as:

1. The author, followed by a newline.

2. The date, followed by a newline.

3. The number of characters in the log message, followed by a newline.

4. The log message itself, followed by a newline.

This output is human-readable, meaning items like the datestamp are displayed using a textual representation instead of something more obscure (such as the number of nanoseconds since the Tasty Freeze guy drove by). But this output is also machine-parsable—because the log message can contain multiple lines and be unbounded in length, svnlook provides the length of that message before the message itself. This allows scripts and other wrappers around this command to make intelligent decisions about the log message, such as how much memory to allocate for the message, or at least how many bytes to skip in the event that this output is not the last bit of data in the stream.

Another common use of svnlook is to actually view the contents of a revision or transaction tree. The svnlook tree command displays the directories and files in the requested tree. If you supply the --show-ids option, it will also show the filesystem node revision IDs for each of those paths (which is generally of more use to developers than to users):

```
$ svnlook tree path/to/repos --show-ids
/ <0.0.1>
 A/ <2.0.1>
  B/ <4.0.1>
   lambda <5.0.1>
   E/ <6.0.1>
    alpha <7.0.1>
    beta <8.0.1>
   F/ <9.0.1>
  mu <3.0.1>
  C/ <a.0.1>
  D/ <b.0.1>
   gamma <c.0.1>
   G/ <d.0.1>
    pi <e.0.1>
    rho <f.0.1>
    tau <g.0.1>
   H/ <h.0.1>
    chi <i.0.1>
    omega <k.0.1>
    psi <j.0.1>
 iota <1.0.1>
```

Once you've seen the layout of directories and files in your tree, you can use commands like svnlook cat, svnlook propget, and svnlook proplist to dig into the details of those files and directories.

svnlook can perform a variety of other queries, displaying subsets of bits of information we've mentioned previously, reporting which paths were modified in a given revision or transaction, showing textual and property differences made to files and directories, and so on. The following is a brief description of the current list of subcommands accepted by svnlook, and the output of those subcommands:

author
> Print the tree's author.

cat
> Print the contents of a file in the tree.

changed
> List all files and directories that changed in the tree.

date
> Print the tree's datestamp.

diff
> Print unified diffs of changed files.

dirs-changed
> List the directories in the tree that were themselves changed, or whose file children were changed.

history
> Display interesting points in the history of a versioned path (places where modifications or copies occurred).

info
> Print the tree's author, datestamp, log message character count, and log message.

log
> Print the tree's log message.

propget
> Print the value of a property on a path in the tree.

proplist
> Print the names and values of properties set on paths in the tree.

tree
> Print the tree listing, optionally revealing the filesystem node revision IDs associated with each path.

uuid
> Print the tree's unique user ID (UUID).

youngest
> Print the youngest revision number.

svnadmin

The svnadmin program is the repository administrator's best friend. Besides providing the ability to create Subversion repositories, this program allows you to perform several maintenance operations on those repositories. The syntax of svnadmin is similar to that of svnlook:

```
$ svnadmin help
general usage: svnadmin SUBCOMMAND REPOS_PATH  [ARGS & OPTIONS ...]
Type "svnadmin help <subcommand>" for help on a specific subcommand.
```

```
Available subcommands:
  create
  deltify
  dump
  help (?, h)
...
```

We already mentioned svnadmin's create subcommand (see "Repository Creation and Configuration" earlier in this chapter). Most of the others we cover in more detail later in this chapter. For now, let's just take a quick glance at what each of the available subcommands offers:

create
> Creates a new Subversion repository.

deltify
> Run over a specified revision range, performing predecessor deltification on the paths changed in those revisions. If no revisions are specified, this command will simply deltify the HEAD revision.

dump
> Dumps the contents of the repository, bounded by a given set of revisions, using a portable dump format.

hotcopy
> Makes a hot copy of a repository. You can run this command at any time and make a safe copy of the repository, regardless of whether other processes are using the repository.

list-dblogs
> Lists the paths of Berkeley DB log files associated with the repository. This list includes all log files—those still in use by Subversion, as well as those no longer in use.

list-unused-dblogs
> Lists the paths of Berkeley DB log files associated with, but no longer used by, the repository. You may safely remove these log files from the repository layout, possibly archiving them for use in the event that you ever need to perform a catastrophic recovery of the repository.

load
> Loads a set of revisions into a repository from a stream of data that uses the same portable dump format generated by the dump subcommand.

lstxns
> List the names of uncommitted Subversion transactions that currently exist in the repository.

recover

> Perform recovery steps on a repository that is in need of such, generally after a fatal error has occurred that prevented a process from cleanly shutting down its communication with the repository.

rmtxns

> Cleanly remove Subversion transactions from the repository (conveniently fed by output from the lstxns subcommand).

setlog

> Replace the current value of the svn:log (commit log message) property on a given revision in the repository with a new value.

verify

> Verify the contents of the repository. This includes, among other things, checksum comparisons of the versioned data stored in the repository.

svndumpfilter

Since Subversion stores everything in an opaque database system, attempting manual tweaks is unwise, if not quite difficult. And once data has been stored in your repository, Subversion generally doesn't really provide an easy way to remove that data.[*] Inevitably, however, there will be times when you would like to manipulate the history of your repository. You might need to strip out all instances of a file that was accidentally added to the repository (and shouldn't be there for whatever reason). Or, perhaps you have multiple projects sharing a single repository, and you decide to split them up into their own repositories. To accomplish tasks such as this, administrators need a more manageable and malleable representation of the data in their repositories—the Subversion repository dump format.

The Subversion repository dump format is a human-readable representation of the changes that you've made to your versioned data over time. You use the svnadmin dump command to generate the dump data, and svnadmin load to populate a new repository with it (see "Migrating a Repository" later in this chapter). The great thing about the human-readability aspect of the dump format is that, if you aren't careless about it, you can manually inspect and modify it. Of course, the downside is that if you have two years' worth of repository activity encapsulated in what is likely to be a very large dumpfile, it could take you a long, long time to manually inspect and modify it.

While it won't be the most commonly used tool at the administrator's disposal, svndumpfilter provides a very particular brand of useful functionality—the ability to quickly and easily modify that dumpfile data by acting as a path-based filter. Simply

---

[*] That, by the way, is a feature, not a bug.

give it either a list of paths you wish to keep, or a list of paths you wish to not keep, then pipe your repository dump data through this filter. The result will be a modified stream of dump data that contains only the versioned paths you (explicitly or implicitly) requested.

The syntax of svndumpfilter is as follows:

```
$ svndumpfilter help
general usage: svndumpfilter SUBCOMMAND [ARGS & OPTIONS ...]
Type "svndumpfilter help <subcommand>" for help on a specific subcommand.

Available subcommands:
   exclude
   include
   help (?, h)
```

There are only two interesting subcommands. They allow you to make the choice between explicit or implicit inclusion of paths in the stream:

exclude
> Filter out a set of paths from the dump data stream

include
> Allow only the requested set of paths to pass through the dump data stream

Let's look a realistic example of how you might use this program. We discuss elsewhere (see "Choosing a Repository Layout" later in this chapter) the process of deciding how to choose a layout for the data in your repositories—using one repository per project or combining them, arranging stuff within your repository, and so on. But sometimes after new revisions start flying in, you rethink your layout and would like to make some changes. A common change is the decision to move multiple projects which are sharing a single repository into a single repository for each project.

Our imaginary repository contains three projects: calc, calendar, and spreadsheet. They have been living side-by-side in a layout like this:

```
/
    calc/
        trunk/
        branches/
        tags/
    calendar/
        trunk/
        branches/
        tags/
    spreadsheet/
        trunk/
        branches/
        tags/
```

To get these three projects into their own repositories, we first make a dumpfile of the whole repository:

```
$ svnadmin dump /path/to/repos > repos-dumpfile
* Dumped revision 0.
* Dumped revision 1.
* Dumped revision 2.
* Dumped revision 3.
...
$
```

Next, run that dumpfile through the filter, each time including only one of our top-level directories, and resulting in three new dumpfiles:

```
$ cat repos-dumpfile | svndumpfilter include calc > calc-dumpfile
...
$ cat repos-dumpfile | svndumpfilter include calendar > cal-dumpfile
...
$ cat repos-dumpfile | svndumpfilter include spreadsheet > ss-dumpfile
...
$
```

At this point, you have to make a decision. Each of your dumpfiles at this point creates a valid repository, but preserves the paths exactly as they were in the original repository. This means that even though you would have a repository solely for your calc project, that repository still has a top-level directory named *calc*. If you want your *trunk*, *tags*, and *branches* directories to live in root of your repository, you might wish to edit your dumpfiles, tweaking the Node-path and Copyfrom-path headers to no longer have that first *calc/* path component. Also, you should remove the section of dump data that creates the *calc* directory. It will look something like:

```
Node-path: calc
Node-action: add
Node-kind: dir
Content-length: 0
```

All that remains now is to create your three new repositories, and load each dumpfile into the right repository:

```
$ svnadmin create calc; svnadmin load calc < calc-dumpfile
<<< Started new transaction, based on original revision 1
     * adding path : Makefile ... done.
     * adding path : button.c ... done.
...
$ svnadmin create calendar; svnadmin load calendar < cal-dumpfile
<<< Started new transaction, based on original revision 1
     * adding path : Makefile ... done.
     * adding path : cal.c ... done.
...
$ svnadmin create spreadsheet; svnadmin load spreadsheet < ss-dumpfile
<<< Started new transaction, based on original revision 1
     * adding path : Makefile ... done.
     * adding path : ss.c ... done.
...
```

```
$
```

Both of svndumpfilter's subcommands accept options for deciding how to deal with
empty revisions. If a given revision contained only changes to paths that were filtered out, that now-empty revision could be considered uninteresting or even
unwanted. So, to give the user control over what to do with those revisions,
svndumpfilter provides the following command-line options:

--drop-empty-revs
> Do not generate empty revisions at all—just omit them.

--renumber-revs
> If empty revisions are dropped (using the --drop-empty-revs option), change the
> revision numbers of the remaining revisions so that there are no gaps in the
> numeric sequence.

--preserve-revprops
> If empty revisions are not dropped, preserve the revision properties (log mes-
> sage, author, date, custom properties, etc.) for those empty revisions. Other-
> wise, empty revisions will only contain the original datestamp, and a generated
> log message that indicates that this revision was emptied by svndumpfilter.

While svndumpfilter can be very useful, and a huge timesaver, there are unfortunately a couple of gotchas. First, this utility is overly sensitive to path semantics. Pay
attention to whether paths in your dumpfile are specified with or without leading
slashes. You should look at the Node-path and Copyfrom-path headers:

```
...
Node-path: spreadsheet/Makefile
...
```

If the paths lack leading slashes, you should not include leading slashes in the paths
you pass to svndumpfilter include and svndumpfilter exclude (and if they do, you
should). Further, if your dumpfile has an inconsistent usage of leading slashes for
some reason,* you should probably normalize those paths to either all have, or all
lack, leading slashes.

Also, copied paths can give you some trouble. Subversion supports copy operations
in the repository, where a new path is created by copying some already existing path.
It is possible that at some point in the lifetime of your repository, you might have
copied a file or directory from some location that svndumpfilter is excluding, to a
location that it is including. In order to make the dump data self-sufficient,
svndumpfilter still needs to show the addition of the new path—including the contents of any files created by the copy—and not represent that addition as a copy from
a source that won't exist in your filtered dump data stream. But, because the Subver-

---

* While svnadmin dump has a consistent leading slash policy—to not include them—other programs that generate dump data might not be so consistent.

sion repository dump format only shows what was changed in each revision, the contents of the copy source might not be readily available. If you suspect that you have any copies of this sort in your repository, you might want to rethink your set of included/excluded paths.

svnshell.py

The Subversion source tree also comes with a shell-like interface to the repository. The svnshell.py Python script (located in *tools/examples/* in the source tree) uses Subversion's language bindings to connect to the repository and filesystem libraries. You must have those language bindings properly compiled and installed for this script to work.

Once started, the program behaves similarly to a shell program, allowing you to browse the various directories in your repository. Initially, you are positioned in the root directory of the HEAD revision of the repository, and presented with a command prompt. You can use the help command at any time to display a list of available commands and what they do:

```
$ svnshell.py /path/to/repos
<rev: 2 />$ help
Available commands:
    cat FILE      : dump the contents of FILE
    cd DIR        : change the current working directory to DIR
    exit          : exit the shell
    ls [PATH]     : list the contents of the current directory
    lstxns        : list the transactions available for browsing
    setrev REV    : set the current revision to browse
    settxn TXN    : set the current transaction to browse
    youngest      : list the youngest browsable revision number
<rev: 2 />$
```

Navigating the directory structure of your repository is done in the same way you would navigate a regular Unix or Windows shell—using the cd command. At all times, the command prompt will show you what revision (prefixed by rev:) or transaction (prefixed by txn:) you are currently examining, and at what path location in that revision or transaction. You can change your current revision or transaction with the setrev and settxn commands, respectively. As in a Unix shell, you can use the ls command to display the contents of the current directory, and you can use the cat command to display the contents of a file (see Example 5-1).

Example 5-1. Using svnshell to navigate the repository

```
<rev: 2 />$ ls
   REV    AUTHOR  NODE-REV-ID    SIZE        DATE NAME
-----------------------------------------------------------------------
     1    sally <    2.0.1>          Nov 15 11:50 A/
     2    harry <    1.0.2>      56 Nov 19 08:19 iota
<rev: 2 />$ cd A
<rev: 2 /A>$ ls
```

Example 5-1. Using svnshell to navigate the repository (continued)

```
   REV   AUTHOR  NODE-REV-ID    SIZE          DATE NAME
--------------------------------------------------------------------
     1    sally <      4.0.1>         Nov 15 11:50 B/
     1    sally <      a.0.1>         Nov 15 11:50 C/
     1    sally <      b.0.1>         Nov 15 11:50 D/
     1    sally <      3.0.1>      23 Nov 15 11:50 mu
<rev: 2 /A>$ cd D/G
<rev: 2 /A/D/G>$ ls
   REV   AUTHOR  NODE-REV-ID    SIZE          DATE NAME
--------------------------------------------------------------------
     1    sally <      e.0.1>      23 Nov 15 11:50 pi
     1    sally <      f.0.1>      24 Nov 15 11:50 rho
     1    sally <      g.0.1>      24 Nov 15 11:50 tau
<rev: 2 /A>$ cd ../..
<rev: 2 />$ cat iota
This is the file 'iota'.
Added this text in revision 2.

<rev: 2 />$ setrev 1; cat iota
This is the file 'iota'.

<rev: 1 />$ exit
$
```

As you can see in the previous example, multiple commands may be specified at a single command prompt, separated by a semicolon. Also, the shell understands the notions of relative and absolute paths, and will properly handle the . and .. special path components.

The youngest command displays the youngest revision. This is useful for determining the range of valid revisions you can use as arguments to the setrev command—you are allowed to browse all the revisions (recalling that they are named with integers) between 0 and the youngest, inclusively. Determining the valid browsable transactions isn't quite as pretty. Use the lstxns command to list the transactions that you are able to browse. The list of browsable transactions is the same list that svnadmin lstxns returns, and the same list that is valid for use with svnlook's --transaction option.

Once you've finished using the shell, you can exit cleanly by using the exit command. Alternatively, you can supply an end-of-file character—Control-D (though some Win32 Python distributions use the Windows Control-Z convention instead).

Berkeley DB utilities

All of your versioned filesystem's structure and data live in a set of Berkeley DB database tables within the *db* subdirectory of your repository. This subdirectory is a regular Berkeley DB environment directory, and can therefore be used in conjunction with any of Berkeley's database tools (you can see the documentation for these tools at SleepyCat's website, *http://www.sleepycat.com/*).

For day-to-day Subversion use, these tools are unnecessary. Most of the functionality typically needed for Subversion repositories has been duplicated in the svnadmin tool. For example, svnadmin list-unused-dblogs and svnadmin list-dblogs perform a subset of what is provided by Berkeley's db_archive command, and svnadmin recover reflects the common use-cases of the db_recover utility.

There are still a few Berkeley DB utilities that you mind find useful. The db_dump and db_load programs write and read, respectively, a custom file format which describes the keys and values in a Berkeley DB database. Since Berkeley databases are not portable across machine architectures, this format is a useful way to transfer those databases from machine to machine, irrespective of architecture or operating system. Also, the db_stat utility can provide useful information about the status of your Berkeley DB environment, including detailed statistics about the locking and storage subsystems.

Repository Cleanup

Your Subversion repository will generally require very little attention once it is configured to your liking. However, there are times when some manual assistance from an administrator might be in order. The svnadmin utility provides some helpful functionality to assist you in performing tasks such as:

- modifying commit log messages
- removing dead transactions
- recovering wedged repositories
- migrating repository contents to a different repository

Perhaps the most commonly used of svnadmin's subcommands is setlog. When a transaction is committed to the repository and promoted to a revision, the descriptive log message associated with that new revision (and provided by the user) is stored as an unversioned property attached to the revision itself. In other words, the repository remembers only the latest value of the property, and discards previous ones.

Sometimes a user will have an error in her log message (a misspelling or some misinformation, perhaps). If the repository is configured (using the pre-revprop-change and post-revprop-change hooks; see "Hook Scripts") to accept changes to this log message after the commit is finished, then the user can fix her log message remotely using the svn program's propset command (see Chapter 9). However, because of the potential to lose information forever, Subversion repositories are not, by default, configured to allow changes to unversioned properties—except by an administrator.

If a log message needs to be changed by an administrator, this can be done using svnadmin setlog. This command changes the log message (the svn:log property) on a given revision of a repository, reading the new value from a provided file:

```
$ echo "Here is the new, correct log message" > newlog.txt
$ svnadmin setlog myrepos newlog.txt -r 388
```

The svnadmin setlog command alone is still bound by the same protections against modifying unversioned properties as a remote client is: the pre- and post-revprop-change hooks are still triggered, and must therefore be set up to accept changes of this nature. But an administrator can get around these protections by passing the --bypass-hooks option to svnadmin setlog command.

 Remember: by bypassing the hooks, you are likely avoiding such things as email notifications of property changes, backup systems which track unversioned property changes, and so on. In other words, be very careful about what you are changing, and how you change it.

Another common use of svnadmin is to query the repository for outstanding—possibly dead—Subversion transactions. In the event that a commit should fail, the transaction is usually cleaned up. That is, the transaction itself is removed from the repository, and any data associated with (and only with) that transaction is removed as well. Occasionally, though, a failure occurs in such a way that the cleanup of the transaction never happens. This could happen for several reasons: perhaps the client operation was inelegantly terminated by the user, or a network failure might have occurred in the middle of an operation, etc. Regardless of the reason, these dead transactions serve only to clutter the repository and consume resources.

You can use svnadmin's lstxns command to list the names of the currently outstanding transactions:

```
$ svnadmin lstxns myrepos
19
3a1
a45
$
```

Each item in the resultant output can then be used with svnlook (and its --transaction option) to determine who created the transaction, when it was created, what types of changes were made in the transaction—in other words, whether or not the transaction is a safe candidate for removal! If so, the transaction's name can be passed to svnadmin rmtxns, which will perform the cleanup of the transaction. In fact, the rmtxns subcommand can take its input directly from the output of lstxns!

```
$ svnadmin rmtxns myrepos `svnadmin lstxns myrepos`
$
```

If you use these two subcommands like this, you should consider making your repository temporarily inaccessible to clients. That way, no one can begin a legitimate transaction before you start your cleanup. Example 5-2 is a little bit of shell-scripting that can quickly generate information about each outstanding transaction in your repository.

Example 5-2. txn-info.sh (reporting outstanding transactions)

```
#!/bin/sh

### Generate informational output for all outstanding transactions in
### a Subversion repository.

SVNADMIN=/usr/local/bin/svnadmin
SVNLOOK=/usr/local/bin/svnlook

REPOS="${1}"
if [ "x$REPOS" = x ] ; then
  echo "usage: $0 REPOS_PATH"
  exit
fi

for TXN in `${SVNADMIN} lstxns ${REPOS}`; do
  echo "---[ Transaction ${TXN} ]-------------------------------------------"
  ${SVNLOOK} info "${REPOS}" --transaction "${TXN}"
done
```

You can run the previous script using /path/to/txn-info.sh /path/to/repos. The output is basically a concatenation of several chunks of svnlook info output (see "svnlook" earlier in this chapter), and will look something like:

```
$ txn-info.sh myrepos
---[ Transaction 19 ]-------------------------------------
sally
2001-09-04 11:57:19 -0500 (Tue, 04 Sep 2001)
0
---[ Transaction 3a1 ]-------------------------------------
harry
2001-09-10 16:50:30 -0500 (Mon, 10 Sep 2001)
39
Trying to commit over a faulty network.
---[ Transaction a45 ]-------------------------------------
sally
2001-09-12 11:09:28 -0500 (Wed, 12 Sep 2001)
0
$
```

Usually, if you see a dead transaction that has no log message attached to it, this is the result of a failed update (or update-like) operation. These operations use Subversion transactions under the hood to mimic working copy state. Since they are never intended to be committed, Subversion doesn't require a log message for those transactions. Transactions that do have log messages attached are almost certainly failed commits of some sort. Also, a transaction's datestamp can provide interesting information—for example, how likely is it that an operation begun nine months ago is still active?

In short, transaction cleanup decisions need not be made unwisely. Various sources of information—including Apache's error and access logs, the logs of successful Subversion commits, and so on—can be employed in the decision-making process. Finally, an administrator can often simply communicate with a seemingly dead transaction's owner (via email, for example) to verify that the transaction is, in fact, in a zombie state.

Managing Disk Space

While the cost of storage has dropped incredibly in the past few years, disk usage is still a valid concern for administrators seeking to version large amounts of data. Every additional byte consumed by the live repository is a byte that needs to be backed up offsite, perhaps multiple times as part of rotating backup schedules. Since the primary storage mechanism of a Subversion repository is a complex database system, it is useful to know what pieces of data need to remain on the live site, which need to be backed up, and which can be safely removed.

Until recently, the largest offender of disk space usage, with respect to Subversion repositories, was the logfiles to which Berkeley DB performs its pre-writes before modifying the actual database files. These files capture all the actions taken along the route of changing the database from one state to another—while the database files reflect at any given time some state, the logfiles contain all the many changes along the way between states. As such, they can start to accumulate quite rapidly.

Fortunately, beginning with the 4.2 release of Berkeley DB, the database environment has the ability to remove its own unused logfiles without any external procedures. Any repositories created using an svnadmin that is compiled against Berkeley DB Version 4.2 or greater will be configured for this automatic log file removal. If you don't want this feature enabled, simply pass the --bdb-log-keep option to the svnadmin create command. If you forget to do this, or change your mind at a later time, simple edit the DB_CONFIG file found in your repository's db directory, comment out the line which contains the set_flags DB_LOG_AUTOREMOVE directive, and then run svnadmin recover on your repository to force the configuration changes to take effect. See "Berkeley DB Configuration" earlier in this chapter for more information about database configuration.

Without some sort of automatic log file removal in place, log files accumulate as you use your repository. This is actually a sort of feature of the database system—you should be able to recreate your entire database using nothing but the log files—so these files can be useful for catastrophic database recovery. Typically, though, you archive the log files that are no longer in use by Berkeley DB, and then remove them from disk to conserve space. Use the `svnadmin` `list-unused-dblogs` command to list the unused logfiles:

```
$ svnadmin list-unused-dblogs /path/to/repos
/path/to/repos/log.0000000031
/path/to/repos/log.0000000032
/path/to/repos/log.0000000033

$ svnadmin list-unused-dblogs /path/to/repos | xargs rm
## disk space reclaimed!
```

To keep the size of the repository as small as possible, Subversion uses *deltification* (or, *deltified storage*) within the repository itself. Deltification involves encoding the representation of a chunk of data as a collection of differences against some other chunk of data. If the two pieces of data are very similar, this deltification results in storage savings for the deltified chunk—rather than taking up space equal to the size of the original data, it only takes up enough space to say, "I look just like this other piece of data over here, except for the following couple of changes." Specifically, each time a new version of a file is committed to the repository, Subversion encodes the previous version (actually, several previous versions) as a delta against the new version. The result is that most of the repository data that tends to be sizable—namely, the contents of versioned files—is stored at a much smaller size than the original fulltext representation of that data.

 Because all of the Subversion repository data that is subject to deltification is stored in a single Berkeley DB database file, reducing the size of the stored values will not necessarily reduce the size of the database file itself. Berkeley DB will, however, keep internal records of unused areas of the database file, and use those areas first before growing the size of the database file. Thus, while deltification doesn't produce immediate space savings, it can drastically slow future growth of the database.

Repository Recovery

To protect the data in your repository, the database back-end uses a locking mechanism. This mechanism ensures that portions of the database are not simultaneously modified by multiple database accessors, and that each process sees the data in the correct state when that data is being read from the database. When a process needs to change something in the database, it first checks for the existence of a lock on the target data. If the data is not locked, the process locks the data, makes the change it wants to make, and then unlocks the data. Other processes are forced to wait until that lock is removed before they are permitted to continue accessing that section of the database.

In the course of using your Subversion repository, fatal errors (such as running out of disk space or available memory) or interruptions can prevent a process from having the chance to remove the locks it has placed in the database. The result is that the back-end database system gets wedged. When this happens, any attempts to access the repository hang indefinitely (since each new accessor is waiting for a lock to go away—which isn't going to happen).

First, if your repository locks up, don't panic. Subversion's filesystem takes advantage of database transactions and checkpoints and pre-write journaling to ensure that only the most catastrophic of events* can permanently destroy a database environment. A sufficiently paranoid repository administrator will be making off-site backups of the repository data in some fashion, but don't call your system administrator to restore a backup tape just yet.

Secondly, use the following recipe to attempt to unwedge your repository:

1. Make sure that there are no processes accessing (or attempting to access) the repository. For networked repositories, this means shutting down the Apache HTTP Server, too.

2. Become the user who owns and manages the repository. This is important, as recovering a repository while running as the wrong user can tweak the permissions of the repository's files in such a way that your repository will still be inaccessible even after it is unwedged.

3. Run the command svnadmin recover /path/to/repos. You should see output such as this:

   ```
   Please wait; recovering the repository may take some time...
   Recovery completed.
   The latest repos revision is 19.
   ```

   This command may take many minutes to complete.

4. Restart the Subversion server.

This procedure fixes almost every case of repository lock-up. Make sure that you run this command as the user that owns and manages the database, not just as root. Part of the recovery process might involve recreating from scratch various database files (shared memory regions, for example). Recovering as root creates those files such that they are owned by root, which means that even after you restore connectivity to your repository, regular users can't access it.

If the previous procedure, for some reason, does not successfully unwedge your repository, you should do two things. First, move your broken repository out of the way and restore your latest backup of it. Then, send an email to the Subversion user list (at *users@subversion.tigris.org*) describing your problem in detail. Data integrity is an extremely high priority to the Subversion developers.

---

* E.g., hard drive + huge electromagnet = disaster.

Migrating a Repository

A Subversion filesystem has its data spread throughout various database tables in a fashion generally understood by (and of interest to) only the Subversion developers themselves. However, circumstances may arise that call for all, or some subset, of that data to be collected into a single portable, flat-file format. Subversion provides such a mechanism, implemented in a pair of svnadmin subcommands: dump and load.

The most common reason to dump and load a Subversion repository is due to changes in Subversion itself. As Subversion matures, there are times when certain changes made to the back-end database schema cause Subversion to be incompatible with previous versions of the repository. The recommended course of action when you are upgrading across one of those compatibility boundaries is a relatively simple process:

1. Using your *current* version of svnadmin, dump your repositories to dump files.

2. Upgrade to the new version of Subversion.

3. Move your old repositories out of the way, and create new empty ones in their place using your *new* svnadmin.

4. Again using your *new* svnadmin, load your dump files into their respective, just-created repositories.

5. Finally, be sure to copy any customizations from your old repositories to the new ones, including *DB_CONFIG* files and hook scripts. Pay attention to the release notes for the new release of Subversion to see if any changes since your last upgrade affect those hooks or configuration options.

svnadmin dump outputs a range of repository revisions that are formatted using Subversion's custom filesystem dump format. The dump format is printed to the standard output stream, while informative messages are printed to the standard error stream. This allows you to redirect the output stream to a file while watching the status output in your terminal window. For example:

```
$ svnlook youngest myrepos
26
$ svnadmin dump myrepos > dumpfile
* Dumped revision 0.
* Dumped revision 1.
* Dumped revision 2.
...
* Dumped revision 25.
* Dumped revision 26.
```

At the end of the process, you have a single file (*dumpfile* in the previous example) that contains all the data stored in your repository in the requested range of revisions. Note that svnadmin dump is reading revision trees from the repository just like any other reader process would (svn checkout, for example.) So it's safe to run this command at any time.

The other subcommand in the pair, svnadmin load, parses the standard input stream as a Subversion repository dump file, and effectively replays those dumped revisions into the target repository for that operation. It also gives informative feedback, this time using the standard output stream:

```
$ svnadmin load newrepos < dumpfile
<<< Started new txn, based on original revision 1
     * adding path : A ... done.
     * adding path : A/B ... done.
     ...
------- Committed new rev 1 (loaded from original rev 1) >>>

<<< Started new txn, based on original revision 2
     * editing path : A/mu ... done.
     * editing path : A/D/G/rho ... done.

------- Committed new rev 2 (loaded from original rev 2) >>>

...

<<< Started new txn, based on original revision 25
     * editing path : A/D/gamma ... done.

------- Committed new rev 25 (loaded from original rev 25) >>>

<<< Started new txn, based on original revision 26
     * adding path : A/Z/zeta ... done.
     * editing path : A/mu ... done.

------- Committed new rev 26 (loaded from original rev 26) >>>
```

Note that because svnadmin uses standard input and output streams for the repository dump and load process, people who are feeling especially saucy can try things such as this (perhaps even using different versions of svnadmin on each side of the pipe):

```
$ svnadmin create newrepos
$ svnadmin dump myrepos | svnadmin load newrepos
```

We mentioned previously that svnadmin dump outputs a range of revisions. Use the --revision option to specify a single revision to dump, or a range of revisions. If you omit this option, all the existing repository revisions are dumped:

```
$ svnadmin dump myrepos --revision 23 > rev-23.dumpfile
$ svnadmin dump myrepos --revision 100:200 > revs-100-200.dumpfile
```

As Subversion dumps each new revision, it outputs only enough information to allow a future loader to re-create that revision based on the previous one. In other words, for any given revision in the dump file, only the items that were changed in that revision appears in the dump. The only exception to this rule is the first revision that is dumped with the current svnadmin dump command.

By default, Subversion doesn't express the first dumped revision as merely differences to be applied to the previous revision. For one thing, there is no previous revision in the dump file! Secondly, Subversion cannot know the state of the repository into which the dump data is to be loaded (if it ever, in fact, occurs). To ensure that the output of each execution of svnadmin dump is self-sufficient, the first dumped revision is, by default, a full representation of every directory, file, and property in that revision of the repository.

However, you can change this default behavior. If you add the --incremental option when you dump your repository, svnadmin will compare the first dumped revision against the previous revision in the repository, the same way it treats every other revision that gets dumped. It will then output the first revision exactly as it does the rest of the revisions in the dump range—mentioning only the changes that occurred in that revision. The benefit of this is that you can create several small dump files that can be loaded in succession, instead of one large one, like so:

```
$ svnadmin dump myrepos --revision 0:1000 > dumpfile1
$ svnadmin dump myrepos --revision 1001:2000 --incremental > dumpfile2
$ svnadmin dump myrepos --revision 2001:3000 --incremental > dumpfile3
```

These dump files could be loaded into a new repository with the following command sequence:

```
$ svnadmin load newrepos < dumpfile1
$ svnadmin load newrepos < dumpfile2
$ svnadmin load newrepos < dumpfile3
```

Another neat trick you can perform with this --incremental option involves appending to an existing dump file a new range of dumped revisions. For example, you might have a post-commit hook that simply appends the repository dump of the single revision that triggered the hook. Or you might have a script that runs nightly to append dump file data for all the revisions that were added to the repository since the last time the script ran. Used like this, svnadmin's dump and load commands can be a valuable means by which to backup changes to your repository over time, in case of a system crash or some other catastrophic event.

The dump format can also be used to merge the contents of several different repositories into a single repository. By using the --parent-dir of svnadmin load, you can specify a new virtual root directory for the load process. That means if you have dumpfiles for three repositories, say *calc-dumpfile*, *cal-dumpfile*, and *ss-dumpfile*, you can first create a new repository to hold them all:

```
$ svnadmin create /path/to/projects
$
```

Then, make new directories in the repository that encapsulate the contents of each of the three previous repositories:

```
$ svn mkdir -m "Initial project roots" \
      file:///path/to/projects/calc \
```

```
        file:///path/to/projects/calendar \
        file:///path/to/projects/spreadsheet
Committed revision 1.
$
```

Lastly, load the individual dumpfiles into their respective locations in the new repository:

```
$ svnadmin load /path/to/projects --parent-dir calc < calc-dumpfile
...
$ svnadmin load /path/to/projects --parent-dir calendar < cal-dumpfile
...
$ svnadmin load /path/to/projects --parent-dir spreadsheet < ss-dumpfile
...
$
```

We want to mention one final way to use the Subversion repository dump format—conversion from a different storage mechanism or version control system altogether. Because the dump file format is, for the most part, human-readable (resembling an RFC-822 format, the same type of format used for most email). it should be relatively easy to describe generic sets of changes—each of which should be treated as a new revision—using this file format. In fact, the cvs2svn.py utility (see "Converting a Repository from CVS to Subversion" in Appendix A) uses the dump format to represent the contents of a CVS repository so that those contents can be moved in a Subversion repository.

Repository Backup

Despite numerous advances in technology since the birth of the modern computer, one thing unfortunately rings true with crystalline clarity—sometimes, things go very, very awry. Power outages, network connectivity dropouts, corrupt RAM, and crashed hard drives are but a taste of the evil that Fate is poised to unleash on even the most conscientious administrator. And so we arrive at a very important topic—how to make backup copies of your repository data.

There are generally two types of backup methods available for Subversion repository administrators—incremental and full. We discussed in an earlier section of this chapter how to use svnadmin dump --incremental to perform an incremental backup (see "Migrating a Repository"). Essentially, the idea is to only back up at a given time the changes to the repository since the last time you made a backup.

A full backup of the repository is quite literally a duplication of the entire repository directory (which includes the Berkeley database environment). Now, unless you temporarily disable all other access to your repository, simply doing a recursive directory copy runs the risk of generating a faulty backup, since someone might be currently writing to the database.

Fortunately, Sleepycat's Berkeley DB documents describe a certain order in which database files can be copied that will guarantee a valid backup copy. And better still, you don't have to implement that algorithm yourself, because the Subversion development team has already done so. The hot-backup.py script is found in the *tools/backup/* directory of the Subversion source distribution. Given a repository path and a backup location, hot-backup.py—which is really just a more intelligent wrapper around the svnadmin hotcopy command—performs the necessary steps for backing up your live repository—without requiring that you bar public repository access at all—and then cleans out the dead Berkeley log files from your live repository.

Even if you also have an incremental backup, you might want to run this program on a regular basis. For example, you might consider adding hot-backup.py to a program scheduler (such as cron on Unix systems). Or, if you prefer fine-grained backup solutions, you could have your post-commit hook script call hot-backup.py (see "Hook Scripts" earlier in this chapter), which then causes a new backup of your repository to occur with every new revision created. Simply add the following to the *hooks/post-commit* script in your live repository directory:

```
(cd /path/to/hook/scripts; ./hot-backup.py ${REPOS} /path/to/backups &)
```

The resulting backup is a fully functional Subversion repository, able to be dropped in as a replacement for your live repository should something go horribly wrong.

There are benefits to both types of backup methods. The easiest is by far the full backup, which always results in a perfect working replica of your repository. Again, this means that should something bad happen to your live repository, you can restore from the backup with a simple recursive directory copy. Unfortunately, if you are maintaining multiple backups of your repository, these full copies each eat up just as much disk space as your live repository.

Incremental backups using the repository dump format are excellent to have on hand if the database schema changes between successive versions of Subversion itself. Since a full repository dump and load are generally required to upgrade your repository to the new schema, it's very convenient to already have half of that process (the dump part) finished. Unfortunately, the creation of—and restoration from—incremental backups takes longer, as each commit is effectively replayed into either the dumpfile or the repository.

In either backup scenario, repository administrators need to be aware of how modifications to unversioned revision properties affect their backups. Because these changes do not themselves generate new revisions, they will not trigger post-commit hooks, and may not even trigger the pre-revprop-change and post-revprop-change hooks.* And because you can change revision properties without respect to chronological order—you can change any revision's properties at any time—an incremental backup of the latest few revisions might not catch a property modification to a revision that was included as part of a previous backup.

---

* svnadmin setlog can be called in a way that bypasses the hook interface altogether.

Generally speaking, only the truly paranoid would need to backup their entire repository, say, every time a commit occurred. However, assuming that a given repository has some other redundancy mechanism in place with relatively fine granularity (such as per-commit emails), a hot backup of the database might be something that a repository administrator would want to include as part of a system-wide nightly backup. For most repositories, archived commit emails alone provide sufficient redundancy as restoration sources, at least for the most recent few commits. But it's your data—protect it as much as you'd like.

Often, the best approach to repository backups is a diversified one. You can leverage combinations of full and incremental backups, plus archives of commit emails. The Subversion developers, for example, back up the Subversion source code repository after every new revision is created, and keep an archive of all the commit and property change notification emails. Your solution might be similar, but should be catered to your needs and that delicate balance of convenience with paranoia. And while all of this might not save your hardware from the iron fist of Fate,* it should certainly help you recover from those trying times.

Adding Projects

Once your repository is created and configured, all that remains is to begin using it. If you have a collection of existing data that is ready to be placed under version control, you will more than likely want to use the svn client program's import subcommand to accomplish that. Before doing this, though, you should carefully consider your long-term plans for the repository. In this section, we offer some advice on how to plan the layout of your repository, and how to arrange your data in that layout.

Choosing a Repository Layout

While Subversion allows you to move around versioned files and directories without any loss of information, doing so can still disrupt the workflow of those who access the repository often and come to expect things to be at certain locations. Try to peer into the future a bit; plan ahead before placing your data under version control. By laying out the contents of your repositories in an effective manner the first time, you can prevent a load of future headaches.

There are a few things to consider when setting up Subversion repositories. Let's assume that as repository administrator, you will be responsible for supporting the version control system for several projects. The first decision is whether to use a single repository for multiple projects, or to give each project its own repository, or some compromise of these two.

---

* You know—the collective term for all of her fickle fingers.

There are benefits to using a single repository for multiple projects, most obviously the lack of duplicated maintenance. A single repository means that there is one set of hook scripts, one thing to routinely back up, one thing to dump and load if Subversion releases an incompatible new version, and so on. Also, you can move data between projects easily, and without losing any historical versioning information.

The downside of using a single repository is that different projects may have different commit mailing lists or different authentication and authorization requirements. Also, remember that Subversion uses repository-global revision numbers. Some folks don't like the fact that even though no changes have been made to their project lately, the youngest revision number for the repository keeps climbing because other projects are actively adding new revisions.

A middle-ground approach can be taken, too. For example, projects can be grouped by how well they relate to each other. You could have a few repositories with a handful of projects in each repository. That way, projects that are likely to want to share data can do so easily, and as new revisions are added to the repository, at least the developers know that those new revisions are at least remotely related to everyone who uses that repository.

After deciding how to organize your projects with respect to repositories, you'll probably want to think about directory hierarchies in the repositories themselves. Because Subversion uses regular directory copies for branching and tagging (see Chapter 4), the Subversion community recommends that you choose a repository location for each *project root*—the topmost directory that contains data related to that project—and then create three subdirectories beneath that root: *trunk*, meaning the directory under which the main project development occurs; *branches*, which is a directory in which to create various named branches of the main development line; and *tags*, which is a directory of branches that are created, and perhaps destroyed, but never changed.

For example, your repository might look like:

```
/
    calc/
        trunk/
        tags/
        branches/
    calendar/
        trunk/
        tags/
        branches/
    spreadsheet/
        trunk/
        tags/
        branches/
    ...
```

Note that it doesn't matter where in your repository each project root is located. If you have only one project per repository, the logical place to put each project root is at the root of that project's respective repository. If you have multiple projects, you might want to arrange them in groups inside the repository, perhaps putting projects with similar goals or shared code in the same subdirectory, or maybe just grouping them alphabetically. Such an arrangement might look like:

```
/
    utils/
        calc/
            trunk/
            tags/
            branches/
        calendar/
            trunk/
            tags/
            branches/
        ...
    office/
        spreadsheet/
            trunk/
            tags/
            branches/
        ...
```

Lay out your repository in whatever way you see fit. Subversion does not expect or enforce a layout schema—in its eyes, a directory is a directory is a directory. Ultimately, you should choose the repository arrangement that meets the needs of the people who work on the projects that live there.

Creating the Layout and Importing Initial Data

After deciding how to arrange the projects in your repository, you'll probably want to actually populate the repository with that layout and with initial project data. There are a couple of ways to do this in Subversion. You could use the svn mkdir command (see Chapter 9) to create each directory in your skeletal repository layout, one by one. A quicker way to accomplish the same task is to use the svn import command (see "svn import" in Chapter 3). By first creating the layout in a temporary location on your drive, you can import the whole layout tree into the repository in a single commit:

```
$ mkdir tmpdir
$ cd tmpdir
$ mkdir projectA
$ mkdir projectA/trunk
$ mkdir projectA/branches
$ mkdir projectA/tags
$ mkdir projectB
$ mkdir projectB/trunk
$ mkdir projectB/branches
```

```
$ mkdir projectB/tags
...
$ svn import . file:///path/to/repos --message 'Initial repository layout'
Adding         projectA
Adding         projectA/trunk
Adding         projectA/branches
Adding         projectA/tags
Adding         projectB
Adding         projectB/trunk
Adding         projectB/branches
Adding         projectB/tags
...
Committed revision 1.
$ cd ..
$ rm -rf tmpdir
$
```

You can verify the results of the import by running the svn list command:

```
$ svn list --verbose file:///path/to/repos
1 harry May 08 21:48 projectA/
1 harry May 08 21:48 projectB/
&hellip;
$
```

Once you have your skeletal layout in place, you can begin importing actual project data into your repository, if any such data exists yet. Once again, there are several ways to do this. You could use the svn import command. You could check out a working copy from your new repository, move and arrange project data inside the working copy, and use the svn add and svn commit commands. But once we start talking about such things, we're no longer discussing repository administration. If you aren't already familiar with the svn client program, see Chapter 3.

Summary

By now you should have a basic understanding of how to create, configure, and maintain Subversion repositories. We introduced you to the various tools that assist you with this task. Throughout the chapter, we noted common administration pitfalls, and suggestions for avoiding them.

All that remains is for you to decide what exciting data to store in your repository, and finally, how to make it available over a network. The next chapter is all about networking.

## CHAPTER 6

Server Configuration

A Subversion repository can be accessed simultaneously by clients running on the same machine on which the repository resides using the file:/// method. But the typical Subversion setup involves a single server machine being accessed from clients on computers all over the office—or, perhaps, all over the world.

This section describes how to get your Subversion repository exposed outside its host machine for use by remote clients. We cover Subversion's currently available server mechanisms, discussing the configuration and use of each. After reading this section, you should be able to decide which networking setup is right for your needs, and understand how to enable such a setup on your host computer.

Overview

Subversion was designed with an abstract network layer. This means that a repository can be programmatically accessed by any sort of server process, and the client repository access API allows programmers to write plugins that speak relevant network protocols. In theory, Subversion can sport an infinite number of network implementations. In practice, there are only two servers at the time of writing.

Apache is an extremely popular webserver; using the mod_dav_svn module, Apache can access a repository and make it available to clients via WebDAV/DeltaV protocol, which is an extension of HTTP. In the other corner is svnserve: a small, standalone server program that speaks a custom protocol with clients. Table 6-1 presents a comparison of the two servers.

Note that Subversion, as an open-source project, does not officially endorse any server as primary or official. Neither network implementation is treated as a second-class citizen; each server has distinct advantages and disadvantages. In fact, it's possible for different servers to run in parallel, each accessing your repositories in its own way, and each without hindering the other (see "Supporting Multiple Repository

Access Methods" later in this chapter). Here's a brief overview and comparison of the two available Subversion servers—as an administrator, it's up to you to choose whatever works best for you and your users.

Table 6-1. Network server comparison

Feature	Apache + mod_dav_svn	svnserve
Authentication options	HTTP(S) basic auth, X.509 certificates, LDAP, NTLM, or any other mechanism available to Apache httpd	CRAM-MD5 or SSH
User account options	private "users" file	private "users" file, or existing system (SSH) accounts
Authorization options	blanket read/write access, or per-directory access control	blanket read/write access
Encryption	via optional SSL	via optional SSH tunnel
Interoperability	partially usable by other WebDAV clients	not interoperable
Web viewing	limited built-in support, or via 3rd-party tools such as ViewCVS	via 3rd-party tools such as ViewCVS
Speed	somewhat slower	somewhat faster
Initial setup	somewhat complex	fairly simple

Network Model

This section is a general discussion of how a Subversion client and server interact with one another, regardless of the network implementation you're using. After reading, you'll have a good understanding of how a server can behave and the different ways in which a client can be configured to respond.

Requests and Responses

The Subversion client spends most of its time managing working copies. When it needs information from a repository, however, it makes a network request, and the server responds with an appropriate answer. The details of the network protocol are hidden from the user; the client attempts to access a URL, and depending on the URL schema, a particular protocol is used to contact the server (see Chapter 2). Users can run svn --version to see which URL schemas and protocols the client knows how to use.

When the server process receives a client request, it typically demands that the client identify itself. It issues an authentication challenge to the client, and the client responds by providing *credentials* back to the server. Once authentication is complete, the server responds with the original information the client asked for. Notice that this system is different from systems such as CVS, where the client preemptively offers credentials (logs in) to the server before ever making a request. In Subversion, the server pulls credentials by challenging the client at the appropriate moment, rather than the client pushing them. This makes certain operations more elegant. For example, if a server is configured to allow anyone in the world to read a repository, then the server will never issue an authentication challenge when a client attempts to svn checkout.

If the client's network request writes new data to the repository (e.g., svn commit), then a new revision tree is created. If the client's request was authenticated, then the authenticated user's name is stored as the value of the svn:author property on the new revision (see "Unversioned Properties" in Chapter 5). If the client was not authenticated (in other words, the server never issued an authentication challenge), then the revision's svn:author property is empty.*

Client Credentials Caching

Many servers are configured to require authentication on every request. This can become a big annoyance to users, who are forced to type their passwords over and over again.

Happily, the Subversion client has a remedy for this: a built-in system for caching authentication credentials on disk. By default, whenever the commandline client successfully authenticates itself to a server, it saves the credentials in the user's private runtime configuration area—in *~/.subversion/auth/* on Unix-like systems or *%APPDATA%/Subversion/auth/* on Windows. (The runtime area is covered further in "Runtime Configuration Area" in Chapter 7.) Successful credentials are cached on disk, keyed on a combination of hostname, port, and authentication realm.

When the client receives an authentication challenge, it first looks for the appropriate credentials in the disk cache; if not present, or if the cached credentials fail to authenticate, then the client simply prompts the user for the information.

The security-paranoid people may be thinking to themselves: "Caching passwords on disk? That's terrible! You should never do that!" But, please, remain calm. First, the *auth/* caching area is permission-protected, so only the user (owner) can read data from it, not the world at large. If that's still not safe enough for you, you can disable credential caching. To disable caching for a single command, pass the --no-auth-cache option:

```
$ svn commit -F log_msg.txt --no-auth-cache
Authentication realm: <svn://host.example.com:3690> example realm
Username:  joe
Password for 'joe':

Adding          newfile
Transmitting file data .
Committed revision 2324.

# password was not cached, so a second commit still prompts us
```

---

* This problem is actually a FAQ, resulting from a misconfigured server setup.

```
$ svn rm newfile
$ svn commit -F new_msg.txt
Authentication realm: <svn://host.example.com:3690> example realm
Username: joe
[...]
```

Or, if you want to disable credential caching permanently, you can edit your runtime *config* file (located next to the *auth/* directory). Simply set `store-auth-creds` to no, and no credentials will be cached on disk, ever.

```
[auth]
store-auth-creds = no
```

Sometimes users will want to remove specific credentials from the disk cache. To do this, you need to navigate into the *auth/* area and manually delete the appropriate cache file. Credentials are cached in individual files; if you look inside each file, you will see keys and values. The `svn:realmstring` key describes the particular server realm that the file is associated with:

```
$ ls ~/.subversion/auth/svn.simple/
5671adf2865e267db74f09ba6f872c28
3893ed123b39500bca8a0b382839198e
5c3c22968347b390f349ff340196ed39

$ cat ~/.subversion/auth/svn.simple/5671adf2865e267db74f09ba6f872c28

K 8
username
V 3
joe
K 8
password
V 4
blah
K 15
svn:realmstring
V 45
<https://svn.domain.com:443> Joe's repository
END
```

Once you have located the proper cache file, just delete it.

One last word about client authentication behavior: a bit of explanation about the --username and --password options is needed. Many client subcommands accept these options; however, it is important to understand using these options does not automatically send credentials to the server. As discussed earlier, the server pulls credentials from the client when it deems necessary; the client cannot push them at will. If a username and/or password are passed as options, they will only be presented to the server if the server requests them.[*] Typically, these options are used when:

---

[*] Again, a common mistake is to misconfigure a server so that it never issues an authentication challenge. When users pass --username and --password options to the client, they're surprised to see that they're never used, i.e., new revisions still appear to have been committed anonymously!

- The user wants to authenticate as a different user than her system login name.
- A script wants to authenticate without using cached credentials.

Here is a final summary that describes how a Subversion client behaves when it receives an authentication challenge:

1. Check whether the user specified any credentials as command-line options, via --username and/or --password. If not, or if these options fail to authenticate successfully, then

2. Look up the server's realm in the runtime *auth/* area, to see if the user already has the appropriate credentials cached. If not, or if the cached credentials fail to authenticate, then

3. Resort to prompting the user.

If the client successfully authenticates by any of the methods listed previously, it will attempt to cache the credentials on disk (unless the user has disabled this behavior, as mentioned earlier).

svnserve; A Custom Server

The svnserve program is a lightweight server, capable of speaking to clients over TCP/IP using a custom, stateful protocol. Clients contact an svnserve server by using URLs that begin with the svn:// or svn+ssh:// schema. This section explains the different ways of running svnserve, how clients authenticate themselves to the server, and how to configure appropriate access control to your repositories.

Invoking the Server

There a few different ways to invoke the svnserve program. If invoked with no options, you'll see nothing but a help message. However, if you're planning to have inetd launch the process, then you can pass the -i (--inetd) option:

```
$ svnserve -i
( success ( 1 2 ( ANONYMOUS ) ( edit-pipeline ) ) )
```

When invoked with the --inetd option, svnserve attempts to speak with a Subversion client via *stdin* and *stdout* using a custom protocol. This is the standard behavior for a program being run via inetd. The IANA has reserved port 3690 for the Subversion protocol, so on a Unix-like system you can add lines to */etc/services* like these (if they don't already exist):

```
svn           3690/tcp    # Subversion
svn           3690/udp    # Subversion
```

And if your system is using a classic Unix-like inetd daemon, you can add this line to */etc/inetd.conf*:

```
svn stream tcp nowait svnowner /usr/local/bin/svnserve svnserve -i
```

Make sure *svnowner* is a user who has appropriate permissions to access your repositories. Now, when a client connection comes into your server on port 3690, inetd spawns an svnserve process to service it.

A second option is to run svnserve as a standalone daemon process. Use the -d option for this:

```
$ svnserve -d
$                    # svnserve is now running, listening on port 3690
```

When running svnserve in daemon mode, you can use the --listen-port= and --listen-host= options to customize the exact port and hostname to bind to.

There's still a third way to invoke svnserve, and that's in tunnel mode, with the -t option. This mode assumes that a remote-service program such as RSH or SSH has successfully authenticated a user and is now invoking a private svnserve process as that user. The svnserve program behaves normally (communicating via *stdin* and *stdout*), and assumes that the traffic is being automatically redirected over some sort of tunnel back to the client. When svnserve is invoked by a tunnel agent like this, be sure that the authenticated user has full read and write access to the repository database files. (See Chapter 6.) It's essentially the same as a local user accessing the repository via file:/// URLs.

Servers and Permissions: A Word of Warning

First, remember that a Subversion repository is a collection of BerkeleyDB database files; any process that accesses the repository directly needs to have proper read and write permissions on the entire repository. If you're not careful, this can lead to a number of headaches. Be sure to read "Supporting Multiple Repository Access Methods."

Secondly, when configuring svnserve, Apache httpd, or any other server process, keep in mind that you might not want to launch the server process as the user root (or as any other user with unlimited permissions). Depending on the ownership and permissions of the repositories you're exporting, it's often prudent to use a different—perhaps custom—user. For example, many administrators create a new user named svn, grant that user exclusive ownership and rights to the exported Subversion repositories, and only run their server processes as that user.

Once the svnserve program is running, it makes every repository on your system available to the network. A client needs to specify an *absolute* path in the repository URL. For example, if a repository is located at */usr/local/repositories/project1*, then a client would reach it via *svn://host.example.com/usr/local/repositories/project1*. To increase security, you can pass the -r option to svnserve, which restricts it to exporting only repositories below that path:

```
$ svnserve -d -r /usr/local/repositories
...
```

Using the -r option effectively modifies the location that the program treats as the root of the remote filesystem space. Clients then use URLs that have that path portion removed from them, leaving much shorter (and much less revealing) URLs:

```
$ svn checkout svn://host.example.com/project1
...
```

Built-In Authentication and Authorization

When a client connects to an svnserve process, the following things happen:

- The client selects a specific repository.
- The server processes the repository's *conf/svnserve.conf* file, and begins to enforce any authentication and authorization policies defined therein.
- Depending on the situation and authorization policies:
  - The client may be allowed to make requests anonymously, without ever receiving an authentication challenge.
  - The client may be challenged for authentication at any time.
  - If operating in tunnel mode, the client will declare itself to be already externally authenticated.

At the time of writing, the server only knows how to send a CRAM-MD5 (see RFC 2195) authentication challenge. In essence, the server sends a bit of data to the client. The client uses its password to encrypt the data with the MD5 hash algorithm, and sends it back. The server performs the same computation with the stored password to verify that the result is identical. At no point does the actual password travel over the network.

It's also possible, of course, for the client to be externally authenticated via a tunnel agent, such as SSH. In that case, the server simply examines the user it's running as, and uses it as the authenticated username.

As you've already guessed, a repository's *svnserve.conf* file is the central mechanism for controlling authentication and authorization policies. The file has the same format as other configuration files (see "Runtime Configuration Area" in Chapter 7): section names are marked by square brackets ([and]), comments begin with hashes (#), and each section contains specific variables that can be set (variable = value). Let's walk through this file and learn how to use them.

Create a "users" file and realm

For now, the [general] section of the *svnserve.conf* has all the variables you need. Begin by defining a file which contains usernames and passwords, and an authentication realm:

```
[general]
password-db = userfile
realm = example realm
```

The realm is a name that you define. It tells clients to which authentication namespace they're connecting; the Subversion client displays it in the authentication prompt, and uses it as a key (along with the server's hostname and port) for caching credentials on disk (see "Client Credentials Caching" earlier in this chapter). The password-db variable points to a separate file that contains a list of usernames and passwords, using the same familiar format. For example:

```
[users]
harry = foopassword
sally = barpassword
```

The value of password-db can be an absolute or relative path to the users file. For many admins, it's easy to keep the file right in the *conf/* area of the repository, alongside *svnserve.conf*. On the other hand, it's possible you may want to have two or more repositories share the same users file; in that case, the file should probably live in a more public place. The repositories sharing the users file should also be configured to have the same realm, since the list of users essentially defines an authentication realm. Wherever the file lives, be sure to set the file's read and write permissions appropriately. If you know which user(s) svnserve will run as, restrict read access to the user file as necessary.

Set access controls

There are two more variables to set in the *svnserve.conf* file: they determine what unauthenticated (anonymous) and authenticated users are allowed to do. The variables anon-access and auth-access can be set to the values none, read, or write. Setting the value to none restricts all access of any kind; read allows read-only access to the repository, and write allows complete read/write access to the repository. For example:

```
[general]
password-db = userfile
realm = example realm

# anonymous users can only read the repository
anon-access = read

# authenticated users can both read and write
auth-access = write
```

The example settings are, in fact, the default values of the variables, should you forget to define them. If you want to be even more conservative, you can block anonymous access completely:

```
[general]
password-db = userfile
realm = example realm

# anonymous users aren't allowed
anon-access = none
```

```
# authenticated users can both read and write
auth-access = write
```

Notice that svnserve only understands blanket access control. A user either has universal read/write access, universal read access, or no access. There is no detailed control over access to specific paths within the repository. For many projects and sites, this level of access control is more than adequate. However, if you need per-directory access control, you'll need to use Apache instead of svnserve as your server process.

SSH Authentication and Authorization

svnserve's built-in authentication can be very handy, because it avoids the need to create real system accounts. On the other hand, some administrators already have well-established SSH authentication frameworks in place. In these situations, all of the project's users already have system accounts and the ability to SSH into the server machine.

It's easy to use SSH in conjunction with svnserve. The client simply uses the svn+ssh:// URL schema to connect:

```
$ whoami
harry

$ svn list svn+ssh://host.example.com/repos/project
harry@host.example.com's password:  *****

foo
bar
baz
...
```

What's happening here is that the Subversion client is invoking a local ssh process, connecting to host.example.com, authenticating as user harry, then spawning a private svnserve process on the remote machine, running as user *harry*. The svnserve command is being invoked in tunnel mode (-t) and all network protocol is being tunneled over the encrypted connection by ssh, the tunnel-agent. svnserve is aware that it's running as user *harry*, and if the client performs a commit, the authenticated username will be attributed as the author of the new revision.

When running over a tunnel, authorization is primarily controlled by operating system permissions to the repository's database files; it's very much the same as if Harry were accessing the repository directly via a file:/// URL. If multiple system users are going to be accessing the repository directly, you may want to place them into a common group, and you'll need to be careful about umasks. (Be sure to read "Supporting Multiple Repository Access Methods," later in this chapter.) But even in the case of tunneling, the *svnserve.conf* file can still be used to block access, by simply setting auth-access = read or auth-access = none.

You'd think that the story of SSH tunneling would end here, but it doesn't. Subversion allows you to create custom tunnel behaviors in your run-time *config* file (see "Runtime Configuration Area.") For example, suppose you want to use RSH instead of SSH. In the [tunnels] section of your *config* file, simply define it like this:

```
[tunnels]
rsh = rsh
```

And now, you can use this new tunnel definition by using a URL schema that matches the name of your new variable: svn+rsh://host/path. When using the new URL schema, the Subversion client will actually be running the command rsh host svnserve -t behind the scenes. If you include a username in the URL (for example, svn+rsh://username@host/path) the client will also include that in its command (rsh username@host svnserve -t.) But you can define new tunneling schemes to be much more clever than that:

```
[tunnels]
joessh = $JOESSH /opt/alternate/ssh -p 29934
```

This example demonstrates a couple of things. First, it shows how to make the Subversion client launch a very specific tunneling binary (the one located at */opt/alternate/ssh*) with specific options. In this case, accessing a svn+joessh:// URL would invoke the particular SSH binary with -p 29934 as arguments—useful if you want the tunnel program to connect to a non-standard port.

Second, it shows how to define a custom environment variable that can override the name of the tunneling program. Setting the SVN_SSH environment variable is a convenient way to override the default SSH tunnel agent. But if you need to have several different overrides for different servers, each perhaps contacting a different port or passing a different set of options, you can use the mechanism demonstrated in this example. Now if we were to set the JOESSH environment variable, its value would override the entire value of the tunnel variable—$JOESSH would be executed instead of */opt/alternate/ssh -p 29934*.

httpd; The Apache HTTP Server

The Apache HTTP Server is a heavy duty network server that Subversion can leverage. Via a custom module, httpd makes Subversion repositories available to clients via the WebDAV/DeltaV protocol, which is an extension to HTTP 1.1 (see *http:// www.webdav.org/* for more information.) This protocol takes the ubiquitous HTTP protocol that is at the core of the World Wide Web, and adds writing—specifically, versioned writing—capabilities. The result is a standardized, robust system that is conveniently packaged as part of the Apache 2.0 software, is supported by numerous operating systems and third-party products, and which doesn't require network administrators to open up yet another custom port.[*] While an Apache-Subversion

---

[*] They really hate doing that.

server has more features than svnserve, it's also a bit more difficult to set up. With flexibility often comes more complexity.

Much of the following discussion includes references to Apache configuration directives. While some examples are given of the use of these directives, describing them in full is outside the scope of this chapter. The Apache team maintains excellent documentation, publicly available on their website at *http://httpd.apache.org*. For example, a general reference for the configuration directives is located at *http://httpd.apache.org/docs-2.0/mod/directives.html*.

Also, as you make changes to your Apache setup, it is likely that somewhere along the way a mistake will be made. If you are not already familiar with Apache's logging subsystem, you should become aware of it. In your *httpd.conf* file are directives that specify the on-disk locations of the access and error logs generated by Apache (the CustomLog and ErrorLog directives, respectively). Subversion's mod_dav_svn uses Apache's error logging interface as well. You can always browse the contents of those files for information that might reveal the source of a problem that is not clearly noticeable otherwise.

Why Apache 2?

If you're a system administrator, it's very likely that you're already running the Apache web server and have some prior experience with it. At the time of writing, Apache 1.3 is by far the most popular version of Apache. The world has been somewhat slow to upgrade to the Apache 2.X series for various reasons: some people fear change, especially changing something as critical as a web server. Other people depend on plug-in modules that only work against the Apache 1.3 API, and are waiting for a 2.X port. Whatever the reason, many people begin to worry when they first discover that Subversion's Apache module is written specifically for the Apache 2 API.

The proper response to this problem is: don't worry about it. It's easy to run Apache 1.3 and Apache 2 side by side; simply install them to separate places, and use Apache 2 as a dedicated Subversion server that runs on a port other than 80. Clients can access the repository by placing the port number into the URL:

```
$ svn checkout http://host.example.com:7382/repos/project
...
```

Prerequisites

To network your repository over HTTP, you basically need four components, available in two packages. You'll need Apache httpd 2.0, the mod_dav DAV module that comes with it, Subversion, and the mod_dav_svn filesystem provider module distributed with Subversion. Once you have all of those components, the process of networking your repository is as simple as:

- Getting httpd 2.0 up and running with the mod_dav module
- Installing the mod_dav_svn plugin to mod_dav, which uses Subversion's libraries to access the repository
- Configuring your *httpd.conf* file to export (or expose) the repository

You can accomplish the first two items either by compiling httpd and Subversion from source code, or by installing prebuilt binary packages of them on your system. For the most up-to-date information on how to compile Subversion for use with the Apache HTTP Server, as well as how to compile and configure Apache itself for this purpose, see the *INSTALL* file in the top level of the Subversion source code tree.

Basic Apache Configuration

Once you have all the necessary components installed on your system, all that remains is the configuration of Apache via its *httpd.conf* file. Instruct Apache to load the mod_dav_svn module using the LoadModule directive. This directive must precede any other Subversion-related configuration items. If your Apache was installed using the default layout, your mod_dav_svn module should have been installed in the *modules* subdirectory of the Apache install location (often */usr/local/apache2*). The LoadModule directive has a simple syntax, mapping a named module to the location of a shared library on disk:

```
LoadModule dav_svn_module     modules/mod_dav_svn.so
```

Note that if mod_dav was compiled as a shared object (instead of statically linked directly to the httpd binary), you'll need a similar LoadModule statement for it, too. Be sure that it comes before the mod_dav_svn line:

```
LoadModule dav_module         modules/mod_dav.so
LoadModule dav_svn_module     modules/mod_dav_svn.so
```

At a later location in your configuration file, you now need to tell Apache where you keep your Subversion repository (or repositories). The Location directive has an XML-like notation, starting with an opening tag, and ending with a closing tag, with various other configuration directives in the middle. The purpose of the Location directive is to instruct Apache to do something special when handling requests that are directed at a given URL or one of its children. In the case of Subversion, you want Apache to simply hand off support for URLs that point at versioned resources to the DAV layer. You can instruct Apache to delegate the handling of all URLs whose path portions (the part of the URL that follows the server's name and the optional port number) begin with */repos/* to a DAV provider whose repository is located at */absolute/path/to/repository* using the following *httpd.conf* syntax:

```
<Location /repos>
  DAV svn
  SVNPath /absolute/path/to/repository
</Location>
```

If you plan to support multiple Subversion repositories that will reside in the same parent directory on your local disk, you can use an alternative directive, the SVNParentPath directive, to indicate that common parent directory. For example, if you know you will be creating multiple Subversion repositories in a directory */usr/local/svn* that would be accessed via URLs like *http://my.server.com/svn/repos1*, *http://my.server.com/svn/repos2*, and so on, you could use the *httpd.conf* configuration syntax in the following example:

```
<Location /svn>
  DAV svn

  # any "/svn/foo" URL will map to a repository /usr/local/svn/foo
  SVNParentPath /usr/local/svn
</Location>
```

Using the previous syntax, Apache will delegate the handling of all URLs whose path portions begin with */svn/* to the Subversion DAV provider, which will then assume that any items in the directory specified by the SVNParentPath directive are actually Subversion repositories. This is a particularly convenient syntax in that, unlike the use of the *SVNPath* directive, you don't have to restart Apache in order to create and network new repositories.

Be sure that when you define your new Location, it doesn't overlap with other exported Locations. For example, if your main DocumentRoot to */www*, do not export a Subversion repository in <Location /www/repos>. If a request comes in for the URI */www/repos/foo.c*, Apache won't know whether to look for a file *repos/foo.c* in the DocumentRoot, or whether to delegate mod_dav_svn to return *foo.c* from the Subversion repository.

At this stage, you should strongly consider the question of permissions. If you've been running Apache for some time now as your regular web server, you probably already have a collection of content—web pages, scripts, and such. These items have already been configured with a set of permissions that allows them to work with Apache, or more appropriately, that allows Apache to work with those files. Apache, when used as a Subversion server, also needs the correct permissions to read and write to your Subversion repository. (See Chapter 6.)

You have to determine a permission system setup that satisfies Subversion's requirements without messing up any previously existing web page or script installations. This might mean changing the permissions on your Subversion repository to match those in use by other things that Apache serves for you, or it could mean using the User and Group directives in *httpd.conf* to specify that Apache should run as the user

---

Server Names and the COPY Request

Subversion makes use of the COPY request type to perform server-side copies of files and directories. As part of the sanity checking done by the Apache modules, the source of the copy is expected to be located on the same machine as the destination of the copy. To satisfy this requirement, you might need to tell mod_dav the name you use as the hostname of your server. Generally, you can use the ServerName directive in *httpd.conf* to accomplish this:

```
ServerName svn.example.com
```

If you are using Apache's virtual hosting support via the NameVirtualHost directive, you may need to use the ServerAlias directive to specify additional names that your server is known by. Again, refer to the Apache documentation for full details.

---

and group that owns your Subversion repository. There is no single correct way to set up your permissions, and each administrator will have different reasons for doing things a certain way. Just be aware that permission-related problems are perhaps the most common oversight when configuring a Subversion repository for use with Apache.

Authentication Options

At this point, if you configured *httpd.conf* to contain something such as:

```
<Location /svn>
  DAV svn
  SVNParentPath /usr/local/svn
</Location>
```

...then your repository is anonymously accessible to the world. Until you configure some authentication and authorization policies, the Subversion repositories you make available via the *Location* directive will be generally accessible to everyone. In other words:

- Anyone can use their Subversion client to checkout a working copy of a repository URL (or any of its subdirectories).

- Anyone can interactively browse the repository's latest revision simply by pointing their web browser to the repository URL.

- Anyone can commit to the repository.

Basic HTTP authentication

The easiest way to authenticate an client is via the HTTP Basic authentication mechanism, which simply uses a username and password to verify that a user is who she says she is. Apache provides an htpasswd utility for managing the list of acceptable usernames and passwords, those to whom you wish to grant special access to your Subversion repository. Let's grant commit access to Sally and Harry. First, we need to add them to the password file:

```
$ ### First time: use -c to create the file
$ ### Use -m to use MD5 encryption of the password, which is more secure
$ htpasswd -cm /etc/svn-auth-file harry
New password: *****
Re-type new password: *****
Adding password for user harry
$ htpasswd /etc/svn-auth-file -m sally
New password: *******
Re-type new password: *******
Adding password for user sally
$
```

Next, you need to add some more *httpd.conf* directives inside your Location block to tell Apache what to do with your new password file. The AuthType directive specifies the type of authentication system to use. In this case, we want to specify the Basic authentication system. AuthName is an arbitrary name that you give for the authentication domain. Most browsers will display this name in the pop-up dialog box when the browser is querying the user for his name and password. Finally, use the AuthUserFile directive to specify the location of the password file you created using htpasswd.

After adding these three directives, your <Location> block should look something like this:

```
<Location /svn>
  DAV svn
  SVNParentPath /usr/local/svn
  AuthType Basic
  AuthName "Subversion repository"
  AuthUserFile /etc/svn-auth-file
</Location>
```

This <Location> block is not yet complete, and will not do anything useful. It's merely telling Apache that whenever authorization is required, Apache should harvest a username and password from the Subversion client. What's missing here, however, are directives that tell Apache *which* sorts of client requests require authorization. Wherever authorization is required, Apache will demand authentication as well. The simplest thing to do is protect all requests. Adding Require valid-user tells Apache that all requests require an authenticated user:

```
<Location /svn>
  DAV svn
  SVNParentPath /usr/local/svn
  AuthType Basic
  AuthName "Subversion repository"
  AuthUserFile /etc/svn-auth-file
  Require valid-user
</Location>
```

Be sure to read the next section ("Authorization Options" earlier in this chapter) for more detail on the Require directive and other ways to set authorization policies.

One word of warning: HTTP Basic Auth passwords pass in very nearly plain-text over the network, and thus are extremely insecure. If you're worried about password snooping, it may be best to use some sort of SSL encryption, so that clients authenticate via https:// instead of http://; at a bare minimum, you can configure Apache to use a self-signed server certificate.* Consult Apache's documentation (and OpenSSL documentation) about how to do that.

SSL certificate management

Businesses that need to expose their repositories for access outside the company firewall should be conscious of the possibility that unauthorized parties could be sniffing their network traffic. SSL makes that kind of unwanted attention less likely to result in sensitive data leaks.

If a Subversion client is compiled to use OpenSSL, then it gains the ability to speak to an Apache server via https:// URLs. The Neon library used by the Subversion client is not only able to verify server certificates, but can also supply client certificates when challenged. When the client and server have exchanged SSL certificates and successfully authenticated one another, all further communication is encrypted via a session key.

It's beyond the scope of this book to describe how to generate client and server certificates, and how to configure Apache to use them. Many other books, including Apache's own documentation, describe this task. But what *can* be covered here is how to manage server and client certificates from an ordinary Subversion client.

When speaking to Apache via https://, a Subversion client can receive two different types of information:

- A server certificate
- A demand for a client certificate

If the client receives a server certificate, it needs to verify that it trusts the certificate: is the server really who it claims to be? The OpenSSL library does this by examining the signer of the server certificate, or *certifying authority* (CA). If OpenSSL is unable to automatically trust the CA, or if some other problem occurs (such as an expired certificate or hostname mismatch), the Subversion commandline client asks you whether you want to trust the server certificate anyway:

```
$ svn list https://host.example.com/repos/project
```

---

* While self-signed server certificates are still vulnerable to a man-in-the-middle attack, such an attack is still much more difficult for a casual observer to pull off, compared to sniffing unprotected passwords.

```
Error validating server certificate for 'https://home.example.com:443':
 - The certificate is not issued by a trusted authority. Use the
   fingerprint to validate the certificate manually!
Certificate information:
 - Hostname: host.example.com
 - Valid: from Jan 30 19:23:56 2004 GMT until Jan 30 19:23:56 2006 GMT
 - Issuer: CA, example.com, Sometown, California, US
 - Fingerprint: 7d:e1:a9:34:33:39:ba:6a:e9:a5:c4:22:98:7b:76:5c:92:a0:9c:7b

(R)eject, accept (t)emporarily or accept (p)ermanently?
```

This dialogue should look familiar; it's essentially the same question you've probably seen coming from your web browser (which is just another HTTP client, like Subversion!). If you choose the (p)ermanent option, the server certificate will be cached in your private run-time *auth/* area in just the same way your username and password are cached (see "Client Credentials Caching.") If cached, Subversion automatically remembers to trust this certificate in future negotiations.

Your run-time *servers* file also gives you the ability to make your Subversion client automatically trust specific CAs, either globally or on a per-host basis. Simply set the `ssl-authority-files` variable to a semicolon-separated list of PEM-encoded CA certificates:

```
[global]
ssl-authority-files = /path/to/CAcert1.pem;/path/to/CAcert2.pem
```

Many OpenSSL installations also have a predefined set of default CAs that are nearly universally trusted. To make the Subversion client automatically trust these standard authorities, set the `ssl-trust-default-ca` variable to true.

When talking to Apache, a Subversion client might also receive a challenge for a client certificate. Apache is asking the client to identify itself: is the client really who he says he is? If all goes correctly, the Subversion client sends back a private certificate signed by a CA that Apache trusts. A client certificate is usually stored on disk in encrypted format, protected by a local password. When Subversion receives this challenge, it asks you for both a path to the certificate and the password that protects it:

```
$ svn list https://host.example.com/repos/project

Authentication realm: https://host.example.com:443
Client certificate filename: /path/to/my/cert.p12
Passphrase for '/path/to/my/cert.p12':  ********
...
```

Notice that the client certificate is a p12 file. To use a client certificate with Subversion, it must be in PKCS#12 format, which is a portable standard. Most web browsers are already able to import and export certificates in that format. Another option is to use the OpenSSL commandline tools to convert existing certificates into PKCS#12.

Again, the runtime *servers* file allows you to automate this challenge on a per-host basis. Either or both pieces of information can be described in runtime variables:

```
[groups]
examplehost = host.example.com

[examplehost]
ssl-client-cert-file = /path/to/my/cert.p12
ssl-client-cert-password = somepassword
```

Once you've set the `ssl-client-cert-file` and `ssl-client-cert-password` variables, the Subversion client can automatically respond to a client certificate challenge without prompting you.[*]

Authorization Options

At this point, you've configured authentication, but not authorization. Apache is able to challenge clients and confirm identities, but it has not been told how to allow or restrict access to the clients bearing those identities. This section describes two strategies for controlling access to your repositories.

Blanket access control

The simplest form of access control is to authorize certain users for either read-only access to a repository, or read/write access to a repository.

You can restrict access on all repository operations by adding the `Require valid-user` directive to your `<Location>` block. Using our previous example, this would mean that only clients that claimed to be either `harry` or `sally`, and which provided the correct password for their respective username, would be allowed to do anything with the Subversion repository:

```
<Location /svn>
  DAV svn
  SVNParentPath /usr/local/svn

  # how to authenticate a user
  AuthType Basic
  AuthName "Subversion repository"
  AuthUserFile /path/to/users/file

  # only authenticated users may access the repository
  Require valid-user
</Location>
```

Sometimes you don't need to run such a tight ship. For example, Subversion's own source code repository at *http://svn.collab.net/repos/svn* allows anyone in the world to

---

[*] More security-conscious folk might not want to store the client certificate password in the runtime *servers* file.

perform read-only repository tasks (such as checking out working copies and browsing the repository with a web browser), but restricts all write operations to authenticated users. To do this type of selective restriction, you can use the Limit and LimitExcept configuration directives. Like the Location directive, these blocks have starting and ending tags, and you would nest them inside your <Location> block.

The parameters present on the Limit and LimitExcept directives are HTTP request types that are affected by that block. For example, if you wanted to disallow all access to your repository except the currently supported read-only operations, you would use the LimitExcept directive, passing the GET, PROPFIND, OPTIONS, and REPORT request type parameters. Then the previously mentioned Require valid-user directive would be placed inside the <LimitExcept> block instead of just inside the <Location> block:

```
<Location /svn>
  DAV svn
  SVNParentPath /usr/local/svn

  # how to authenticate a user
  AuthType Basic
  AuthName "Subversion repository"
  AuthUserFile /path/to/users/file

  # For any operations other than these, require an authenticated user.
  <LimitExcept GET PROPFIND OPTIONS REPORT>
    Require valid-user
  </LimitExcept>
</Location>
```

These are only a few simple examples. For more in-depth information about Apache access control and the Require directive, take a look at the Security section of the Apache documentation's tutorials collection at *http://httpd.apache.org/docs-2.0/misc/tutorials.html*.

Per-directory access control

It's possible to set up finer-grained permissions using a second Apache httpd module, mod_authz_svn. This module grabs the various opaque URLs passing from client to server, asks mod_dav_svn to decode them, and then possibly vetoes requests based on access policies defined in a configuration file.

If you've built Subversion from source code, mod_authz_svn is automatically built and installed alongside mod_dav_svn. Many binary distributions install it automatically as well. To verify that it's installed correctly, make sure it comes right after mod_dav_svn's LoadModule directive in *httpd.conf*:

```
LoadModule dav_module        modules/mod_dav.so
LoadModule dav_svn_module    modules/mod_dav_svn.so
LoadModule authz_svn_module  modules/mod_authz_svn.so
```

To activate this module, you need to configure your Location block to use the AuthzSVNAccessFile directive, which specifies a file containing the permissions policy for paths within your repositories. (In a moment, we'll discuss the format of that file.)

Apache is flexible, so you have the option to configure your block in one of three general patterns. To begin, choose one of these basic configuration patterns. (The examples below are very simple; look at Apache's own documentation for much more detail on Apache authentication and authorization options.)

The simplest block is to allow open access to everyone. In Example 6-1, Apache never sends authentication challenges, so all users are treated as anonymous.

Example 6-1. A sample configuration for anonymous access

```
<Location /repos>
  DAV svn
  SVNParentPath /usr/local/svn

  # our access control policy
  AuthzSVNAccessFile /path/to/access/file
</Location>
```

On the opposite end of the paranoia scale, you can configure your block to demand authentication from everyone. All clients must supply credentials to identify themselves. In Example 6-2, your block unconditionally requires authentication via the Require valid-user directive, and defines a means to authenticate.

Example 6-2. A sample configuration for authenticated access

```
<Location /repos>
  DAV svn
  SVNParentPath /usr/local/svn

  # our access control policy
  AuthzSVNAccessFile /path/to/access/file

  # only authenticated users may access the repository
  Require valid-user

  # how to authenticate a user
  AuthType Basic
  AuthName "Subversion repository"
  AuthUserFile /path/to/users/file
</Location>
```

A third very popular pattern is to allow a combination of authenticated and anonymous access. For example, many administrators want to allow anonymous users to read certain repository directories, but want only authenticated users to read (or write) more sensitive areas. In this setup, all users start out accessing the repository anonymously. If your access control policy demands a real username at any point, Apache will demand authentication from the client. In Example 6-3, you use both the Satisfy Any and Require valid-user directives together.

Example 6-3. A sample configuration for mixed authenticated/anonymous access

```
<Location /repos>
  DAV svn
  SVNParentPath /usr/local/svn

  # our access control policy
  AuthzSVNAccessFile /path/to/access/file

  # try anonymous access first, resort to real
  # authentication if necessary.
  Satisfy Any
  Require valid-user

  # how to authenticate a user
  AuthType Basic
  AuthName "Subversion repository"
  AuthUserFile /path/to/users/file
</Location>
```

Once your basic Location block is configured, you can create an access file and define some authorization rules in it.

The syntax of the access file is the same familiar one used by svnserve.conf and the runtime configuration files. Lines that start with hash (#) are ignored. In its simplest form, each section names a repository and path within it, and the authenticated usernames are the option names within each section. The value of each option describes the user's level of access to the repository path: either r (read-only) or rw (read-write). If the user is not mentioned at all, no access is allowed.

To be more specific: the value of the section-names are either of the form [reposname:path] or the form [path]. If you're using the SVNParentPath directive, then it's important to specify the repository names in your sections. If you omit them, then a section like [/some/dir] will match the path *some/dir* in *every* repository. If you're using the SVNPath directive, however, then it's fine to only define paths in your sections—after all, there's only one repository:

```
[calc:/branches/calc/bug-142]
harry = rw
sally = r
```

In this first example, user harry has full read and write access on the */branches/calc/bug-142* directory in the calc repository, but user sally has read-only access. Any other users are blocked from accessing this directory.

Of course, permissions inherit from parent to child directory. That means that we can specify a subdirectory with a different access policy for Sally:

```
[calc:/branches/calc/bug-142]
harry = rw
sally = r
```

```
# give sally write access only to the 'testing' subdir
[calc:/branches/calc/bug-142/testing]
sally = rw
```

Now Sally can write to the testing subdirectory of the branch, but can still only read other parts. Harry, meanwhile, continues to have complete read-write access to the whole branch.

It's also possible to explicitly deny permission to someone via inheritance rules, by setting the username variable to nothing:

```
[calc:/branches/calc/bug-142]
harry = rw
sally = r

[calc:/branches/calc/bug-142/secret]
harry =
```

In this example, Harry has read-write access to the entire *bug-142* tree, but has absolutely no access at all to the *secret* subdirectory within it.

By default, nobody has any access to the repository at all. That means that if you're starting with an empty file, you'll probably want to give at least read permission to all users at the root of the repository. You can do this by using the asterisk variable (*), which means all users:

```
[/]
* = r
```

This is a common setup; notice that there's no repository name mentioned in the section name. This makes all repositories world-readable to all users, whether you're using SVNPath or SVNParentPath. Once all users have read access to the repositories, you can give explicit rw permission to certain users on specific subdirectories within specific repositories.

The asterisk variable (*) is also worth special mention here: it's the *only* pattern that matches an anonymous user. If you've configured your Location block to allow a mixture of anonymous and authenticated access, all users start out accessing Apache anonymously. mod_authz_svn looks for a * value defined for the path being accessed; if it can't find one, then Apache demands real authentication from the client.

The access file also allows you to define whole groups of users, much as the Unix */etc/group* file:

```
[groups]
calc-developers = harry, sally, joe
paint-developers = frank, sally, jane
everyone = harry, sally, joe, frank, sally, jane
```

Groups can be granted access control just like users. Distinguish them with an ampersand (@) prefix:

```
[calc:/projects/calc]
@calc-developers = rw
```

```
[paint:/projects/paint]
@paint-developers = rw
jane = r
```

...and that's pretty much all there is to it.

Extra Goodies

We've covered most of the authentication and authorization options for Apache and mod_dav_svn. But Apache also provides a few other nice features.

Repository browsing

One of the most useful benefits of an Apache/WebDAV configuration for your Subversion repository is that the youngest revisions of your versioned files and directories are immediately available for viewing via a regular web browser. Since Subversion uses URLs to identify versioned resources, those URLs used for HTTP-based repository access can be typed directly into a Web browser. Your browser will issue a GET request for that URL, and, based on whether that URL represents a versioned directory or file, mod_dav_svn will respond with a directory listing or with file contents.

Since the URLs do not contain any information about which version of the resource you wish to see, mod_dav_svn will always answer with the youngest version. This functionality has the wonderful side effect of allowing you to pass around Subversion URLs to your peers as references to documents, and those URLs will always point at the latest manifestation of that document. Of course, you can even use the URLs as hyperlinks from other web sites, too.

You will generally get more use out of URLs to versioned files—after all, that's where the interesting content tends to lie. But you might have occasion to browse a Subversion directory listing, where you'll quickly note that the generated HTML used to display that listing is very basic, and certainly not intended to be aesthetically pleasing (or even interesting). To enable customization of these directory displays, Subversion provides an XML index feature. A single SVNIndexXSLT directive in your repository's Location block of *httpd.conf* will instruct mod_dav_svn to generate XML output when displaying a directory listing, and to reference the XSLT stylesheet of your choice:

```
<Location /svn>
  DAV svn
  SVNParentPath /usr/local/svn
  SVNIndexXSLT "/svnindex.xsl"
  ...
</Location>
```

Using the SVNIndexXSLT directive and a creative XSLT stylesheet, you can make your directory listings match the color schemes and imagery used in other parts of your website. Or, if you'd prefer, you can use the sample stylesheets provided in the Subversion source distribution's *tools/xslt/* directory. Keep in mind that the path provided to the SVNIndexXSLT directory is actually a URL path—browsers need to be able to read your stylesheets in order to make use of them!

Can I View Older Revisions?

With an ordinary web browser? In one word: nope. At least, not with mod_dav_svn as your only tool.

Your web browser only speaks ordinary HTTP. That means it only knows how to GET public URLs, which represent the latest versions of files and directories. According to the WebDAV/DeltaV spec, each server defines a private URL syntax for older versions of resources, and that syntax is opaque to clients. To find an older version of a file, a client must follow a specific procedure to discover the proper URL; the procedure involves issuing a series of WebDAV PROPFIND requests and understanding DeltaV concepts. This is something your web browser simply can't do.

So to answer the question, one obvious way to see older revisions of files and directories is by passing the --revision argument to the svn list and svn cat commands. To browse old revisions with your web browser, however, you can use third-party software. A good example of this is ViewCVS (*http://viewcvs.sourceforge.net/*). ViewCVS was originally written to display CVS repositories through the web, and the latest bleeding-edge versions (at the time of this writing) are able to understand Subversion repositories as well.

Other features

Several of the features already provided by Apache in its role as a robust web server can be leveraged for increased functionality or security in Subversion as well. Subversion communicates with Apache using Neon, which is a generic HTTP/WebDAV library with support for such mechanisms as SSL (the Secure Sockets Layer, discussed earlier) and Deflate compression (the same algorithm used by the gzip and PKZIP programs to shrink files into smaller chunks of data). You need only to compile support for the features you desire into Subversion and Apache, and properly configure the programs to use those features.

Deflate compression places a small burden on the client and server to compress and decompress network transmissions as a way to minimize the size of the actual transmission. In cases where network bandwidth is in short supply, this kind of compression can greatly increase the speed at which communications between server and client can be sent. In extreme cases, this minimized network transmission could be the difference between an operation timing out or completing successfully.

Less interesting, but equally useful, are other features of the Apache and Subversion relationship, such as the ability to specify a custom port (instead of the default HTTP port 80) or a virtual domain name by which the Subversion repository should be accessed, or the ability to access the repository through a proxy. These things are all supported by Neon, so Subversion gets that support for free.

Finally, because `mod_dav_svn` is speaking a semi-complete dialect of WebDAV/DeltaV, it's possible to access the repository via third-party DAV clients. Most modern operating systems (Win32, OS X, and Linux) have the built-in ability to mount a DAV server as a standard network share. This is a complicated topic; for details, read Appendix C.

Supporting Multiple Repository Access Methods

You've seen how a repository can be accessed in many different ways. But is it possible—or safe—for your repository to be accessed by multiple methods simultaneously? The answer is yes, provided you use a bit of foresight.

At any given time, these processes may require read and write access to your repository:

- Regular system users using a Subversion client (as themselves) to access the repository directly via `file:///` URLs
- Regular system users connecting to SSH-spawned private `svnserve` processes (running as themselves) that access the repository
- An `svnserve` process—either a daemon or one launched by `inetd`—running as a particular fixed user
- An Apache `httpd` process, running as a particular fixed user

The most common problem administrators run into is repository ownership and permissions. Does every process (or user) in the previous list have the rights to read and write the Berkeley DB files? Assuming you have a Unix-like operating system, a straightforward approach might be to place every potential repository user into a new `svn` group, and make the repository wholly owned by that group. But even that's not enough, because a process may write to the database files using an unfriendly umask—one that prevents access by other users.

The next step beyond setting up a common group for repository users is to force every repository-accessing process to use a sane umask. For users accessing the repository directly, you can make the svn program into a wrapper script that first sets `umask 002` and then runs the real svn client program. You can write a similar wrapper script for the `svnserve` program, and add a `umask 002` command to Apache's own startup script, *apachectl*. For example:

```
$ cat /usr/local/bin/svn

#!/bin/sh
```

```
umask 002
/usr/local/subversion/bin/svn "$@"
```

Another common problem is often encountered on Unix-like systems. As a repository is used, BerkeleyDB occasionally creates new logfiles to journal its actions. Even if the repository is wholly owned by the svn group, these newly created files won't necessarily be owned by that same group, which then creates more permissions problems for your users. A good workaround is to set the group SUID bit on the repository's *db* directory. This causes all newly created logfiles to have the same group owner as the parent directory.

Once you've jumped through these hoops, your repository should be accessible by all the necessary processes. It may seem a bit messy and complicated, but the problems of having multiple users sharing write access to common files are classic ones that are not often elegantly solved.

Fortunately, most repository administrators will never *need* to have such a complex configuration. Users who wish to access repositories that live on the same machine are not limited to using file:// access URLs—they can typically contact the Apache HTTP server or svnserve using localhost for the server name in their http:// or svn:// URLs. And, to maintain multiple server processes for your Subversion repositories is likely to be more of a headache than necessary. We recommend you choose the server that best meets your needs, and stick with it!

The svn+ssh:// Server Checklist

It can be quite tricky to get a bunch of users with existing SSH accounts to share a repository without permissions problems. If you're confused about all the things that you (as an admininstrator) need to do on a Unix-like system, here's a quick checklist that resummarizes some points discussed in this section:

- All of your SSH users need to be able to read and write to the repository. Put all the SSH users into a single group. Make the repository wholly owned by that group, and set the group permissions to read/write.
- Your users need to use a sane umask when accessing the repository. Make sure that svnserve (*/usr/local/bin/svnserve*, or wherever it lives in $PATH) is actually a wrapper script that sets umask 002 and executes the real svnserve binary.
- When BerkeleyDB creates new logfiles, they need to be owned by the group as well, so make sure you run chmod g+s on the repository's *db* directory.

## CHAPTER 7

Advanced Topics

If you read this book chapter by chapter, by now, you should have acquired enough knowledge to use the Subversion client to perform the most common version control operations. You understand how to check out a working copy from a Subversion repository. You are comfortable with submitting and receiving changes using the svn commit and svn update functions. You probably even developed a reflex that causes you to run the svn status command almost unconsciously. For all intents and purposes, you are ready to use Subversion in a typical environment.

But the Subversion feature set doesn't stop at common version control operations.

This chapter highlights some of Subversion's features that aren't regularly used. In it, we discuss Subversion's property (or metadata) support, and how to modify Subversion's default behaviors by tweaking its runtime configuration area. We describe how you can use externals definitions to instruct Subversion to pull data from multiple repositories, and we cover in detail some of the additional client- and server-side tools that are part of the Subversion distribution.

Before reading this chapter, you should be familiar with the basic file and directory versioning capabilities of Subversion. If you haven't already read about those, or if you need a refresher, we recommend that you check out Chapters 2 and 3. Once you've mastered the basics and consumed this chapter, you'll be a Subversion power-user!

Runtime Configuration Area

The user can control many optional behaviors that Subversion provides. Users can apply these options to all Subversion operations. So, rather than forcing users to remember command-line arguments for specifying these options, and to use them for each and every operation they perform, Subversion uses configuration files, segregated into a Subversion configuration area.

The Subversion *configuration area* is a two-tiered hierarchy of option names and their values. Usually, this boils down to a special directory that contains *configuration files* (the first tier), which are just text files in standard INI format (with sections providing the second tier). These files can be easily edited using your favorite text editor (such as Emacs or vi), and contain directives read by the client to determine which of several optional behaviors the user prefers.

Configuration Area Layout

The first time that the svn command-line client is executed, it creates a per-user configuration area. On Unix-like systems, this area appears as a directory named *.subversion* in the user's home directory. On Win32 systems, Subversion creates a folder named *Subversion*, typically inside the *Application Data* area of the user's profile directory (which, by the way, is usually a hidden directory). However, on this platform the exact location differs from system to system, and is dictated by the Windows registry.[*] We will refer to the per-user configuration area using its Unix name, *.subversion*.

In addition to the per-user configuration area, Subversion also recognizes the existence of a system-wide configuration area. This gives system administrators the ability to establish defaults for all users on a given machine. Note that the system-wide configuration area does not alone dictate mandatory policy—the settings in the per-user configuration area override those in the system-wide one, and command-line arguments supplied to the svn program have the final word on behavior. On Unix-like platforms, the system-wide configuration area is expected to be the */etc/subversion* directory; on Windows machines, it again looks for a *Subversion* directory inside the common Application Data location (again, as specified by the Windows Registry). Unlike the per-user case, the svn program does not attempt to create the system-wide configuration area.

The configuration area currently contains three files—two configuration files (*config* and *servers*) and a *README.txt* file which describes the INI format. At the time of their creation, the files contain default values for each of the supported Subversion options, mostly commented out and grouped with textual descriptions about how the values for the key affect Subversion's behavior. To change a certain behavior, you need only to load the appropriate configuration file into a text editor, and modify the desired option's value. If you wish to have the default configuration settings restored, you can simply remove (or rename) your configuration directory, and then run some innocuous svn command, such as svn --version. A new configuration directory with the default contents will be created.

---

[*] The APPDATA environment variable points to the *Application Data* area, so you can always refer to this folder as *%APPDATA%\Subversion*.

The per-user configuration area also contains a cache of authentication data. The *auth* directory holds a set of subdirectories that contain pieces of cached information used by Subversion's various supported authentication methods. This directory is created in such a way that only the user herself has permission to read its contents.

Configuration and the Windows Registry

In addition to the usual INI-based configuration area, Subversion clients running on Windows platforms may also use the Windows Registry to hold the configuration data. The option names and their values are the same as in the INI files. The file/section hierarchy is preserved as well, though addressed in a slightly different fashion—in this schema, files and sections are just levels in the registry key tree.

Subversion looks for system-wide configuration values under the HKEY_LOCAL_MACHINE\Software\Tigris.org\Subversion key. For example, the global-ignores option, which is in the miscellany section of the *config* file, would be found at HKEY_LOCAL_MACHINE\Software\Tigris.org\Subversion\Config\Miscellany\global-ignores. Per-user configuration values should be stored under HKEY_CURRENT_USER\Software\Tigris.org\Subversion.

Registry-based configuration options are parsed *before* their file-based counterparts, so are overridden by values found in the configuration files. In other words, configuration priority is granted in the following order on a Windows system:

1. Command-line options
2. The per-user INI files
3. The per-user Registry values
4. The system-wide INI files
5. The system-wide Registry values

Also, the Windows Registry doesn't really support the notion of something being commented out. However, Subversion will ignore any option key whose name begins with a hash (#) character. This allows you to effectively comment out a Subversion option without deleting the entire key from the Registry, obviously simplifying the process of restoring that option.

The svn command-line client never attempts to write to the Windows Registry, and will not attempt to create a default configuration area there. You can create the keys you need using the REGEDIT program. Alternatively, you can create a *.reg* file, and then double-click on that file from the Explorer shell, which merges the data into your registry (see Example 7-1).

Example 7-1. Sample registration entries (.reg) file

```
REGEDIT4

[HKEY_LOCAL_MACHINE\Software\Tigris.org\Subversion\Servers\groups]

[HKEY_LOCAL_MACHINE\Software\Tigris.org\Subversion\Servers\global]
"#http-proxy-host"=""
"#http-proxy-port"=""
"#http-proxy-username"=""
"#http-proxy-password"=""
"#http-proxy-exceptions"=""
"#http-timeout"="0"
"#http-compression"="yes"
"#neon-debug-mask"=""
"#ssl-authority-files"=""
"#ssl-trust-default-ca"=""
"#ssl-client-cert-file"=""
"#ssl-client-cert-password"=""

[HKEY_CURRENT_USER\Software\Tigris.org\Subversion\Config\auth]
"#store-auth-creds"="no"

[HKEY_CURRENT_USER\Software\Tigris.org\Subversion\Config\helpers]
"#editor-cmd"="notepad"
"#diff-cmd"=""
"#diff3-cmd"=""
"#diff3-has-program-arg"=""

[HKEY_CURRENT_USER\Software\Tigris.org\Subversion\Config\miscellany]
"#global-ignores"="*.o *.lo *.la #*# .*.rej *.rej .*~ *~ .#*"
"#log-encoding"=""
"#use-commit-times"=""
"#template-root"=""
"#enable-auto-props"=""

[HKEY_CURRENT_USER\Software\Tigris.org\Subversion\Config\tunnels]

[HKEY_CURRENT_USER\Software\Tigris.org\Subversion\Config\auto-props]
```

The previous example shows the contents of a *.reg* file that contains some of the most commonly used configuration options and their default values. Note the presence of both system-wide (for network proxy-related options) and per-user settings (editor programs and password storage, among others). Also note that all the options are effectively commented out. You need only to remove the hash (#) character from the beginning of the option names, and set the values as you desire.

Configuration Options

In this section, we discuss the specific runtime configuration options that are currently supported by Subversion.

Servers

The *servers* file contains Subversion configuration options related to the network layers. There are two special section names in this file—groups and global. The groups section is essentially a cross-reference table. The keys in this section are the names of other sections in the file; their values are *globs*—textual tokens which possibly contain wildcard characters—that are compared against the hostnames of the machine to which Subversion requests are sent:

```
[groups]
beanie-babies = *.red-bean.com
collabnet = svn.collab.net

[beanie-babies]
...

[collabnet]
...
```

When Subversion is used over a network, it attempts to match the name of the server it is trying to reach with a group name under the groups section. If a match is made, Subversion then looks for a section in the *servers* file whose name is the matched group's name. From that section it reads the actual network configuration settings.

The global section contains the settings that are meant for all of the servers not matched by one of the globs under the groups section. The options available in this section are exactly the same as those valid for the other server sections in the file (except, of course, the special groups section), and are as follows:

http-proxy-host

> This specifies the hostname of the proxy computer through which your HTTP-based Subversion requests must pass. It defaults to an empty value, which means that Subversion does not attempt to route HTTP requests through a proxy computer, and instead attempts to contact the destination machine directly.

http-proxy-port

> This specifies the port number on the proxy host to use. It defaults to an empty value.

http-proxy-username

> This specifies the username to supply to the proxy machine. It defaults to an empty value.

http-proxy-password

> This specifies the password to supply to the proxy machine. It defaults to an empty value.

http-timeout

> This specifies the amount of time, in seconds, to wait for a server response. If you experience problems with a slow network connection causing Subversion operations to timeout, you should increase the value of this option. The default

value is 0, which instructs the underlying HTTP library, Neon, to use its default
timeout setting.

http-compression

> This specifies whether or not Subversion should attempt to compress network
> requests made to DAV-ready servers. The default value is yes (though compres-
> sion will only occur if that capability is compiled into the network layer). Set this
> to no to disable compression, such as when debugging network transmissions.

neon-debug-mask

> This is an integer mask that the underlying HTTP library, Neon, uses for choos-
> ing what type of debugging output to yield. The default value is 0, which silences
> all debugging output. For more information about how Subversion makes use of
> Neon, see Chapter 8.

ssl-authority-files

> A semicolon delimited list of paths to files containing certificates of the certifi-
> cate authorities (or CAs) that are accepted by the Subversion client when access-
> ing the repository over HTTPS.

ssl-trust-default-ca

> Set this variable to yes if you want Subversion to trust the set of default CAs that
> ship with OpenSSL automatically.

ssl-client-cert-file

> If host (or set of hosts) requries an SSL client certificate, you normally are
> prompted for a path to your certificate. By setting this variable to that same path,
> Subversion can find your client certificate automatically without prompting you.
> There's no standard place to store your certificate on disk; Subversion grabs it
> from any path you specify.

ssl-client-cert-password

> If your SSL client certificate file is encrypted by a passphrase, Subversion will
> prompt you for the passphrase whenever the certificate is used. If you find this
> annoying (and don't mind storing the password in the *servers* file), then you can
> set this variable to the certificate's passphrase. You won't be prompted anymore.

Config

The *config* file contains the rest of the currently available Subversion run-time
options, those not related to networking. There are only a few options in use at this
time, but they are again grouped into sections in expectation of future additions.

The auth section contains settings related to Subversion's authentication and authorization against the repository. It contains:

store-auth-creds

> This instructs Subversion to cache, or not to cache, authentication credentials
> that are supplied by the user in response to server authentication challenges. The
> default value is yes. Set this to no to disable this on-disk credential caching. You

can override this option for a single instance of the svn command using the --no-auth-cache command-line parameter (for those subcommands that support it). For more information, see "Client Credentials Caching" in Chapter 6.

The helpers section controls which external applications Subversion uses to accomplish its tasks. Valid options in this section are as follows:

editor-cmd

> This specifies the program Subversion will use to query the user for a log message during a commit operation, such as when using svn commit without either the --message (-m) or --file (-F) options. This program is also used with the svn propedit command—a temporary file is populated with the current value of the property the user wishes to edit, and the edits take place right in the editor program (see "Properties"). This option's default value is empty. If the option is not set, Subversion will fall back to checking the environment variables SVN_EDITOR, VISUAL, and EDITOR (in that order) for an editor command.

diff-cmd

> This specifies the absolute path of a differencing program, used when Subversion generates diff output (such as when using the svn diff command). By default Subversion uses an internal differencing library—setting this option causes it to perform this task using an external program.

diff3-cmd

> This specifies the absolute path of a three-way differencing program. Subversion uses this program to merge changes made by the user with those received from the repository. By default Subversion uses an internal differencing library—setting this option will cause it to perform this task using an external program.

diff3-has-program-arg

> This flag should be set to true if the program specified by the diff3-cmd option accepts a --diff-program command-line parameter.

The tunnels section allows you to define new tunnel schemes for use with svnserve and svn:// client connections. For more details, see "SSH Authentication and Authorization."

The miscellany section is where everything that doesn't belong elsewhere winds up.* In this section, you can find:

global-ignores

> When running the svn status command, Subversion lists unversioned files and directories along with the versioned ones, annotating them with a ? character (see "svn status" in Chapter 3). Sometimes, it can be annoying to see uninteresting, unversioned items—for example, object files that result from a program's compilation—in this display. The global-ignores option is a list of whitespace-

---

* Anyone for potluck dinner?

delimited globs which describe the names of files and directories that Subversion should not display unless they are versioned. The default value is *.o *.lo *.la #*# .*.rej *.rej .*~ *~ .#*.

You can override this option for a single instance of the svn status command by using the --no-ignore command-line flag. For information on more fine-grained control of ignored items, see "svn:ignore" later in this chapter.

enable-auto-props

This instructs Subversion to set properties automatically on newly added or imported files. The default value is no, so set this to yes to enable auto-props.

The auto-props section controls the Subversion client's ability to automatically set properties on files when they are added or imported. It contains any number of key-value pairs in the format PATTERN = PROPNAME=PROPVALUE where PATTERN is a regular expression that matches a set of filenames and the rest of the line is the property and its value. Multiple matches on a file will result in multiple propsets for that file; however, there is no guarantee that auto-props will be applied in the order in which they are listed in the config file, so you can't have one rule override another. You can find several examples of auto-props usage in the *config* file. Lastly, don't forget to set enable-auto-props to yes if you want to enable auto-props.

log-encoding

This variable sets the default character set encoding for commit log messages. It's a permanent form of the --encoding option (see "svn Switches" in Chapter 9). The Subversion repository stores log messages in UTF8, and assumes that your log message is written using your operating system's native locale. You should specify a different encoding if your commit messages are written in any other encoding.

use-commit-times

Normally your working copy files have timestamps that reflect the last time they were touched by any process, i.e., by your own editor or by some svn subcommand. This is generally convenient for people developing software, because build systems often look at timestamps as a way of deciding which files need to be recompiled.

In other situations, however, it's sometimes nice for the working copy files to have timestamps that reflect the last time they were changed in the repository. The svn export command always places these last-commit timestamps on trees that it produces. By setting this config variable to yes, the svn checkout, svn update, svn switch, and svn revert commands also sets last-commit timestamps on files that they touch.

Properties

We covered in detail how Subversion stores and retrieves various versions of files and directories in its repository. Entire chapters have been devoted to this most fundamental piece of functionality provided by the tool. And, if the versioning support stopped there, Subversion would still be complete from a version control perspective. But it doesn't stop there.

In addition to versioning your directories and files, Subversion provides interfaces for adding, modifying, and removing versioned metadata on each of your versioned directories and files. We refer to this metadata as *properties*, and they can be thought of as two-column tables that map property names to arbitrary values attached to each item in your working copy. Generally speaking, the names and values of the properties can be whatever you want them to be, with the constraint that the names must be human-readable text. And the best part about these properties is that they, too, are versioned, just like the textual contents of your files. You can modify, commit, and revert property changes as easily as committing textual changes. And you receive other people's property changes as you update your working copy.

Other Properties in Subversion

Properties show up elsewhere in Subversion, too. Just as files and directories may have arbitrary property names and values attached to them, each revision as a whole may have arbitrary properties attached to it. The same constraints apply—human-readable, text names and anything-you-want, binary values—except that revision properties are not versioned. See "Unversioned Properties" in Chapter 5 for more information on these unversioned properties.

In this section, we examine the utility—both to users of Subversion, and to Subversion itself—of property support. You'll learn about the property-related svn subcommands, and how property modifications affect your normal Subversion workflow. Hopefully, you'll be convinced that Subversion properties can enhance your version control experience.

Why Properties?

Properties can be very useful additions to your working copy. In fact, Subversion itself uses properties to house special information, and as a way to denote that certain special processing might be needed. Likewise, you can use properties for your own purposes. Of course, anything you can do with properties you could also do using regular versioned files, but consider the following example of Subversion property use.

Say you wish to design a website that houses many digital photos, and displays them with captions and a datestamp. Now, your set of photos is constantly changing, so you'd like to have as much of this site automated as possible. These photos can be quite large, so, as is common with sites of this nature, you want to provide smaller thumbnail images to your site visitors. You can do this with traditional files. That is, you can have your *image123.jpg* and an *image123-thumbnail.jpg* side-by-side in a directory. Or, if you want to keep the filenames the same, you might have your thumbnails in a different directory, like *thumbnails/image123.jpg*. You can also store your captions and datestamps in a similar fashion, again separated from the original image file. Soon, your tree of files is a mess, and grows in multiples with each new photo added to the site.

Now consider the same setup using Subversion's file properties. Imagine having a single image file, *image123.jpg*, and then properties set on that file named caption, datestamp, and even thumbnail. Now your working copy directory looks much more manageable—in fact, it looks like there are nothing but image files in it. But your automation scripts know better. They know that they can use svn (or better yet, they can use the Subversion language bindings—see "Using Languages Other than C and C++" in Chapter 8) to dig out the extra information that your site needs to display without having to read an index file or play path manipulation games.

How (and if) you use Subversion properties is up to you. As we mentioned, Subversion has it own uses for properties, which we discuss a little later in this chapter. But first, let's discuss how to manipulate options using the svn program.

Manipulating Properties

The svn command affords a few ways to add or modify file and directory properties. For properties with short, human-readable values, perhaps the simplest way to add a new property is to specify the property name and value on the command-line of the propset subcommand:

```
$ svn propset copyright '(c) 2003 Red-Bean Software' calc/button.c
property 'copyright' set on 'calc/button.c'
$
```

But we've been touting the flexibility that Subversion offers for your property values. And if you are planning to have a multiline textual, or even binary, property value, you probably do not want to supply that value on the command line. So the propset subcommand takes a --file (-F) option for specifying the name of a file which contains the new property value:

```
$ svn propset license -F /path/to/LICENSE calc/button.c
property 'license' set on 'calc/button.c'
$
```

In addition to the propset command, the svn program supplies the propedit command. This command uses the configured editor program (see "Config" earlier in this chapter) to add or modify properties. When you run the command, svn invokes your editor program on a temporary file that contains the current value of the property (or which is empty, if you are adding a new property). Then, you just modify that value in your editor program until it represents the new value you wish to store for the property, save the temporary file, and then exit the editor program. If Subversion detects that you've actually changed the existing value of the property, it will accept that as the new property value. If you exit your editor without making any changes, no property modification occurs:

```
$ svn propedit copyright calc/button.c  ### exit the editor without changes
No changes to property 'copyright' on 'calc/button.c'
$
```

We should note that, as with other svn subcommands, those related to properties can act on multiple paths at once. This enables you to modify properties on whole sets of files with a single command. For example, we could have done:

```
$ svn propset copyright '(c) 2002 Red-Bean Software' calc/*
property 'copyright' set on 'calc/Makefile'
property 'copyright' set on 'calc/button.c'
property 'copyright' set on 'calc/integer.c'
...
$
```

All of this property adding and editing isn't really very useful if you can't easily get the stored property value. So the svn program supplies two subcommands for displaying the names and values of properties stored on files and directories. The svn proplist command lists the names of properties that exist on a path. Once you know the names of the properties on the node, you can request their values individually using svn propget. This command, given a path (or set of paths) and a property name, prints the value of the property to the standard output stream:

```
$ svn proplist calc/button.c
Properties on 'calc/button.c':
  copyright
  license
$ svn propget copyright calc/button.c
(c) 2003 Red-Bean Software
```

There's even a variation of the proplist command that lists both the name and value of all of the properties. Simply supply the --verbose (-v) option:

```
$ svn proplist --verbose calc/button.c
Properties on 'calc/button.c':
  copyright : (c) 2003 Red-Bean Software
  license : ========================================================
=========
Copyright (c) 2003 Red-Bean Software.  All rights reserved.

Redistribution and use in source and binary forms, with or without
modification, are permitted provided that the following conditions
are met:
```

```
1. Redistributions of source code must retain the above copyright
notice, this list of conditions, and the recipe for Fitz's famous
red-beans-and-rice.
...
```

The last property-related subcommand is propdel. Since Subversion allows you to store properties with empty values, you can't remove a property altogether using propedit or propset. For example, this command does *not* yield the desired effect:

```
$ svn propset license '' calc/button.c
property 'license' set on 'calc/button.c'
$ svn proplist --verbose calc/button.c
Properties on 'calc/button.c':
  copyright : (c) 2003 Red-Bean Software
  license :
$
```

You need to use the propdel command to delete properties altogether. The syntax is similar to the other property commands:

```
$ svn propdel license calc/button.c
property 'license' deleted from ''.
$ svn proplist --verbose calc/button.c
Properties on 'calc/button.c':
  copyright : (c) 2003 Red-Bean Software
$
```

Now that you are familiar with all of the property-related svn subcommands, let's see how property modifications affect the usual Subversion workflow. As we mentioned earlier, file and directory properties are versioned, just like your file contents. As a result, Subversion provides the same opportunities for merging—in cleanly or conflicting fashions—someone else's modifications into your own.

And as with file contents, your property changes are local modifications, only made permanent when you commit them to the repository with svn commit. Your property changes can be easily unmade, too—the svn revert command restores your files and directories to their unedited states, contents, properties, and all. Also, you can receive interesting information about the state of your file and directory properties by using the svn status and svn diff commands:

```
$ svn status calc/button.c
 M      calc/button.c
$ svn diff calc/button.c
Property changes on: calc/button.c
_____
Name: copyright
   + (c) 2003 Red-Bean Software

$
```

Notice how the status subcommand displays M in the second column instead of the first. That is because we have modified the properties on *calc/button.c*, but not modified its textual contents. Had we changed both, we would have seen M in the first column, too (see "svn status" in Chapter 3).

You might also have noticed the nonstandard way that Subversion currently displays property differences. You can still run svn diff and redirect the output to create a usable patch file. The patch program will ignore property patches—as a rule, it ignores any noise it can't understand. This does unfortunately mean that to fully apply a patch generated by svn diff, any property modifications will need to be applied by hand.

As you can see, the presence of property modifications has no outstanding effect on the typical Subversion workflow. Your general patterns of updating your working copy, checking the status of your files and directories, reporting on the modifications you have made, and committing those modifications to the repository are completely immune to the presence or absence of properties. The svn program has some additional subcommands for actually making property changes, but that is the only noticeable asymmetry.

Special Properties

Subversion has no particular policy regarding properties—you can use them for any purpose. Subversion asks only that you not use property names that begin with the prefix svn:. That's the namespace that it sets aside for its own use. In fact, Subversion defines certain properties that have magical effects on the files and directories to which they are attached. In this section, we untangle the mystery, and describe how these special properties make your life just a little easier.

svn:executable

The svn:executable property controls a versioned file's filesystem-level execute permission bit in a semi-automated way. This property has no defined values—its mere presence indicates a desire that Subversion keeps the execute permission bit enabled. Removing this property restores full control of the execute bit back to the operating system.

On many operating systems, the ability to execute a file as a command is governed by the presence of an execute permission bit. This bit usually defaults to being disabled, and must be explicitly enabled by the user for each file that needs it. In a working copy, new files are being created all the time as new versions of existing files are received during an update. This means that you might enable the execute bit on a file, then update your working copy, and if that file was changed as part of the update, its execute bit might get disabled. So, Subversion provides the svn:executable property as a way to keep the execute bit enabled.

This property has no effect on filesystems that have no concept of an executable permission bit, such as FAT32 and NTFS. (For example, the Windows filesystems use file extensions such as .EXE, .BAT, and .COM to denote executable files. Also, although it has no defined values, Subversion will force its value to * when setting this property. Finally, this property is valid only on files, not on directories.

svn:mime-type

The `svn:mime-type` property serves many purposes in Subversion. Besides being a general-purpose storage location for a file's Multipurpose Internet Mail Extensions (MIME) classification, the value of this property determines some behavioral characteristics of Subversion itself.

For example, if a file's `svn:mime-type` property is set to a non-text MIME type (generally, something that doesn't begin with `text/`, although there are exceptions), Subversion assumes that the file contains binary—that is, not human-readable—data. One of the benefits that Subversion typically provides is contextual, line-based merging of changes received from the server during an update into your working file. But for files believed to contain binary data, there is no concept of a line. So, for those files, Subversion does not attempt to perform contextual merges during updates. Instead, any time you have locally modified a binary working copy file that is also being updated, your file is renamed with a *.orig* extension, and then Subversion stores a new working copy file that contains the changes received during the update, but not your own local modifications, at the original filename. This behavior is really for the protection of the user against failed attempts at performing contextual merges on files that simply cannot be contextually merged.

Also, if the `svn:mime-type` property is set, then the Subversion Apache module uses its value to populate the `Content-type:` HTTP header when responding to GET requests. This gives a crucial clue about how to display a file when perusing your repository with a web browser.

svn:ignore

The `svn:ignore` property contains a list of file patterns that certain Subversion operations will ignore. Perhaps the most commonly used special property, it works in conjunction with the `global-ignores` runtime configuration option (see "Config" earlier in this chapter) to filter unversioned files and directories out of commands like `svn status`, `svn add`, and `svn import`.

The rationale behind the `svn:ignore` property is easily explained. Subversion does not assume that every file or subdirectory in a working copy directory is intended for version control. Resources must be explicitly placed under Subversion's management using the `svn add` or `svn import` commands. As a result, there are often many resources in a working copy that are not versioned.

Now, the `svn status` command displays as part of its output every unversioned file or subdirectory in a working copy that is not already filtered out by the `global-ignores` option (or its built-in default value). This is done so that users can see if perhaps they've forgotten to add a resource to version control.

But Subversion cannot possibly guess the names of every resource that should be ignored. Also, quite often there are things that should be ignored in *every* working copy of a particular repository. To force every user of that repository to add patterns for those resources to their runtime configuration areas would be not just a burden, but has the potential to clash with the configuration needs of other working copies that the user has checked out.

The solution is to store ignore patterns that are unique to the resources likely to appear in a given directory with the directory itself. Common examples of unversioned resources that are basically unique to a directory, yet likely to appear there, include output from program compilations. Or—to use an example more appropriate to this book—the HTML, PDF, or PostScript files generated as the result of a conversion of some source DocBook XML files to a more legible output format.

Ignore Patterns for CVS Users

The Subversion svn:ignore property is very similar in syntax and function to the CVS *.cvsignore* file. In fact, if you are migrating a CVS working copy to Subversion, you can directly migrate the ignore patterns by using the *.cvsignore* file as input file to the svn propset command:

```
$ svn propset svn:ignore -F .cvsignore .
property 'svn:ignore' set on '.'
$
```

There are, however, some differences in the ways that CVS and Subversion handle ignore patterns. The two systems use the ignore patterns at some different times, and there are slight discrepancies in what the ignore patterns apply to. Also, Subversion does not recognize the use of the ! pattern as a reset back to having no ignore patterns at all.

For this purpose, the svn:ignore property is the solution. Its value is a multiline collection of file patterns, one pattern per line. The property is set on the directory in which you wish the patterns to be applied.[*] For example, say you have the following output from svn status:

```
$ svn status calc
 M      calc/button.c
?       calc/calculator
?       calc/data.c
?       calc/debug_log
?       calc/debug_log.1
?       calc/debug_log.2.gz
?       calc/debug_log.3.gz
```

---

[*] The patterns are strictly for that directory—they do not carry recursively into subdirectories.

In this example, you have made some property modifications to *button.c*, but in your working copy you also have some unversioned files, in this case, the latest *calculator* program that you've compiled from your source code, a source file named *data.c*, and a set of debugging output log files. Now, you know that your build system always results in the *calculator* program being generated.* And you know that your test suite always leaves those debugging log files lying around. These facts are true for all working copies, not just your own. And you know that you aren't interested in seeing those things every time you run svn status. So you use svn propedit svn:ignore calc to add some ignore patterns to the *calc* directory. For example, you might add this as the new value of the svn:ignore property:

```
calculator
debug_log*
```

After you've added this property, you have a local property modification on the *calc* directory. But notice what else is different about your svn status output:

```
$ svn status
 M      calc
 M      calc/button.c
 ?      calc/data.c
```

Now, all the cruft is missing from the output! Of course, those files are still in your working copy. Subversion is simply not reminding you that they are present and unversioned. And now with all the trivial noise removed from the display, you are left with more interesting items—such as that source code file that you probably forgot to add to version control.

If you want to see the ignored files, you can pass the --no-ignore option to subversion:

```
$ svn status --no-ignore
 M      calc/button.c
 I      calc/calculator
 ?      calc/data.c
 I      calc/debug_log
 I      calc/debug_log.1
 I      calc/debug_log.2.gz
 I      calc/debug_log.3.gz
```

The list of patterns to ignore is also used by svn add and svn import. Both of these operations involve asking Subversion to begin managing some set of files and directories. Rather than force the user to pick and choose which files in a tree she wishes to start versioning, Subversion uses the ignore patterns to determine which files should not be swept into the version control system as part of a larger recursive addition or import operation.

* Isn't that the whole point of a build system?

svn:keywords

Subversion has the ability to substitute *keywords*—pieces of useful, dynamic information about a versioned file—into the contents of the file itself. Keywords generally describe information about the last time the file was known to be modified. Because this information changes each time the file changes, and more importantly, just *after* the file changes, it is a hassle for any process except the version control system to keep the data completely up-to-date. Left to human authors, the information would inevitably grow stale.

Assume you have a document in which you would like to display the last date on which it was modified. You could burden every author of that document to, just before committing their changes, also tweak the part of the document that describes when it was last changed. But, sooner or later, someone would forget to do that. Instead, simply ask Subversion to perform keyword substitution on the LastChangedDate keyword. You control where the keyword is inserted into your document by placing a *keyword anchor* at the desired location in the file. This anchor is just a string of text formatted as *$KeywordName$*.

Subversion defines the list of keywords available for substitution. That list contains the following five keywords, some of which have shorter aliases that you can also use:

LastChangedDate
> This keyword describes the last time the file was known to have been changed in the repository, and looks something like $LastChangedDate: 2002-07-22 21:42:37 -0700 (Mon, 22 Jul 2002) $. It may be abbreviated as Date.

LastChangedRevision
> This keyword describes the last known revision in which this file changed in the repository, and looks something like $LastChangedRevision: 144 $. It may be abbreviated as Rev.

LastChangedBy
> This keyword describes the last known user to change this file in the repository, and looks something like $LastChangedBy: harry $. It may be abbreviated as Author.

HeadURL
> This keyword describes the full URL to the latest version of the file in the repository, and looks something like $HeadURL: http://svn.collab.net/repos/trunk/ README $. It may be abbreviated as URL.

Id
> This keyword is a compressed combination of the other keywords. Its substitution looks something like $Id: ch07,v 1.9 2004/05/29 04:01:38 reg Exp free2 $id Exp $id $, and is interpreted to mean that the file *calc.c* was last changed in revision 148 on the evening of July 28, 2002 by the user sally.

Simply adding keyword anchor text to your file does nothing special. Subversion never attempts to perform textual substitutions on your file contents unless explicitly asked to do so. After all, you might be writing a document* about how to use keywords, and you don't want Subversion to substitute your beautiful examples of un-substituted keyword anchors!

To tell Subversion whether or not to substitute keywords on a particular file, we again turn to the property-related subcommands. The svn:keywords property, when set on a versioned file, controls which keywords will be substituted on that file. The value is a space-delimited list of the keyword names or aliases found in the previous table.

For example, say you have a versioned file named *weather.txt* that looks like this:

```
Here is the latest report from the front lines.
$LastChangedDate$
$Rev$
Cumulus clouds are appearing more frequently as summer approaches.
```

With no svn:keywords property set on that file, Subversion will do nothing special. Now, let's enable substitution of the LastChangedDate keyword:

```
$ svn propset svn:keywords "LastChangedDate Author" weather.txt
property 'svn:keywords' set on 'weather.txt'
$
```

Now you have made a local property modification on the *weather.txt* file. There are no changes to the file's contents (unless you made some of your own prior to setting the property). Notice that the file contained a keyword anchor for the Rev keyword, yet we did not include that keyword in the property value we set. Subversion will happily ignore requests to substitute keywords that are not present in the file, and will not substitute keywords that are not present in the svn:keywords property value.

Keywords and Spurious Differences

The user-visible result of keyword substitution might lead you to think that every version of a file with that feature in use differs from the previous version in at least the area where the keyword anchor was placed. However, this is actually not the case. While checking for local modifications during svn diff, and before transmitting those local modifications during svn commit, Subversion unsubstitutes any keywords that it previously substituted. The result is that the versions of the file that are stored in the repository contain only the real modifications that users make to the file.

---

* ... or maybe even a section of a book ...

Immediately after you commit this property change, Subversion updates your working file with the new substitute text. Instead of seeing your keyword anchor $LastChangedDate$, you'll see its substituted result. That result also contains the name of the keyword, and continues to be bounded by the dollar sign ($) characters. And as we predicted, the Rev keyword was not substituted because we didn't ask for it to be:

```
Here is the latest report from the front lines.
$LastChangedDate: 2002-07-22 21:42:37 -0700 (Mon, 22 Jul 2002) $
$Rev$
Cumulus clouds are appearing more frequently as summer approaches.
```

If someone else now commits a change to *weather.txt*, your copy of that file continues to display the same substituted keyword value as before—until you update your working copy. At that time the keywords in your *weather.txt* file are resubstituted with information that reflects the most recent known commit to that file.

svn:eol-style

Unless otherwise noted using a versioned file's svn:mime-type property, Subversion assumes the file contains human-readable data. Generally speaking, Subversion only uses this knowledge to determine if contextual difference reports for that file are possible. Otherwise, to Subversion, bytes are bytes.

This means that by default, Subversion doesn't pay any attention to the type of *end-of-line (EOL) markers* used in your files. Unfortunately, different operating systems use different tokens to represent the end of a line of text in a file. For example, the usual line ending token used by software on the Windows platform is a pair of ASCII control characters—carriage return (CR) and line feed (LF). Unix software, however, just uses the LF character to denote the end of a line.

Not all of the various tools on these operating systems are prepared to understand files that contain line endings in a format that differs from the *native line ending style* of the operating system on which they are running. Common results are that Unix programs treat the CR character present in Windows files as a regular character (usually rendered as ^M), and that Windows programs combine all of the lines of a Unix file into one giant line because no carriage return–linefeed (or CRLF) character combination was found to denote the end of lines.

This sensitivity to foreign EOL markers can become frustrating for folks who share a file across different operating systems. For example, consider a source code file, and developers that edit this file on both Windows and Unix systems. If all the developers always use tools that preserve the line ending style of the file, no problems occur.

But in practice, many common tools either fail to read a file with foreign EOL markers properly, or they convert the file's line endings to the native style when the file is saved. If the former is true for a developer, he has to use an external conversion utility (such as dos2unix or its companion, unix2dos) to prepare the file for editing. The latter case requires no extra preparation. But both cases result in a file that differs from the original quite literally on every line! Prior to committing his changes, the user has two choices. Either he can use a conversion utility to restore the modified file to the same line ending style that it was in before his edits were made. Or, he can simply commit the file—new EOL markers and all.

The result of scenarios like these include wasted time and unnecessary modifications to committed files. Wasted time is painful enough. But when commits change every line in a file, this complicates the job of determining which of those lines were changed in a non-trivial way. Where was that bug really fixed? On what line was a syntax error introduced?

The solution to this problem is the svn:eol-style property. When this property is set to a valid value, Subversion uses it to determine what special processing to perform on the file so that the file's line ending style isn't flip-flopping with every commit that comes from a different operating system. The valid values are as follows:

native

> This causes the file to contain the EOL markers that are native to the operating system on which Subversion was run. In other words, if a user on a Windows machine checks out a working copy that contains a file with an svn:eol-style property set to native, that file will contain CRLF EOL markers. A Unix user checking out a working copy that contains the same file will see LF EOL markers in his copy of the file.

> Note that Subversion actually stores the file in the repository using normalized LF EOL markers regardless of the operating system. This is basically transparent to the user, though.

CRLF

> This causes the file to contain CRLF sequences for EOL markers, regardless of the operating system in use.

LF

> This causes the file to contain LF characters for EOL markers, regardless of the operating system in use.

CR

> This causes the file to contain CR characters for EOL markers, regardless of the operating system in use. This line ending style is not very common. It was used on older Macintosh platforms (on which Subversion doesn't even run).

svn:externals

The svn:externals property contains instructions for Subversion to populate a versioned directory with one or more other checked-out Subversion working copies. For more information on this keyword and its use, see "Externals Definitions."

Automatic Property Setting

Properties are a powerful feature of Subversion, acting as key components of many Subversion features discussed elsewhere in this and other chapters—textual diff and merge support, keyword substitution, newline translation, etc. But to get the full benefit of properties, they must be set on the right files and directories. Unfortunately, that can be a step easily forgotten in the routine of things, especially since failing to set a property doesn't usually result in an obvious error condition (at least compared to, say, failing to add a file to version control). To help your properties get applied to the places that need them, Subversion provides a couple of simple but useful features.

Whenever you introduce a file to version control using the svn add or svn import commands, Subversion runs a very basic heuristic to determine if that file consists of human-readable or non-human-readable content. If the latter is the decision made, Subversion will automatically set the svn:mime-type property on that file to application/octet-stream (the generic this is a collection of bytes MIME type). Of course, if Subversion guesses incorrectly, or if you wish to set the svn:mime-type property to something more precise—perhaps image/png or application/x-shockwave-flash—you can always remove or edit that property.

Subversion also provides the auto-props feature, which allows you to create mappings of filename patterns to property names and values. These mappings are made in your runtime configuration area. They again affect adds and imports, and not only can override any default MIME type decision made by Subversion during those operations, they can also set additional Subversion or custom properties, too. For example, you might create a mapping that says that any time you add JPEG files—ones that match the pattern *.jpg—Subversion should automatically set the svn:mime-type property on those files to image/jpeg. Or perhaps any files that match *.cpp should have svn:eol-style set to native, and svn:keywords set to Id. Auto-prop support is perhaps the handiest property related tool in the Subversion toolbox. See "Config" for more about configuring that support.

Externals Definitions

Sometimes it is useful to construct a working copy that is made out of a number of different checkouts. For example, you may want different subdirectories to come from different locations in a repository, or perhaps from different repositories altogether. You could certainly set up such a scenario by hand—using svn checkout to create the sort of nested working copy structure you are trying to achieve. But if this layout is important for everyone who uses your repository, every other user will need to perform the same checkout operations that you did.

Fortunately, Subversion provides support for *externals definitions*. An externals definition is a mapping of a local directory to the URL—and possibly a particular revision—of a versioned resource. In Subversion, you declare externals definitions in groups using the svn:externals property. You can create or modify this property using svn propset or svn propedit, and its value is a multiline table of subdirectories (relative to the versioned directory on which the property is set) and fully qualified, absolute Subversion repository URLs:

```
$ svn propget svn:externals calc
third-party/sounds          http://sounds.red-bean.com/repos
third-party/skins           http://skins.red-bean.com/repositories/skinproj
third-party/skins/toolkit -r21 http://svn.red-bean.com/repos/skin-maker
```

The convenience of the svn:externals property is that once it is set on a versioned directory, everyone who checks out a working copy with that directory also gets the benefit of the externals definition. In other words, once one person has made the effort to define those nested working copy checkouts, no one else has to bother—Subversion, upon checkout of the original working copy, also checks out the external working copies.

Note the previous externals definition example. When someone checks out a working copy of the *calc* directory, Subversion also continues to check out the items found in its externals definition:

```
$ svn checkout http://svn.example.com/repos/calc
A  calc
A  calc/Makefile
A  calc/integer.c
A  calc/button.c
Checked out revision 148.

Fetching external item into calc/third-party/sounds
A  calc/third-party/sounds/ding.ogg
A  calc/third-party/sounds/dong.ogg
A  calc/third-party/sounds/clang.ogg
...
A  calc/third-party/sounds/bang.ogg
A  calc/third-party/sounds/twang.ogg
Checked out revision 14.

Fetching external item into calc/third-party/skins
...
```

If you need to change the externals definition, you can do so using the regular property modification subcommands. When you commit a change to the svn:externals property, Subversion synchronizes the checked-out items against the changed externals definition when you next run svn update. The same thing happens when others update their working copies and receive your changes to the externals definition.

The svn status command also recognizes externals definitions, displaying a status code of X for the disjoint subdirectories into which externals are checked out, and then recursing into those subdirectories to display the status of the external items themselves.

The support that exists for externals definitions in Subversion today can be a little misleading, though. The working copies created via the externals definition support are still disconnected from the primary working copy (on whose versioned directories the `svn:externals` property was actually set). And Subversion still only truly operates on non-disjoint working copies. For example, if you want to commit changes that you've made in one or more of those external working copies, you must run `svn commit` explicitly on those working copies—committing on the primary working copy will not recurse into any external ones.

Also, since the definitions themselves use absolute URLs, moving or copying a directory to which they are attached will not affect what gets checked out as an external (though the relative local target subdirectory will, of course, move with renamed directory). This can be confusing—even frustrating—in certain situtations. For example, if you use externals definitions on a directory in your */trunk* development line that point to other areas of that same line, and then you use `svn copy` to branch that line to some new location */branches/my-branch*, the externals definitions on items in your new branch will still refer to versioned resources in */trunk*. Also, be aware that if you need to re-parent your working copy (using `svn switch --relocate`), externals definitions will *not* also be re-parented.

Vendor Branches

As is especially the case when developing software, the data that you maintain under version control is often closely related to, or perhaps dependent upon, someone else's data. Generally, the needs of your project will dictate that you stay as up-to-date as possible with the data provided by that external entity without sacrificing the stability of your own project. This scenario plays itself out all the time—anywhere that the information generated by one group of people has a direct effect on that which is generated by another group.

For example, software developers might be working on an application which makes use of a third-party library. Subversion has just such a relationship with the Apache Portable Runtime library (see "The Apache Portable Runtime Library" in Chapter 8). The Subversion source code depends on the APR library for all its portability needs. In earlier stages of Subversion's development, the project closely tracked APR's changing API, always sticking to the bleeding edge of the library's code churn. Now that both APR and Subversion have matured, Subversion attempts to synchronize with APR's library API only at well-tested, stable release points.

Now, if your project depends on someone else's information, there are several ways that you could attempt to synchronize that information with your own. Most painfully, you could issue oral or written instructions to all the contributors of your project, telling them to make sure that they have the specific versions of that third-party information that your project needs. If the third-party information is maintained in a Subversion repository, you could also use Subversion's externals definitions to effectively pin down specific versions of that information to some location in your own working copy directory (see "Externals Definitions" earlier in this chapter).

But sometimes you want to maintain custom modifications to third-party data in your own version control system. Returning to the software development example, programmers might need to make modifications to that third-party library for their own purposes. These modifications might include new functionality or bug fixes, maintained internally only until they become part of an official release of the third-party library. Or the changes might never be relayed back to the library maintainers, existing solely as custom tweaks to make the library further suit the needs of the software developers.

Now you face an interesting situation. Your project could house its custom modifications to the third-party data in some disjointed fashion, such as using patch files or full-fledged alternate versions of files and directories. But these quickly become maintenance headaches, requiring some mechanism by which to apply your custom changes to the third-party data, and necessitating regeneration of those changes with each successive version of the third-party data that you track.

The solution to this problem is to use *vendor branches*. A vendor branch is a directory tree in your own version control system that contains information provided by a third-party entity, or vendor. Each version of the vendor's data that you decide to absorb into your project is called a *vendor drop*.

Vendor branches provide two key benefits. First, by storing the currently supported vendor drop in your own version control system, the members of your project never need to question whether they have the right version of the vendor's data. They simply receive that correct version as part of their regular working copy updates. Secondly, because the data lives in your own Subversion repository, you can store your custom changes to it in-place—you have no more need of an automated (or worse, manual) method for swapping in your customizations.

General Vendor Branch Management Procedure

Managing vendor branches generally works like this. You create a top-level directory (such as /vendor) to hold the vendor branches. Then you import the third-party code into a subdirectory of that top-level directory. You then copy that subdirectory into your main development branch (for example, /trunk) at the appropriate location. You always make your local changes in the main development branch. With each new release of the code you are tracking, you bring it into the vendor branch and merge the changes into /trunk, resolving whatever conflicts occur between your local changes and the upstream changes.

Perhaps an example will clarify this algorithm. We'll use a scenario where your development team is creating a calculator program that links against a third-party complex number arithmetic library, libcomplex. Begin with the initial creation of the vendor branch, and the import of the first vendor drop. Let's call our vendor branch directory *libcomplex*, and our code drops will go into a subdirectory of our vendor branch called *current*. And since svn import creates all the intermediate parent directories it needs, we can actually accomplish both of these steps with a single command.

```
$ svn import /path/to/libcomplex-1.0 \
            http://svn.example.com/repos/vendor/libcomplex/current \
            -m 'importing initial 1.0 vendor drop'
…
```

We now have the current version of the libcomplex source code in */vendor/libcomplex/current*. Now, we tag that version and then copy it into the main development branch. Our copy will create a new directory called *libcomplex* in our existing *calc* project directory. It is in this copied version of the vendor data that we will make our customizations.

```
$ svn copy http://svn.example.com/repos/vendor/libcomplex/current  \
            http://svn.example.com/repos/vendor/libcomplex/1.0       \
            -m 'tagging libcomplex-1.0'
…
$ svn copy http://svn.example.com/repos/vendor/libcomplex/1.0  \
            http://svn.example.com/repos/calc/libcomplex          \
            -m 'bringing libcomplex-1.0 into the main branch'
…
```

We check out our project's main branch—which now includes a copy of the first vendor drop—and we get to work customizing the libcomplex code. Before we know it, our modified version of libcomplex is now completely integrated into our calculator program.[*]

A few weeks later, the developers of libcomplex release a new version of their library—version 1.1—that contains some features and functionality that we really want. We'd like to upgrade to this new version, but without losing the customizations we made to the existing version. What we essentially would like to do is replace our current baseline version of libcomplex 1.0 with a copy of libcomplex 1.1, and then reapply the custom modifications we previously made to that library to the new version. But we actually approach the problem from the other direction, applying the changes made to libcomplex between versions 1.0 and 1.1 to our modified copy of it.

To perform this upgrade, we check out a copy of our vendor branch, and replace the code in the *current* directory with the new libcomplex 1.1 source code. We quite literally copy new files on top of existing files, perhaps exploding the libcomplex 1.1 release tarball atop our existing files and directories. The goal here is to make our *current* directory contain only the libcomplex 1.1 code, and to ensure that all that

---

[*] And entirely bug-free, of course!

code is under version control. Oh, and we want to do this with as little version control history disturbance as possible.

After replacing the 1.0 code with 1.1 code, svn status will show files with local modifications as well as, perhaps, some unversioned or missing files. If we did what we were supposed to do, the unversioned files are only those new files introduced in the 1.1 release of libcomplex—we run svn add on those to get them under version control. The missing files are files that were in 1.0 but not in 1.1, and on those paths we run svn remove. Finally, once our *current* working copy contains only the libcomplex 1.1 code, we commit the changes we made to get it looking that way.

Our *current* branch now contains the new vendor drop. We tag the new version (in the same way we previously tagged the version 1.0 vendor drop), and then merge the differences between the tag of the previous version and the new current version into our main development branch.

```
$ cd working-copies/calc
$ svn merge http://svn.example.com/repos/vendor/libcomplex/1.0      \
            http://svn.example.com/repos/vendor/libcomplex/current  \
            libcomplex
… # resolve all the conflicts between their changes and our changes
$ svn commit -m 'merging libcomplex-1.1 into the main branch'
…
```

In the trivial use-case, the new version of our third-party tool would look, from a files-and-directories point of view, just like the previous version. None of the libcomplex source files would have been deleted, renamed, or moved to different locations—the new version would contain only textual modifications against the previous one. In a perfect world, our modifications would apply cleanly to the new version of the library, with absolutely no complications or conflicts.

But things aren't always that simple, and, in fact, it is quite common for source files to get moved around between releases of software. This complicates the process of ensuring that our modifications are still valid for the new version of code, and can quickly degrade into a situation where we have to manually re-create our customizations in the new version. Once Subversion knows about the history of a given source file—including all its previous locations—the process of merging in the new version of the library is pretty simple. But we are responsible for telling Subversion how the source file layout changed from vendor drop to vendor drop.

svn_load_dirs.pl

Vendor drops that contain more than a few deletes, additions, and moves complicate the process of upgrading to each successive version of the third-party data. So Subversion supplies the svn_load_dirs.pl script to assist with this process. This script automates the importing steps we mentioned in the general vendor branch management procedure to make sure that mistakes are minimized. You will still be responsible for using the merge commands to merge the new versions of the third-party data into your main development branch, but svn_load_dirs.pl can help you more quickly and easily arrive at that stage.

In short, svn_load_dirs.pl is an enhancement to svn import that has several important characteristics:

- It can be run any time to bring an existing directory in the repository to exactly match an external directory, performing all the necessary adds and deletes, and optionally performing moves, too.

- It takes care of complicated series of operations between which Subversion requires an intermediate commit—such as before renaming a file or directory twice.

- It will optionally tag the newly imported directory.

- It will optionally add arbitrary properties to files and directories that match a regular expression.

svn_load_dirs.pl takes three mandatory arguments. The first argument is the URL to the base Subversion directory to work in. This argument is followed by the URL—relative to the first argument—into which the current vendor drop will be imported. Finally, the third argument is the local directory to import. Using our previous example, a typical run of svn_load_dirs.pl might look like:

```
$ svn_load_dirs.pl http://svn.example.com/repos/vendor/libcomplex \
                   current                                        \
                   /path/to/libcomplex-1.1
...
```

You can indicate that you want svn_load_dirs.pl to tag the new vendor drop by passing the -t command-line option and specifying a tag name. This tag is another URL relative to the first program argument:

```
$ svn_load_dirs.pl -t libcomplex-1.1                              \
                   http://svn.example.com/repos/vendor/libcomplex \
                   current                                        \
                   /path/to/libcomplex-1.1
...
```

When you run svn_load_dirs.pl, it examines the contents of your existing current vendor drop, and compares them with the proposed new vendor drop. In the trivial case, there will be no files that are in one version and not the other, and the script will perform the new import without incident. If, however, there are discrepancies in the file layouts between versions, svn_load_dirs.pl will prompt you for how you would like to resolve those differences. For example, you will have the opportunity to tell the script that you know that the file *math.c* in Version 1.0 of libcomplex was renamed to *arithmetic.c* in libcomplex 1.1. Any discrepancies not explained by moves are treated as regular additions and deletions.

The script also accepts a separate configuration file for setting properties on files and directories matching a regular expression that are *added* to the repository. This configuration file is specified to svn_load_dirs.pl using the -p command-line option. Each line of the configuration file is a whitespace-delimited set of two or four values: a Perl-style regular expression to match the added path against, a control keyword (either break or cont), and then optionally a property name and value:

```
\.png$          break   svn:mime-type   image/png
\.jpe?g$        break   svn:mime-type   image/jpeg
\.m3u$          cont    svn:mime-type   audio/x-mpegurl
\.m3u$          break   svn:eol-style   LF
.*              break   svn:eol-style   native
```

For each added path, the configured property changes whose regular expression matches the path are applied in order, unless the control specification is break (which means that no more property changes should be applied to that path). If the control specification is cont—an abbreviation for continue—then matching will continue with the next line of the configuration file.

Any whitespace in the regular expression, property name, or property value must be surrounded by either single or double quote characters. You can escape quote characters that are not used for wrapping whitespace by preceding them with a backslash (\) character. The backslash escapes only quotes when parsing the configuration file, so do not protect any other characters beyond what is necessary for the regular expression.

CHAPTER 8

Developer Information

Subversion is an open source software project developed under an Apache-style software license. The project is financially backed by CollabNet, Inc., a California-based software development company. The community that has formed around the development of Subversion always welcomes new members who can donate their time and attention to the project. Volunteers are encouraged to assist in any way they can, whether that means finding and diagnosing bugs, refining existing source code, or fleshing out whole new features.

This chapter is for those who wish to assist in the continued evolution of Subversion by actually getting their hands dirty with the source code. We cover some of the software's more intimate details, the kind of technical nitty-gritty that those developing Subversion itself—or writing entirely new tools based on the Subversion libraries—should be aware of. If you don't foresee yourself participating with the software at such a level, feel free to skip this chapter with confidence that your experience as a Subversion user will not be affected.

Layered Library Design

Subversion has a modular design, implemented as a collection of C libraries. Each library has a well-defined purpose and interface, and most modules are said to exist in one of three main layers—the Repository Layer, the Repository Access (RA) Layer, or the Client Layer. We will examine these layers shortly, but first, see our brief inventory of Subversion's libraries in Table 8-1. For the sake of consistency, we will refer to the libraries by their extensionless Unix library names (e.g.,: libsvn_fs, libsvn_wc, mod_dav_svn).

Table 8-1. A brief inventory of the Subversion libraries

Library	Description
libsvn_client	Primary interface for client programs
libsvn_delta	Tree and text differencing routines

Table 8-1. A brief inventory of the Subversion libraries (continued)

Library	Description
libsvn_fs	The Subversion filesystem library
libsvn_ra	Repository Access commons and module loader
libsvn_ra_dav	The WebDAV Repository Access module
libsvn_ra_local	The local Repository Access module
libsvn_ra_svn	A custom protocol Repository Access module
libsvn_repos	Repository interface
libsvn_subr	Miscellaneous helpful subroutines
libsvn_wc	The working copy management library
mod_authz_svn	Apache authorization module for Subversion repositories access via WebDAV
mod_dav_svn	Apache module for mapping WebDAV operations to Subversion ones

The fact that the word miscellaneous only appears once in Table 8-1 is a good sign. The Subversion development team is serious about making sure that functionality lives in the right layer and libraries. Perhaps the greatest advantage of the modular design is its lack of complexity from a developer's point of view. As a developer, you can quickly formulate that kind of big picture that allows you to pinpoint the location of certain pieces of functionality with relative ease.

Another benefit of modularity is the ability to replace a given module with a whole new library that implements the same API without affecting the rest of the code base. In some sense, this happens within Subversion already. The libsvn_ra_dav, libsvn_ra_local, and libsvn_ra_svn all implement the same interface. And all three communicate with the Repository Layer—libsvn_ra_dav and libsvn_ra_svn do so across a network, and libsvn_ra_local connects to it directly.

The client itself also highlights modularity in the Subversion design. While Subversion currently comes with only a command-line client program, there are already a few other programs being developed by third parties to act as GUIs for Subversion. Again, these GUIs use the same APIs that the stock command-line client does. Subversion's libsvn_client library is the one-stop shop for most of the functionality necessary for designing a working Subversion client (see "Client Layer" later in this chapter).

Repository Layer

When referring to Subversion's Repository Layer, we're generally talking about two libraries—the repository library and the filesystem library. These libraries provide the storage and reporting mechanisms for the various revisions of your version-controlled data. This layer is connected to the Client Layer via the Repository Access Layer, and is, from the perspective of the Subversion user, the stuff at the other end of the line.

The Subversion Filesystem is accessed via the libsvn_fs API, and is not a kernel-level filesystem that one would install in an operating system (like the Linux ext2 or NTFS), but a virtual filesystem. Rather than storing files and directories as real files and directories (as in, the kind you can navigate through using your favorite shell program), it uses a database system for its back-end storage mechanism. Currently, the database system in use is Berkeley DB.[*] However, there has been considerable interest by the development community in giving future releases of Subversion the ability to use other back-end database systems, perhaps through a mechanism such as Open Database Connectivity (ODBC).

The filesystem API exported by libsvn_fs contains the kinds of functionality you would expect from any other filesystem API: you can create and remove files and directories, copy and move them around, modify file contents, and so on. It also has features that are not quite as common, such as the ability to add, modify, and remove metadata (properties) on each file or directory. Furthermore, the Subversion Filesystem is a versioning filesystem, which means that as you make changes to your directory tree, Subversion remembers what your tree looked like before those changes. And before the previous changes. And the previous ones. And so on, all the way back through versioning time to (and just beyond) the moment you first started adding things to the filesystem.

All the modifications you make to your tree are done within the context of a Subversion transaction. The following is a simplified general routine for modifying your filesystem:

1. Begin a Subversion transaction.
2. Make your changes (adds, deletes, property modifications, etc.).
3. Commit your transaction.

Once you have committed your transaction, your filesystem modifications are permanently stored as historical artifacts. Each of these cycles generates a single new revision of your tree, and each revision is forever accessible as an immutable snapshot of the way things were.

Most of the functionality provided by the filesystem interface comes as an action that occurs on a filesystem path. That is, from outside of the filesystem, the primary mechanism for describing and accessing the individual revisions of files and directories comes through the use of path strings like */foo/bar*, just as if you were addressing files and directories through your favorite shell program. You add new files and directories by passing their paths-to-be to the right API functions. You query for information about them by the same mechanism.

---

[*] The choice of Berkeley DB brought several automatic features that Subversion needed, such as data integrity, atomic writes, recoverability, and hot backups.

The Transaction Distraction

The notion of a Subversion transaction, especially given its close proximity to the database code in libsvn_fs, can become easily confused with the transaction support provided by the underlying database itself. Both types of transaction exist to provide atomicity and isolation. In other words, transactions give you the ability to perform a set of actions in an all or nothing fashion—either all the actions in the set complete with success, or they all get treated as if *none* of them ever happened—and in a way that does not interfere with other processes acting on the data.

Database transactions generally encompass small operations related specifically to the modification of data in the database itself (such as changing the contents of a table row). Subversion transactions are larger in scope, encompassing higher-level operations like making modifications to a set of files and directories which are intended to be stored as the next revision of the filesystem tree. If that isn't confusing enough, consider this: Subversion uses a database transaction during the creation of a Subversion transaction (so that if the creation of Subversion transaction fails, the database will look as if we had never attempted that creation in the first place)!

Fortunately for users of the filesystem API, the transaction support provided by the database system itself is hidden almost entirely from view (as should be expected from a properly modularized library scheme). It is only when you start digging into the implementation of the filesystem itself that such things become visible (or interesting).

Unlike most filesystems, though, a path alone is not enough information to identify a file or directory in Subversion. Think of a directory tree as a two-dimensional system, where a node's siblings represent a sort of left-and-right motion, and descending into subdirectories a downward motion. Figure 8-1 shows a typical representation of a tree as exactly that.

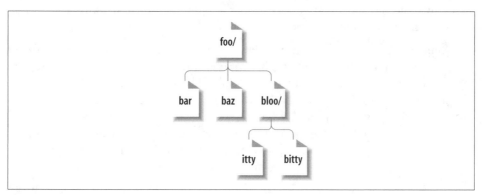

Figure 8-1. Files and directories in two dimensions

Of course, the Subversion filesystem has a nifty third dimension that most filesystems do not have—time!* In the filesystem interface, nearly every function that has a path argument also expects a root argument. This svn_fs_root_t argument describes either a revision or a Subversion transaction (which is usually just a revision-to-be), and provides that third-dimensional context needed to understand the difference between /foo/bar in revision 32, and the same path as it exists in revision 98. Figure 8-2 shows revision history as an added dimension to the Subversion filesystem universe.

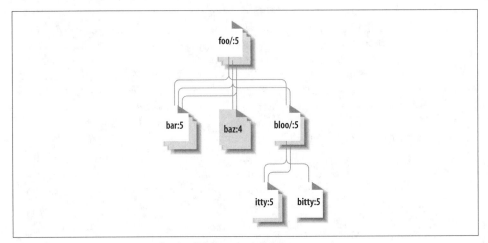

Figure 8-2. Revisioning time—the third dimension!

As we mentioned earlier, the libsvn_fs API looks and feels like any other filesystem, except that it has this wonderful versioning capability. It was designed to be usable by any program interested in a versioning filesystem. Not coincidentally, Subversion itself is interested in that functionality. But while the filesystem API should be sufficient for basic file and directory versioning support, Subversion wants more—and that is where libsvn_repos comes in.

The Subversion repository library (libsvn_repos) is basically a wrapper library around the filesystem functionality. This library is responsible for creating the repository layout, making sure that the underlying filesystem is initialized, and so on. libsvn_repos also implements a set of hooks—scripts that are executed by the repository code when certain actions take place. These scripts are useful for notification, authorization, or whatever purposes the repository administrator desires. This type of functionality, and other utility provided by the repository library, is not strictly related to implementing a versioning filesystem, which is why it was placed into its own library.

---

* We understand that this may come as a shock to sci-fi fans who have long been under the impression that time was actually the *fourth* dimension, and we apologize for any emotional trauma induced by our assertion of a different theory.

Developers who wish to use the libsvn_repos API find that it is not a complete wrapper around the filesystem interface. That is, only certain major events in the general cycle of filesystem activity are wrapped by the repository interface. Some of these include the creation and commit of Subversion transactions, and the modification of revision properties. These particular events are wrapped by the repository layer because they have hooks associated with them. In the future, other events may be wrapped by the repository API. All of the remaining filesystem interaction continues to occur directly with libsvn_fs API, though.

For example, Example 8-1 is a code segment that illustrates the use of both the repository and filesystem interfaces to create a new revision of the filesystem in which a directory is added. Note that in this example (and all others throughout this book), the SVN_ERR macro simply checks for a non-successful error return from the function it wraps, and returns that error if it exists.

Example 8-1. Using the repository layer

```
/* Create a new directory at the path NEW_DIRECTORY in the Subversion
   repository located at REPOS_PATH.  Perform all memory allocation in
   POOL.  This function will create a new revision for the addition of
   NEW_DIRECTORY.  */
static svn_error_t *
make_new_directory (const char *repos_path,
                    const char *new_directory,
                    apr_pool_t *pool)
{
  svn_error_t *err;
  svn_repos_t *repos;
  svn_fs_t *fs;
  svn_revnum_t youngest_rev;
  svn_fs_txn_t *txn;
  svn_fs_root_t *txn_root;
  const char *conflict_str;

  /* Open the repository located at REPOS_PATH.  */
  SVN_ERR (svn_repos_open (&repos, repos_path, pool));

  /* Get a pointer to the filesystem object that is stored in
     REPOS.  */
  fs = svn_repos_fs (repos);

  /* Ask the filesystem to tell us the youngest revision that
     currently exists.  */
  SVN_ERR (svn_fs_youngest_rev (&youngest_rev, fs, pool));

  /* Begin a new transaction that is based on YOUNGEST_REV.  We are
     less likely to have our later commit rejected as conflicting if we
     always try to make our changes against a copy of the latest snapshot
     of the filesystem tree.  */
  SVN_ERR (svn_fs_begin_txn (&txn, fs, youngest_rev, pool));

  /* Now that we have started a new Subversion transaction, get a root
```

Example 8-1. Using the repository layer (continued)

```
   object that represents that transaction.  */
SVN_ERR (svn_fs_txn_root (&txn_root, txn, pool));

/* Create our new directory under the transaction root, at the path
   NEW_DIRECTORY.  */
SVN_ERR (svn_fs_make_dir (txn_root, new_directory, pool));

/* Commit the transaction, creating a new revision of the filesystem
   which includes our added directory path.  */
err = svn_repos_fs_commit_txn (&conflict_str, repos,
                                   &youngest_rev, txn, pool);
if (! err)
  {
    /* No error?  Excellent!  Print a brief report of our success.  */
    printf ("Directory '%s' was successfully added as new revision "
            "'%" SVN_REVNUM_T_FMT "'.\n", new_directory, youngest_rev);
  }
else if (err->apr_err == SVN_ERR_FS_CONFLICT)
  {
    /* Uh-oh.  Our commit failed as the result of a conflict
       (someone else seems to have made changes to the same area
       of the filesystem that we tried to modify).  Print an error
       message.  */
    printf ("A conflict occurred at path '%s' while attempting "
            "to add directory '%s' to the repository at '%s'.\n",
            conflict_str, new_directory, repos_path);
  }
else
  {
    /* Some other error has occurred.  Print an error message.  */
    printf ("An error occurred while attempting to add directory '%s' "
            "to the repository at '%s'.\n",
            new_directory, repos_path);
  }

/* Return the result of the attempted commit to our caller.  */
return err;
}
```

In the previous code segment, calls were made to both the repository and filesystem interfaces. We could just as easily have committed the transaction using svn_fs_commit_txn. But the filesystem API knows nothing about the repository library's hook mechanism. If you want your Subversion repository to automatically perform some set of non-Subversion tasks every time you commit a transaction (such as sending an email that describes all the changes made in that transaction to your developer mailing list), you need to use the libsvn_repos-wrapped version of that function—svn_repos_fs_commit_txn. This function actually first run the pre-commit hook script if one exists, then commit the transaction, and finally runs a post-commit hook script. The hooks provide a special kind of reporting mechanism that does not really belong in the core filesystem library itself. (For more information regarding Subversion's repository hooks, see "Hook Scripts" in Chapter 5).

The hook mechanism requirement is but one of the reasons for the abstraction of a separate repository library from the rest of the filesystem code. The libsvn_repos API provides several other important utilities to Subversion. These include the abilities to:

- Create, open, destroy, and perform recovery steps on a Subversion repository and the filesystem included in that repository
- Describe the differences between two filesystem trees
- Query for the commit log messages associated with all (or some) of the revisions in which a set of files was modified in the filesystem
- Generate a human-readable dump of the filesystem, a complete representation of the revisions in the filesystem
- Parse that dump format, loading the dumped revisions into a different Subversion repository

As Subversion continues to evolve, the repository library grows with the filesystem library to offer increased functionality and configurable option support.

Repository Access Layer

If the Subversion Repository Layer is at the other end of the line, the Repository Access Layer is the line itself. Charged with marshalling data between the client libraries and the repository, this layer includes the libsvn_ra module loader library, the RA modules themselves (which currently includes libsvn_ra_dav, libsvn_ra_local, and libsvn_ra_svn), and any additional libraries needed by one or more of those RA modules, such as the mod_dav_svn Apache module with which libsvn_ra_dav communicates or libsvn_ra_svn's server, svnserve.

Since Subversion uses URLs to identify its repository resources, the protocol portion of the URL schema (usually file:, http:, https:, or svn:) is used to determine which RA module will handle the communications. Each module registers a list of the protocols it knows how to speak so that the RA loader can, at runtime, determine which module to use for the task at hand. You can determine which RA modules are available to the Subversion command-line client, and what protocols they claim to support, by running svn --version:

```
$ svn --version
svn, version 1.0.1 (r9023)
   compiled Mar 17 2004, 09:31:13

Copyright (C) 2000-2004 CollabNet.
Subversion is open source software, see http://subversion.tigris.org/
This product includes software developed by CollabNet (http://www.Collab.Net/).

The following repository access (RA) modules are available:

* ra_dav : Module for accessing a repository via WebDAV (DeltaV) protocol.
```

```
  - handles 'http' schema
  - handles 'https' schema
* ra_local : Module for accessing a repository on local disk.
  - handles 'file' schema
* ra_svn : Module for accessing a repository using the svn network protocol.
  - handles 'svn' schema
```

RA-DAV (repository access using HTTP/DAV)

The libsvn_ra_dav library is designed for use by clients that are being run on different machines than the servers with which they communicating, specifically machines reached using URLs that contain the http: or https: protocol portions. To understand how this module works, we should first mention a couple of other key components in this particular configuration of the Repository Access Layer—the powerful Apache HTTP Server, and the Neon HTTP/WebDAV client library.

Subversion's primary network server is the Apache HTTP Server. Apache is a time-tested, extensible open-source server process that is ready for serious use. It can sustain a high network load and runs on many platforms. The Apache server supports a number of different standard authentication protocols, and can be extended through the use of modules to support many others. It also supports optimizations like network pipelining and caching. By using Apache as a server, Subversion gets all of these features for free. And, since most firewalls already allow HTTP traffic to pass through, sysadmins typically don't even have to change their firewall configurations to allow Subversion to work.

Subversion uses HTTP and WebDAV (with DeltaV) to communicate with an Apache server. You can read more about this in the WebDAV section of this chapter, but in short, WebDAV and DeltaV are extensions to the standard HTTP 1.1 protocol that enable sharing and versioning of files over the web. Apache 2.0 comes with mod_dav, an Apache module that understands the DAV extensions to HTTP. Subversion itself supplies mod_dav_svn, though, which is another Apache module that works in conjunction with (really, as a back-end to) mod_dav to provide Subversion's specific implementations of WebDAV and DeltaV.

When communicating with a repository over HTTP, the RA loader library chooses libsvn_ra_dav as the proper access module. The Subversion client makes calls into the generic RA interface, and libsvn_ra_dav maps those calls (which embody rather large-scale Subversion actions) to a set of HTTP/WebDAV requests. Using the Neon library, libsvn_ra_dav transmits those requests to the Apache server. Apache receives these requests (exactly as it does generic HTTP requests that your web browser might make), notices that the requests are directed at a URL that is configured as a DAV location (using the <Location> directive in *httpd.conf*), and hands the request off to its own mod_dav module. When properly configured, mod_dav knows to use Subversion's mod_dav_svn for any filesystem-related needs, as opposed to the generic mod_dav_fs that comes with Apache. So ultimately, the client is communicating with mod_dav_svn, which binds directly to the Subversion Repository Layer.

That was a simplified description of the actual exchanges taking place, though. For example, the Subversion repository might be protected by Apache's authorization directives. This could result in initial attempts to communicate with the repository being rejected by Apache on authorization grounds. At this point, libsvn_ra_dav gets back the notice from Apache that insufficient identification was supplied, and calls back into the Client Layer to get some updated authentication data. If the data is supplied correctly, and the user has the permissions that Apache seeks, libsvn_ra_dav's next automatic attempt at performing the original operation will be granted, and all will be well. If sufficient authentication information cannot be supplied, the request ultimately fails, and the client reports the failure to the user.

By using Neon and Apache, Subversion gets free functionality in several other complex areas, too. For example, if Neon finds the OpenSSL libraries, it allows the Subversion client to attempt to use SSL-encrypted communications with the Apache server (whose own mod_ssl can speak the language). Also, both Neon itself and Apache's mod_deflate can understand the deflate algorithm (the same used by the PKZIP and gzip programs), so requests can be sent in smaller, compressed chunks across the wire. Other complex features that Subversion hopes to support in the future include the ability to automatically handle server-specified redirects (for example, when a repository has been moved to a new canonical URL) and taking advantage of HTTP pipelining.

RA-SVN (custom protocol repository access)

In addition to the standard HTTP/WebDAV protocol, Subversion also provides an RA implementation that uses a custom protocol. The libsvn_ra_svn module implements its own network socket connectivity, and communicates with a stand-alone server—the *svnserve* program—on the machine that hosts the repository. Clients access the repository using the svn:// schema.

This RA implementation lacks most of the advantages of Apache mentioned in the previous section; however, it may be appealing to some sysadmins nonetheless. It is dramatically easier to configure and run; setting up an *svnserve* process is nearly instantaneous. It is also much smaller (in terms of lines of code) than Apache, making it much easier to audit, for security reasons or otherwise. Furthermore, some sysadmins may already have an SSH security infrastructure in place, and want Subversion to use it. Clients using ra_svn can easily tunnel the protocol over SSH.

RA-Local (direct repository access)

Not all communications with a Subversion repository require a powerhouse server process and a network layer. For users who simply wish to access the repositories on their local disk, they may do so using file: URLs and the functionality provided by libsvn_ra_local. This RA module binds directly with the repository and filesystem libraries, so no network communication is required at all.

Subversion requires the server name included as part of the file: URL be either localhost or empty, and that there be no port specification. In other words, your URLs should look like either file://localhost/path/to/repos or file:///path/to/repos.

Also, be aware that Subversion's file: URLs cannot be used in a regular web browser the way typical file: URLs can. When you attempt to view a file: URL in a regular web browser, it reads and displays the contents of the file at that location by examining the filesystem directly. However, Subversion's resources exist in a virtual filesystem (see "Repository Layer" earlier in this chapter), and your browser will not understand how to read that filesystem.

Your RA library here

For those who wish to access a Subversion repository using still another protocol, that is precisely why the Repository Access Layer is modularized! Developers can simply write a new library that implements the RA interface on one side and communicates with the repository on the other. Your new library can use existing network protocols, or you can invent your own. You could use interprocess communication (IPC) calls, or—let's get crazy, shall we?—you could even implement an email-based protocol. Subversion supplies the APIs; you supply the creativity.

Client Layer

On the client side, the Subversion working copy is where all the action takes place. The bulk of functionality implemented by the client-side libraries exists for the sole purpose of managing working copies—directories full of files and other subdirectories which serve as a sort of local, editable reflection of one or more repository locations—and propagating changes to and from the Repository Access layer.

Subversion's working copy library, libsvn_wc, is directly responsible for managing the data in the working copies. To accomplish this, the library stores administrative information about each working copy directory within a special subdirectory. This subdirectory, named *.svn*, is present in each working copy directory and contains various other files and directories which record state and provide a private workspace for administrative action. For those familiar with CVS, this *.svn* subdirectory is similar in purpose to the *CVS* administrative directories found in CVS working copies. For more information about the *.svn* administrative area, see "Inside the Working Copy Administration Area" later in this chapter.

The Subversion client library, libsvn_client, has the broadest responsibility; its job is to mingle the functionality of the working copy library with that of the Repository Access Layer, and then to provide the highest-level API to any application that wishes to perform general revision control actions. For example, the function svn_client_checkout takes a URL as an argument. It passes this URL to the RA layer and opens an authenticated session with a particular repository. It then asks the repository for a certain tree, and sends this tree into the working copy library, which then writes a full working copy to disk (.svn directories and all).

The client library is designed to be used by any application. While the Subversion source code includes a standard command-line client, it should be very easy to write any number of GUI clients on top of the client library. New GUIs (or any new client, really) for Subversion need not be clunky wrappers around the included command-line client—they have full access via the libsvn_client API to same functionality, data, and callback mechanisms that the command-line client uses.

Binding Directly—A Word About Correctness

Why should your GUI program bind directly with a libsvn_client instead of acting as a wrapper around a command-line program? Besides simply being more efficient, this can address potential correctness issues as well. A command-line program (like the one supplied with Subversion) that binds to the client library needs to effectively translate feedback and requested data bits from C types to some form of human-readable output. This type of translation can be lossy. That is, the program may not display all of the information harvested from the API, or may combine bits of information for compact representation.

If you wrap such a command-line program with yet another program, the second program has access only to already interpreted (and as we mentioned, likely incomplete) information, which it must *again* translate into *its* representation format. With each layer of wrapping, the integrity of the original data is potentially tainted more and more, much like the result of making a copy of a copy (of a copy...) of a favorite audio or video cassette.

Using the APIs

Developing applications against the Subversion library APIs is fairly straightforward. All of the public header files live in the *subversion/include* directory of the source tree. These headers are copied into your system locations when you build and install Subversion itself from source. These headers represent the entirety of the functions and types meant to be accessible by users of the Subversion libraries.

The first thing you might notice is that Subversion's datatypes and functions are namespace protected. Every public Subversion symbol name begins with svn_, followed by a short code for the library in which the symbol is defined (such as wc, client, fs, etc.), followed by a single underscore (_) and then the rest of the symbol name. Semi-public functions (used among source files of a given library but not by code outside that library, and found inside the library directories themselves) differ from this naming scheme in that instead of a single underscore after the library code, they use a double underscore (__). Functions that are private to a given source file have no special prefixing, and are declared static. Of course, a compiler isn't interested in these naming conventions, but they definitely help to clarify the scope of a given function or datatype.

The Apache Portable Runtime Library

Along with Subversion's own datatype, you will see many references to datatypes that begin with apr_—symbols from the Apache Portable Runtime (APR) library. APR is Apache's portability library, originally carved out of its server code as an attempt to separate the OS-specific bits from the OS-independent portions of the code. The result was a library that provides a generic API for performing operations that differ mildly—or wildly—from OS to OS. While Apache HTTP Server was obviously the first user of the APR library, the Subversion developers immediately recognized the value of using APR as well. This means that there are practically no OS-specific code portions in Subversion itself. Also, it means that the Subversion client compiles and runs anywhere that the server does. Currently this list includes all flavors of Unix, Win32, BeOS, OS/2, and Mac OS X.

In addition to providing consistent implementations of system calls that differ across operating systems (Subversion uses ANSI system calls and datatypes as much as possible), APR gives Subversion immediate access to many custom datatypes, such as dynamic arrays and hash tables. Subversion uses these types extensively throughout the codebase. But perhaps the most pervasive APR datatype, found in nearly every Subversion API prototype, is the apr_pool_t—the APR memory pool. Subversion uses pools internally for all its memory allocation needs (unless an external library requires a different memory management schema for data passed through its API),* and while a person coding against the Subversion APIs is not required to do the same, they are required to provide pools to the API functions that need them. This means that users of the Subversion API must also link against APR, must call apr_initialize( ) to initialize the APR subsystem, and then must acquire a pool for use with Subversion API calls. See "Programming with Memory Pools" later in this chapter for more information.

URL and Path Requirements

With remote version control operation as the whole point of Subversion's existence, it makes sense that some attention has been paid to internationalization (i18n) support. After all, while remote might mean across the office, it could just as well mean across the globe. To facilitate this, all of Subversion's public interfaces that accept path arguments expect those paths to be canonicalized, and encoded in UTF-8. This means, for example, that any new client binary that drives the libsvn_client interface

---

* Neon and Berkeley DB are examples of such libraries

needs to first convert paths from the locale-specific encoding to UTF-8 before passing those paths to the Subversion libraries, and then reconvert any resultant output paths from Subversion back into the locale's encoding before using those paths for non-Subversion purposes. Fortunately, Subversion provides a suite of functions (see *subversion/include/svn_utf.h*) that can be used by any program to do these conversions.

Also, Subversion APIs require all URL parameters to be properly URI-encoded. So, instead of passing *file:///home/username/My File.txt* as the URL of a file named My File.txt, you need to pass *file:///home/username/My%20File.txt*. Again, Subversion supplies helper functions that your application can use—svn_path_uri_encode and svn_path_uri_decode, for URI encoding and decoding, respectively.

Using Languages Other than C and C++

If you are interested in using the Subversion libraries in conjunction with something other than a C program—such as a Python script or Java application—Subversion has some initial support for this via the Simplified Wrapper and Interface Generator (SWIG). The SWIG bindings for Subversion are located in *subversion/bindings/swig* and are slowly maturing into a usable state. These bindings allow you to call Subversion API functions indirectly, using wrappers that translate the datatypes native to your scripting language into the datatypes needed by Subversion's C libraries.

There is an obvious benefit to accessing the Subversion APIs via a language binding—simplicity. Generally speaking, languages such as Python and Perl are much more flexible and easy to use than C or C++. The sort of high-level datatypes and context-driven type checking provided by these languages are often better at handling information that comes from users. As you know, humans are proficient at botching up input to a program, and scripting languages tend to handle that misinformation more gracefully. Of course, often that flexibility comes at the cost of performance. That is why using a tightly optimized, C-based interface and library suite, combined with a powerful, flexible binding language is so appealing.

Let's look at Example 8-2, which uses Subversion's Python SWIG bindings, and does the same thing as our last example. Note the difference in size and complexity of the function this time!

Example 8-2. Using the repository layer with Python

```
from svn import fs
import os.path

def crawl_filesystem_dir (root, directory, pool):
    """Recursively crawl DIRECTORY under ROOT in the filesystem, and return
    a list of all the paths at or below DIRECTORY.  Use POOL for all
    allocations."""

    # Get the directory entries for DIRECTORY.
```

Example 8-2. Using the repository layer with Python (continued)

```
entries = fs.dir_entries(root, directory, pool)

# Initialize our returned list with the directory path itself.
paths = [directory]

# Loop over the entries
names = entries.keys( )
for name in names:
  # Calculate the entry's full path.
  full_path = os.path.join(basepath, name)

  # If the entry is a directory, recurse.  The recursion will return
  # a list with the entry and all its children, which we will add to
  # our running list of paths.
  if fs.is_dir(fsroot, full_path, pool):
    subpaths = crawl_filesystem_dir(root, full_path, pool)
    paths.extend(subpaths)

  # Else, it is a file, so add the entry's full path to the FILES list.
  else:
    paths.append(full_path)

return paths
```

An implementation in C of the previous example would stretch on quite a bit longer. The same routine in C would need to pay close attention to memory usage, and need to use custom datatypes for representing the hash of entries and the list of paths. Python has hashes and lists (called dictionaries and sequences, respectively) as built-in datatypes, and provides a wonderful selection of methods for operating on those types. And since Python uses reference counting and garbage collection, users of the language don't have to bother themselves with allocating and freeing memory.

In the previous section of this chapter, we mentioned the *libsvn_client* interface, and how it exists for the sole purpose of simplifying the process of writing a Subversion client. Example 8-3 shows how that library can be accessed via the SWIG bindings. In just a few lines of Python, you can check out a fully functional Subversion working copy!

Example 8-3. A simple script to check out a working copy

```
#!/usr/bin/env python
import sys
from svn import util, _util, _client

def usage( ):
  print "Usage: " + sys.argv[0] + " URL PATH\n"
  sys.exit(0)

def run(url, path):
  # Initialize APR and get a POOL.
  _util.apr_initialize( )
```

Example 8-3. A simple script to check out a working copy (continued)

```
pool = util.svn_pool_create(None)

# Checkout the HEAD of URL into PATH (silently)
_client.svn_client_checkout(None, None, url, path, -1, 1, None, pool)

# Cleanup our POOL, and shut down APR.
util.svn_pool_destroy(pool)
_util.apr_terminate( )

if __name__ == '__main__':
  if len(sys.argv) != 3:
    usage( )
  run(sys.argv[1], sys.argv[2])
```

Subversion's language bindings unfortunately tend to lack the level of attention given to the core Subversion modules. However, there have been significant efforts towards creating functional bindings for Python, Perl, and Java. Once you have the SWIG interface files properly configured, generation of the specific wrappers for all the supported SWIG languages (which currently includes versions of C#, Guile, Java, Mzscheme, OCaml, Perl, PHP, Python, Ruby, and Tcl) should theoretically be trivial. Still, some extra programming is required to compensate for complex APIs that SWIG needs some help generalizing. For more information on SWIG itself, see the project's website at *http://www.swig.org/*.

Inside the Working Copy Administration Area

As we mentioned earlier, each directory of a Subversion working copy contains a special subdirectory called *.svn* which houses administrative data about that working copy directory. Subversion uses the information in *.svn* to keep track of things such as:

- Which repository location(s) are represented by the files and subdirectories in the working copy directory
- What revision of each of those files and directories are currently present in the working copy
- Any user-defined properties that might be attached to those files and directories
- Pristine (unedited) copies of the working copy files

While there are several other bits of data stored in the *.svn* directory, we examine only a couple of the most important items.

The Entries File

Perhaps the single most important file in the *.svn* directory is the *entries* file. The entries file is an XML document that contains the bulk of the administrative information about a versioned resource in a working copy directory. It is this one file which tracks the repository URLs, pristine revision, file checksums, pristine text and property timestamps, scheduling and conflict state information, last-known commit information (author, revision, timestamp), local copy history—practically everything that a Subversion client is interested in knowing about a versioned (or to-be-versioned) resource!

Comparing the Administrative Areas of Subversion and CVS

A glance inside the typical *.svn* directory turns up a bit more than what CVS maintains in its *CVS* administrative directories. The entries file contains XML which describes the current state of the working copy directory, and basically serves the purposes of CVS's *Entries*, *Root*, and *Repository* files combined.

Example 8-4 is an example of an actual entries file.

Example 8-4. Contents of a typical .svn/entries file

```
<?xml version="1.0" encoding="utf-8"?>
<wc-entries
   xmlns="svn:">
<entry
   committed-rev="1"
   name="svn:this_dir"
   committed-date="2002-09-24T17:12:44.064475Z"
   url="http://svn.red-bean.com/tests/.greek-repo/A/D"
   kind="dir"
   revision="1"/>
<entry
   committed-rev="1"
   name="gamma"
   text-time="2002-09-26T21:09:02.000000Z"
   committed-date="2002-09-24T17:12:44.064475Z"
   checksum="QSE4vWd9ZMOcMvr7/+YkXQ= ="
   kind="file"
   prop-time="2002-09-26T21:09:02.000000Z"/>
<entry
   name="zeta"
   kind="file"
   schedule="add"
   revision="0"/>
<entry
   url="http://svn.red-bean.com/tests/.greek-repo/A/B/delta"
```

Example 8-4. Contents of a typical .svn/entries file (continued)

```
    name="delta"
    kind="file"
    schedule="add"
    revision="0"/>
<entry
    name="G"
    kind="dir"/>
<entry
    name="H"
    kind="dir"
    schedule="delete"/>
</wc-entries>
```

As you can see, the entries file is essentially a list of entries. Each `<entry>` tag represents one of three things: the working copy directory itself (called the this directory entry, and noted as having an empty value for its name attribute), a file in that working copy directory (noted by having its kind attribute set to `"file"`), or a subdirectory in that working copy (kind here is set to `"dir"`). The files and subdirectories whose entries are stored in this file are either already under version control, or (as in the case of the file named *zeta* above) are scheduled to be added to version control when the user next commits this working copy directory's changes. Each entry has a unique name, and each entry has a node kind.

Developers should be aware of some special rules that Subversion uses when reading and writing its *entries* files. While each entry has a revision and URL associated with it, note that not every `<entry>` tag in the sample file has explicit revision or url attributes attached to it. Subversion allows entries to not explicitly store those two attributes when their values are the same as (in the revision case) or trivially calculable from[*] (in the url case) the data stored in the this directory entry. Note also that for subdirectory entries, Subversion stores only the crucial attributes—name, kind, url, revision, and schedule. In an effort to reduce duplicated information, Subversion dictates that the method for determining the full set of information about a subdirectory is to traverse down into that subdirectory, and read the this directory entry from its own *.svn/entries* file. However, a reference to the subdirectory is kept in its parent's *entries* file, with enough information to permit basic versioning operations in the event that the subdirectory itself is actually missing from disk.

Pristine Copies and Property Files

As mentioned before, the *.svn* directory also holds the pristine text-base versions of files. Those can be found in *.svn/text-base*. The benefits of these pristine copies are multiple—network-free checks for local modifications and difference reporting, net-

---

[*] That is, the URL for the entry is the same as the concatenation of the parent directory's URL and the entry's name.

work-free reversion of modified or missing files, smaller transmission of changes to the server—but comes at the cost of having each versioned file stored at least twice on disk. These days, this seems to be a negligible penalty for most files. However, the situation gets uglier as the size of your versioned files grows. Some attention is being given to making the presence of the text-base an option. Ironically though, it is as your versioned files' sizes get larger that the existence of the text-base becomes more crucial—who wants to transmit a huge file across a network just because they want to commit a tiny change to it?

Similar in purpose to the text-base files are the property files and their pristine prop-base copies, located in *.svn/props* and *.svn/prop-base* respectively. Since directories can have properties, too, there are also *.svn/dir-props* and *.svn/dir-prop-base* files. Each of these property files (working and base versions) uses a simple hash-on-disk file format for storing the property names and values.

WebDAV

WebDAV (shorthand for Web-based Distributed Authoring and Versioning) is an extension of the standard HTTP protocol designed to make the web into a read/write medium, instead of the basically read-only medium that exists today. The theory is that directories and files can be shared—as both readable and writable objects—over the web. RFCs 2518 and 3253 describe the WebDAV/DeltaV extensions to HTTP, and are available (along with a lot of other useful information) at *http://www.webdav.org/*.

A number of operating system file browsers are already able to mount networked directories using WebDAV. On Win32, the Windows Explorer can browse what it calls WebFolders (which are just WebDAV-ready network locations) as if they were regular shared folders. Mac OS X also has this capability, as do the Nautilus and Konqueror browsers (under GNOME and KDE, respectively).

How does all of this apply to Subversion? The mod_dav_svn Apache module uses HTTP, extended by WebDAV and DeltaV, as one of its network protocols. Subversion uses mod_dav_svn to map between Subversion's versioning concepts and those of RFCs 2518 and 3253.

For a more thorough discussion of WebDAV, how it works, and how Subversion uses it, see Appendix C. Among other things, that appendix discusses the degree to which Subversion adheres to the generic WebDAV specification, and how that affects interoperability with generic WebDAV clients.

Programming with Memory Pools

Almost every developer who has used the C programming language has at some point sighed at the daunting task of managing memory usage. Allocating enough memory to use, keeping track of those allocations, freeing the memory when you no longer need it—these tasks can be quite complex. And, of course, failure to do those things properly can result in a program that crashes itself, or worse, crashes the computer. Fortunately, the APR library that Subversion depends on for portability provides the apr_pool_t type, which represents a pool from which the application may allocate memory.

A memory pool is an abstract representation of a chunk of memory allocated for use by a program. Rather than requesting memory directly from the OS using the standard malloc( ) and friends, programs that link against APR can simply request that a pool of memory be created (using the apr_pool_create( ) function). APR will allocate a moderately sized chunk of memory from the OS, and that memory will be instantly available for use by the program. Any time the program needs some of the pool memory, it uses one of the APR pool API functions, like apr_palloc( ), which returns a generic memory location from the pool. The program can keep requesting bits and pieces of memory from the pool, and APR will keep granting the requests. Pools will automatically grow in size to accommodate programs that request more memory than the original pool contained, until of course there is no more memory available on the system.

Now, if this were the end of the pool story, it would hardly have merited special attention. Fortunately, that's not the case. Pools can not only be created; they can also be cleared and destroyed, using apr_pool_clear( ) and apr_pool_destroy( ) respectively. This gives developers the flexibility to allocate several—or several thousand—things from the pool, and then clean up all of that memory with a single function call! Further, pools have hierarchy. You can make subpools of any previously created pool. When you clear a pool, all of its subpools are destroyed; if you destroy a pool, it and its subpools are destroyed.

Before we go further, developers should be aware that they probably will not find many calls to the APR pool functions we just mentioned in the Subversion source code. APR pools offer some extensibility mechanisms, like the ability to have custom user data attached to the pool, and mechanisms for registering cleanup functions that get called when the pool is destroyed. Subversion makes use of these extensions in a somewhat non-trivial way. So, Subversion supplies (and most of its code uses) the wrapper functions svn_pool_create( ), svn_pool_clear( ), and svn_pool_destroy( ).

While pools are helpful for basic memory management, the pool construct really shines in looping and recursive scenarios. Since loops are often unbounded in their iterations, and recursions in their depth, memory consumption in these areas of the code can become unpredictable. Fortunately, using nested memory pools can be a great way to easily manage these potentially hairy situations. Example 8-5 demonstrates the basic use of nested pools in a situation that is fairly common—recursively crawling a directory tree, doing some task to each thing in the tree.

Example 8-5. Effective pool usage

```
/* Recursively crawl over DIRECTORY, adding the paths of all its file
   children to the FILES array, and doing some task to each path
   encountered.  Use POOL for the all temporary allocations, and store
   the hash paths in the same pool as the hash itself is allocated in.  */
static apr_status_t
crawl_dir (apr_array_header_t *files,
           const char *directory,
           apr_pool_t *pool)
{
  apr_pool_t *hash_pool = files->pool;  /* array pool */
  apr_pool_t *subpool = svn_pool_create (pool);  /* iteration pool */
  apr_dir_t *dir;
  apr_finfo_t finfo;
  apr_status_t apr_err;
  apr_int32_t flags = APR_FINFO_TYPE | APR_FINFO_NAME;

  apr_err = apr_dir_open (&dir, directory, pool);
  if (apr_err)
    return apr_err;

  /* Loop over the directory entries, clearing the subpool at the top of
     each iteration.  */
  for (apr_err = apr_dir_read (&finfo, flags, dir);
       apr_err == APR_SUCCESS;
       apr_err = apr_dir_read (&finfo, flags, dir))
    {
      const char *child_path;

      /* Clear the per-iteration SUBPOOL.  */
      svn_pool_clear (subpool);

      /* Skip entries for "this dir" ('.') and its parent ('..').  */
      if (finfo.filetype == APR_DIR)
        {
          if (finfo.name[0] == '.'
              && (finfo.name[1] == '\0'
                  || (finfo.name[1] == '.' && finfo.name[2] == '\0')))
            continue;
        }

      /* Build CHILD_PATH from DIRECTORY and FINFO.name.  */
      child_path = svn_path_join (directory, finfo.name, subpool);

      /* Do some task to this encountered path. */
      do_some_task (child_path, subpool);

      /* Handle subdirectories by recursing into them, passing SUBPOOL
         as the pool for temporary allocations.  */
      if (finfo.filetype == APR_DIR)
        {
          apr_err = crawl_dir (files, child_path, subpool);
          if (apr_err)
```

Example 8-5. Effective pool usage (continued)

```
            return apr_err;
      }

   /* Handle files by adding their paths to the FILES array.  */
   else if (finfo.filetype == APR_REG)
     {
        /* Copy the file's path into the FILES array's pool.  */
        child_path = apr_pstrdup (hash_pool, child_path);

        /* Add the path to the array.  */
        (*((const char **) apr_array_push (files))) = child_path;
     }
 }

/* Destroy SUBPOOL.  */
svn_pool_destroy (subpool);

/* Check that the loop exited cleanly. */
if (apr_err)
  return apr_err;

/* Yes, it exited cleanly, so close the dir. */
apr_err = apr_dir_close (dir);
if (apr_err)
  return apr_err;

return APR_SUCCESS;
}
```

The previous example demonstrates effective pool usage in *both* looping and recursive situations. Each recursion begins by making a subpool of the pool passed to the function. This subpool is used for the looping region, and cleared with each iteration. The result is memory usage is roughly proportional to the depth of the recursion, not to total number of file and directories present as children of the top-level directory. When the first call to this recursive function finally finishes, there is actually very little data stored in the pool that was passed to it. Now imagine the extra complexity that would be present if this function had to alloc( ) and free( ) every single piece of data used!

Pools might not be ideal for every application, but they are extremely useful in Subversion. As a Subversion developer, you'll need to grow comfortable with pools and how to wield them correctly. Memory usage bugs and bloating can be difficult to diagnose and fix regardless of the API, but the pool construct provided by APR has proven a tremendously convenient, time-saving bit of functionality.

Contributing to Subversion

The official source of information about the Subversion project is, of course, the project's website at *http://subversion.tigris.org/*. There you can find information about getting access to the source code and participating on the discussion lists. The Subversion community always welcomes new members. If you are interested in participating in this community by contributing changes to the source code, here are some hints on how to get started.

Join the Community

The first step in community participation is to find a way to stay on top of the latest happenings. To do this most effectively, you will want to subscribe to the main developer discussion list (*dev@subversion.tigris.org*) and commit mail list (*svn@subversion.tigris.org*). By following these lists even loosely, you will have access to important design discussions, be able to see actual changes to Subversion source code as they occur, and be able to witness peer reviews of those changes and proposed changes. These email-based discussion lists are the primary communication media for Subversion development. See the Mailing Lists section of the website for other Subversion-related lists you might be interested in.

But how do you know what needs to be done? It is quite common for a programmer to have the greatest intentions of helping out with the development, yet be unable to find a good starting point. After all, not many folks come to the community having already decided on a particular itch they would like to scratch. But by watching the developer discussion lists, you might see mentions of existing bugs or feature requests fly by that particularly interest you. Also, a great place to look for outstanding, unclaimed tasks is the Issue Tracking database on the Subversion website. There you will find the current list of known bugs and feature requests. If you want to start with something small, look for issues marked as bite-sized.

Get the Source Code

To edit the code, you need to have the code. This means you need to check out a working copy from the public Subversion source repository. As straightforward as that might sound, the task can be slightly tricky. Because Subversion's source code is versioned using Subversion itself, you actually need to bootstrap by getting a working Subversion client via some other method. The most common methods include downloading the latest binary distribution (if such is available for your platform), or downloading the latest source tarball and building your own Subversion client. If you build from source, make sure to read the *INSTALL* file in the top level of the source tree for instructions.

After you have a working Subversion client, you are now poised to checkout a working copy of the Subversion source repository from *http://svn.collab.net/repos/svn/trunk/*: *

```
$ svn checkout http://svn.collab.net/repos/svn/trunk subversion
A   HACKING
A   INSTALL
A   README
A   autogen.sh
A   build.conf
...
```

This command will check out the bleeding-edge, latest version of the Subversion source code into a subdirectory named *subversion* in your current working directory. Obviously, you can adjust that last argument as you see fit. Regardless of what you call the new working copy directory, though, after this operation completes, you will now have the Subversion source code. Of course, you will still need to fetch a few helper libraries (apr, apr-util, etc.)—see the *INSTALL* file in the top level of the working copy for details.

Become Familiar with Community Policies

Now that you have a working copy containing the latest Subversion source code, you will most certainly want to take a cruise through the *HACKING* file in that working copy's top-level directory. The *HACKING* file contains general instructions for contributing to Subversion, including how to properly format your source code for consistency with the rest of the codebase, how to describe your proposed changes with an effective change log message, how to test your changes, and so on. Commit privileges on the Subversion source repository are earned—a government by meritocracy.†
The *HACKING* file is an invaluable resource when it comes to making sure that your proposed changes earn the praises they deserve without being rejected on technicalities.

Make and Test Your Changes

With the code and community policy understanding in hand, you are ready to make your changes. It is best to try to make smaller but related sets of changes, even tackling larger tasks in stages, instead of making huge, sweeping modifications. Your proposed changes will be easier to understand (and therefore easier to review) if you disturb the fewest lines of code possible to accomplish your task properly. After

---

* Note that the URL checked out in the example above ends not with svn, but with a subdirectory thereof called trunk. See our discussion of Subversion's branching and tagging model for the reasoning behind this.

† While this may superficially appear as some sort of elitism, this "earn your commit privileges" notion is about efficiency—whether it costs more in time and effort to review and apply someone else's changes that are likely to be safe and useful, versus the potential costs of undoing changes that are dangerous.

making each set of proposed changes, your Subversion tree should be in a state in which the software compiles with no warnings.

Subversion has a fairly thorough* regression test suite, and your proposed changes are expected to not cause any of those tests to fail. By running make check (in Unix) from the top of the source tree, you can sanity-check your changes. The fastest way to get your code contributions rejected (other than failing to supply a good log message) is to submit changes that cause failure in the test suite.

In the best-case scenario, you will have actually added appropriate tests to that test suite that verify that your proposed changes actually work as expected. In fact, sometimes the best contribution a person can make is solely the addition of new tests. You can write regression tests for functionality that currently works in Subversion as a way to protect against future changes that might trigger failure in those areas. Also, you can write new tests that demonstrate known failures. For this purpose, the Subversion test suite allows you to specify that a given test is expected to fail (called an XFAIL), and so long as Subversion fails in the way that was expected, a test result of XFAIL itself is considered a success. Ultimately, the better the test suite, the less time wasted on diagnosing potentially obscure regression bugs.

Donate Your Changes

After making your modifications to the source code, compose a clear and concise log message to describe those changes and the reasons for them. Then, send an email to the developers list containing your log message and the output of svn diff (from the top of your Subversion working copy). If the community members consider your changes acceptable, someone who has commit privileges (permission to make new revisions in the Subversion source repository) adds your changes to the public source code tree. Recall that permission to directly commit changes to the repository is granted on merit—if you demonstrate comprehension of Subversion, programming competency, and a team spirit, you will likely be awarded that permission.

---

* You might want to grab some popcorn. Thorough, in this instance, translates to somewhere in the neighborhood of 30 minutes of noninteractive machine churn.

## CHAPTER 9

Subversion Complete Reference

This chapter is intended to be a complete reference to using Subversion. This includes the command line client (svn) and all its subcommands, as well as the repository administration programs (svnadmin and svnlook) and their respective subcommands.

The Subversion Command Line Client: svn

To use the command line client, you type svn, the subcommand you wish to use,[*] and any switches or targets that you wish to operate on—there is no specific order that the subcommand and the switches must appear in. For example, all of the following are valid ways to use svn status:

```
$ svn -v status
$ svn status -v
$ svn status -v myfile
```

You can find many more examples of how to use most client commands in Chapter 3 and commands for managing properties in "Properties" in Chapter 7.

svn Switches

While Subversion has different switches for its subcommands, all switches are global—that is, each switch is guaranteed to mean the same thing regardless of the subcommand you use it with. For example, --verbose (-v) always means verbose output, regardless of the subcommand with which you use it.

--auto-props
    Enables auto-props, overriding the enable-auto-props directive in the *config* file.

---

[*] Yes, yes, you don't need a subcommand to use the --version switch, but we'll get to that in just a minute.

`--config-dir` *DIR*

> Instructs Subversion to read configuration information from the specified directory instead of the default location (*.subversion* in the user's home directory).

`--diff-cmd` *CMD*

> Specifies an external program to use to show differences between files. When `svn diff` is invoked, it uses Subversion's internal diff engine, which provides unified diffs by default. If you want to use an external diff program, use `--diff-cmd`. You can pass switches to the diff program with the `--extensions` switch (more on that later in this section).

`--diff3-cmd` *CMD*

> Specifies an external program to use to merge files.

`--dry-run`

> Goes through all the motions of running a command, but makes no actual changes—either on disk or in the repository.

`--editor-cmd` *CMD*

> Specifies an external program to use to edit a log message or a property value.

`--encoding` *ENC*

> Tells Subversion that your commit message is encoded in the charset provided. The default is your operating system's native locale, and you should specify the encoding if your commit message is in any other encoding.

`--extensions (-x)` *ARGS*

> Specifies an argument or arguments that Subversion should pass to an external diff command when providing differences between files. If you wish to pass multiple arguments, you must enclose all of them in quotes (for example, `svn diff --diff-cmd /usr/bin/diff -x "-b -E"`). This switch can *only* be used if you also pass the `--diff-cmd` switch.

`--file (-F)` *FILENAME*

> Uses the contents of the file passed as an argument to this switch for the specified subcommand.

`--force`

> Forces a particular command or operation to run. There are some operations that Subversion prevents you from doing in normal usage, but you can pass the force switch to tell Subversion, "I know what I'm doing as well as the possible repercussions of doing it, so let me at 'em." (This switch is the programmatic equivalent of doing your own electrical work with the power on—if you don't know what you're doing, you're likely to get a nasty shock.)

`--force-log`

> Forces a suspicious parameter passed to the `--message` (`-m`) or `--file` (`-F`) options to be accepted as valid. By default, Subversion produces an error if parameters to these options look as if they might instead be targets of the subcommand. For example, if you pass a versioned file's path to the `--file` (`-F`) option, Subversion will assume you've made a mistake, that the path was instead intended as the

target of the operation, and that you simply failed to provide some other—unversioned—file as the source of your log message. To assert your intent and override these types of errors, pass the `--force-log` option to commands that accept log messages.

--help *(-h or -?)*

If used with one or more subcommands, shows the built-in help text for each subcommand. If used alone, it displays the general client help text.

--ignore-ancestry

Ignore ancestry when calculating differences (rely on path contents alone).

--incremental

Prints output in a format suitable for concatenation.

--message *(-m)* *MESSAGE*

Indicates that you will specify a commit message on the command line, following this switch. For example:

```
$ svn commit -m "They don't make Sunday."
```

--new *ARG*

Uses *ARG* as the newer target.

--no-auth-cache

Prevents caching of authentication information (e.g., username and password) in the Subversion administrative directories.

--no-auto-props

Disable auto-props, overriding the `enable-auto-props` directive in the *config* file.

--no-diff-deleted

Prevents Subversion from printing differences for deleted files. The default behavior when you remove a file is for svn diff to print the same differences that you would see if you had left the file but removed all the content.

--no-ignore

Shows files in the status listing that would normally be omitted since they match a pattern in the `svn:ignore` property. See "Config" in Chapter 7 for more information.

--non-interactive

In the case of an authentication failure, or insufficient credentials, prevents prompting for credentials (e.g., username or password). This is useful if you're running Subversion inside of an automated script and it's more appropriate to have Subversion fail than to prompt for more information.

--non-recursive *(-N)*

Stops a subcommand from recursing into subdirectories. Most subcommands recurse by default, but some subcommands—usually those that have the potential to remove or undo your local modifications—do not.

`--notice-ancestry`

Pays attention to ancestry when calculating differences.

`--old ARG`

Uses *ARG* as the older target.

`--password PASS`

Indicates that you are providing your password for authentication on the command line—otherwise, if it is needed, Subversion prompts you for it.

`--quiet (-q)`

Requests that the client print only essential information while performing an operation.

`--recursive (-R)`

Makes a subcommand recurse into subdirectories. Most subcommands recurse by default.

`--relocate FROM TO [PATH...]`

Used with the `svn switch` subcommand, changes the location of the repository that your working copy references. This is useful if the location of your repository changes and you have an existing working copy that you'd like to continue to use. See `svn switch` for an example.

`--revision (-r) REV`

Indicates that you're going to supply a revision (or range of revisions) for a particular operation. You can provide revision numbers, revision keywords, or dates (in curly braces) as arguments to the revision switch. If you wish to provide a range of revisions, you can provide two revisions separated by a colon. For example:

```
$ svn log -r 1729
$ svn log -r 1729:HEAD
$ svn log -r 1729:1744
$ svn log -r {2001-12-04}:{2002-02-17}
$ svn log -r 1729:{2002-02-17}
```

See "Revision Keywords" for more information.

`--revprop`

Operates on a revision property instead of a Subversion property specific to a file or directory. This switch requires that you pass a revision with the `--revision (-r)` switch. See "Unversioned Properties" in Chapter 5 for more details on unversioned properties.

`--show-updates (-u)`

Causes the client to display information about which files in your working copy are out-of-date. This doesn't actually update any of your files—it just shows you which files will be updated if you run `svn update`.

`--stop-on-copy`

Causes a Subversion subcommand that is traversing the history of a versioned resource to stop harvesting that historical information when a copy—that is, a location in history where that resource was copied from another location in the repository—is encountered.

`--strict`

Causes Subversion to use strict semantics, a notion which is rather vague unless talking about specific subcommands.

`--targets` *FILENAME*

Tells Subversion to get the list of files that you wish to operate on from the filename you provide instead of listing all the files on the command line.

`--username` *NAME*

Indicates that you are providing your username for authentication on the command line—otherwise, if it is needed, Subversion will prompt you for it.

`--verbose` *(-v)*

Requests that the client print out as much information as it can while running any subcommand. This may result in Subversion printing out additional fields, detailed information about every file, or additional information regarding its actions.

`--version`

Prints the client version info. This information not only includes the version number of the client, but also a listing of all repository access modules that the client can use to access a Subversion repository.

`--xml`

Prints output in XML format.

svn Subcommands

svn add
Adds files and directories.

Synopsis

`svn add PATH...`

Description

Adds files and directories to your working copy and schedules them for addition to the repository. They will be uploaded and added to the repository on your next commit. If you add something and change your mind before committing, you can unschedule the addition using `svn revert`.

Alternate Names

None

Changes

Working copy

Switches

```
--targets FILENAME
--non-recursive (-N)
--quiet (-q)
--config-dir DIR
--auto-props
--no-auto-props
```

Examples

To add a file to your working copy:

```
$ svn add foo.c
A         foo.c
```

When adding a directory, the default behavior of svn add is to recurse:

```
$ svn add testdir
A         testdir
A         testdir/a
A         testdir/b
A         testdir/c
A         testdir/d
```

You can add a directory without adding its contents:

```
$ svn add --non-recursive otherdir
A         otherdir
```

---

svn blame

Shows author and revision information in-line for the specified files or URLs.

Synopsis

```
svn blame TARGET...
```

Description

Shows author and revision information in-line for the specified files or URLs. Each line of text is annotated at the beginning with the author (username) and the revision number for the last change to that line.

Alternate Names

praise, annotate, ann

Changes

Nothing

Accesses Repository

Yes

Switches

```
--revision (-r) REV
--username USER
--password PASS
--no-auth-cache
--non-interactive
--config-dir DIR
```

Examples

If you want to see blame-annotated source for *readme.txt* in your test repository:

```
$ svn blame http://svn.red-bean.com/repos/test/readme.txt
     3      sally This is a README file.
     5      harry You should read this.
```

---

svn cat
Outputs the contents of the specified files or URLs.

Synopsis

```
svn cat TARGET...
```

Description

Outputs the contents of the specified files or URLs. For listing the contents of directories, see svn list.

Alternate Names

None

Changes

Nothing

Accesses Repository

Yes

Switches

```
--revision (-r) REV
--username USER
--password PASS
--no-auth-cache
--non-interactive
--config-dir DIR
```

Examples

If you want to view *readme.txt* in your repository without checking it out:

```
$ svn cat http://svn.red-bean.com/repos/test/readme.txt
This is a README file.
You should read this.
```

If your working copy is out of date (or you have local modifications) and you want to see the HEAD revision of a file in your working copy, svn cat will automatically fetch the HEAD revision when you give it a path:

```
$ cat foo.c
This file is in my local working copy
and has changes that I've made.
$ svn cat foo.c
Latest revision fresh from the repository!
```

svn checkout

Checks out a working copy from a repository.

Synopsis

```
svn checkout URL... [PATH]
```

Description

Checks out a working copy from a repository. If *PATH* is omitted, the basename of the URL will be used as the destination. If multiple URLs are given each is checked out into a subdirectory of PATH, with the name of the subdirectory being the basename of the URL.

Alternate Names

co

Changes

Creates a working copy.

Accesses Repository

Yes

Switches

```
--revision (-r) REV
--quiet (-q)
--non-recursive (-N)
--username USER
--password PASS
--no-auth-cache
--non-interactive
--config-dir DIR
```

Examples

Check out a working copy into a directory called *mine*:

```
$ svn checkout file:///tmp/repos/test mine
A  mine/a
A  mine/b
Checked out revision 2.
$ ls
mine
```

Check out two different directories into two separate working copies:

```
$ svn checkout file:///tmp/repos/test  file:///tmp/repos/quiz
A  test/a
A  test/b
Checked out revision 2.
A  quiz/l
A  quiz/m
Checked out revision 2.
$ ls
quiz  test
```

Check out two different directories into two separate working copies, but place both into a directory called *working-copies*:

```
$ svn checkout file:///tmp/repos/test  file:///tmp/repos/quiz working-copies
A  working-copies/test/a
A  working-copies/test/b
Checked out revision 2.
A  working-copies/quiz/l
A  working-copies/quiz/m
Checked out revision 2.
$ ls
working-copies
```

If you interrupt a checkout (or something else interrupts your checkout, such as loss of connectivity, etc.), you can restart it either by issuing the identical checkout command again, or by updating the incomplete working copy:

```
$ svn checkout file:///tmp/repos/test test
A  test/a
A  test/b
^C
svn: The operation was interrupted
svn: caught SIGINT
$ svn checkout file:///tmp/repos/test test
A  test/c
A  test/d
^C
svn: The operation was interrupted
svn: caught SIGINT
$ cd test
$ svn update
A  test/e
A  test/f
Updated to revision 3.
```

svn cleanup

Recursively cleans up the working copy.

Synopsis

```
svn cleanup [PATH...]
```

Description

Recursively cleans up the working copy, removing locks and resuming unfinished operations. If you ever get a working copy locked error, run this command to remove stale locks and get your working copy into a usable state again. See Appendix B.

If, for some reason, an svn update fails due to a problem running an external diff program (e.g., user input or network failure), pass the --diff3-cmd to allow cleanup to complete any merging with your external diff program. You can also specify any configuration directory with the --config-dir switch, but you should need these switches extremely infrequently.

Alternate Names

None

Changes

Working copy

Accesses Repository

No

Switches

```
--diff3-cmd CMD
--config-dir DIR
```

Examples

Well, there's not much to the examples here, as svn cleanup generates no output. If you pass no PATH, . is used:

```
$ svn cleanup
$ svn cleanup /path/to/working-copy
```

---

svn commit

Sends changes from your working copy to the repository.

Synopsis

```
svn commit [PATH...]
```

Description

Sends changes from your working copy to the repository. If you do not supply a log message with your commit by using either the --file or --message switch, svn will launch your editor for you to compose a commit message. See the editor-cmd section in "Config" in Chapter 7."

If you begin a commit and Subversion launches your editor to compose the commit message, you can still abort without committing your changes. If you want to cancel your commit, just quit your editor without saving your commit message and Subversion prompts you either to abort the commit, continue with no message, or edit the message again.

Alternate Names

ci (short for "check in," not co, which is short for "check out")

Changes

Working copy, repository

Accesses Repository

Yes

Switches

```
--message (-m) TEXT
--file (-F) FILE
--quiet (-q)
--non-recursive (-N)
--targets FILENAME
--force-log
--username USER
--password PASS
--no-auth-cache
--non-interactive
--encoding ENC
--config-dir DIR
```

Examples

Commit a simple modification to a file with the commit message on the command line and an implicit target of your current directory (.):

```
$ svn commit -m "added howto section."
Sending        a
Transmitting file data .
Committed revision 3.
```

Commit a modification to the file *foo.c* (explicitly specified on the command line) with the commit message in a file named msg:

```
$ svn commit -F msg foo.c
Sending        foo.c
Transmitting file data .
Committed revision 5.
```

If you want to use a file that's under version control for your commit message with --file, you need to pass the --force-log switch:

```
$ svn commit --file file_under_vc.txt foo.c
svn: The log message file is under version control
svn: Log message file is a versioned file; use '--force-log' to override
$ svn commit --force-log --file file_under_vc.txt foo.c
Sending        foo.c
Transmitting file data .
Committed revision 6.
```

To commit a file scheduled for deletion:

```
$ svn commit -m "removed file 'c'."
Deleting        c
Committed revision 7.
```

---

svn copy
Copies a file or directory in a working copy or in the repository.

Synopsis

```
svn copy SRC DST
```

Description

Copies a file in a working copy or in the repository. *SRC* and *DST* can each be either a working copy (WC) path or URL:

WC -> WC
> Copy and schedule an item for addition (with history).

WC -> URL
> Immediately commit a copy of WC to URL.

URL -> WC
> Check out URL into WC, and schedule it for addition.

URL -> URL
> Complete server-side copy. This is usually used to branch and tag.

You can only copy files within a single repository. Subversion does not support cross-repository copying.

Alternate Names

cp

Changes

Repository if destination is a URL.

Working copy if destination is a WC path.

Accesses Repository

If source or destination is in the repository, or if needed to look up the source revision number.

Switches

```
--message (-m) TEXT
--file (-F) FILE
--revision (-r) REV
--quiet (-q)
--username USER
--password PASS
--no-auth-cache
--non-interactive
```

```
--force-log
--editor-cmd EDITOR
--encoding ENC
--config-dir DIR
```

Examples

Copy an item within your working copy (only schedules the copy—nothing goes into the repository until you commit):

```
$ svn copy foo.txt bar.txt
A         bar.txt
$ svn status
A  +  bar.txt
```

Copy an item in your working copy to a URL in the repository (an immediate commit, so you must supply a commit message):

```
$ svn copy near.txt file:///tmp/repos/test/far-away.txt -m "Remote copy."
Committed revision 8.
```

Copy an item from the repository to your working copy (only schedules the copy—nothing goes into the repository until you commit):

This is the recommended way to resurrect a dead file in your repository!

```
$ svn copy file:///tmp/repos/test/far-away near-here
A         near-here
```

And finally, copying between two URLs:

```
$ svn copy file:///tmp/repos/test/far-away file:///tmp/repos/test/over-there -m
"remote copy."
Committed revision 9.
```

This is the easiest way to tag a revision in your repository—just svn copy that revision (usually HEAD) into your tags directory.

```
$ svn copy file:///tmp/repos/test/trunk file:///tmp/repos/test/tags/0.6.32-prerelease
-m "tag tree"
Committed revision 12.
```

And don't worry if you forgot to tag—you can always specify an older revision and tag anytime:

```
$ svn copy -r 11 file:///tmp/repos/test/trunk file:///tmp/repos/test/tags/0.6.32-
prerelease -m "Forgot to tag at rev 11"
Committed revision 13.
```

---

svn delete

Deletes an item from a working copy or the repository.

Synopsis

```
svn delete PATH...
svn delete URL...
```

Description

Items specified by *PATH* are scheduled for deletion upon the next commit. Files (and directories that have not been committed) are immediately removed from the working copy. The command will not remove any unversioned or modified items; use the --force switch to override this behavior.

Items specified by URL are deleted from the repository via an immediate commit. Multiple URLs are committed atomically.

Alternate Names

del, remove, rm

Changes

Working copy if operating on files, repository if operating on URLs

Accesses Repository

Only if operating on URLs

Switches

```
--force
--force-log
--message (-m) TEXT
--file (-F) FILE
--quiet (-q)
--targets FILENAME
--username USER
--password PASS
--no-auth-cache
--non-interactive
--editor-cmd EDITOR
--encoding ENC
--config-dir DIR
```

Examples

Using svn to delete a file from your working copy merely schedules it to be deleted. When you commit, the file is deleted in the repository:

```
$ svn delete myfile
D         myfile
$ svn commit -m "Deleted file 'myfile'."
Deleting       myfile
Transmitting file data .
Committed revision 14.
```

Deleting a URL, however, is immediate, so you have to supply a log message:

```
$ svn delete -m "Deleting file 'yourfile'" file:///tmp/repos/test/yourfile
Committed revision 15.
```

Here's an example of how to force deletion of a file that has local mods:

```
$ svn delete over-there
svn: Attempting restricted operation for modified resource
```

```
svn: Use --force to override this restriction
svn: 'over-there' has local modifications
$ svn delete --force over-there
D           over-there
```

svn diff

Displays the differences between two paths.

Synopsis

```
svn diff [-r N[:M]] [--old OLD-TGT] [--new NEW-TGT] [PATH...]
svn diff -r N:M URL
svn diff [-r N[:M]] URL1[@N] URL2[@M]
```

Description

Displays the differences between two paths. The three different ways you can use svn diff are as follows:

svn diff [-r N[:M]] [--old OLD-TGT] [--new NEW-TGT] [PATH...] displays the differences between *OLD-TGT* and *NEW-TGT*. If *PATH*s are given, they are treated as relative to *OLD-TGT* and *NEW-TGT* and the output is restricted to differences in only those paths. *OLD-TGT* and *NEW-TGT* may be working copy paths or *URL[@REV]*. *OLD-TGT* defaults to the current working directory and *NEW-TGT* defaults to *OLD-TGT*. N defaults to BASE or, if *OLD-TGT* is a URL, to HEAD. *M* defaults to the current working version or, if *NEW-TGT* is a URL, to HEAD. svn diff -r N sets the revision of *OLD-TGT* to *N*, svn diff -r N:M also sets the revision of *NEW-TGT* to *M*.

svn diff -r N:M URL is shorthand for svn diff -r N:M --old=URL --new=URL.

svn diff [-r N[:M]] URL1[@N] URL2[@M] is shorthand for svn diff [-r N[:M]] --old=URL1 --new=URL2.

If *TARGET* is a URL, then revs N and M can be given either via the --revision or by using @ notation as described earlier.

If *TARGET* is a working copy path, then the --revision switch means:

--revision N:M

The server compares *TARGET@N* and *TARGET@M*.

--revision N

The client compares *TARGET@N* against working copy.

(no --revision)

The client compares base and working copies of *TARGET*.

If the alternate syntax is used, the server compares URL1 and URL2 at revisions N and M respectively. If either N or M are omitted, a value of HEAD is assumed.

By default, svn diff ignores the ancestry of files and merely compares the contents of the two files being compared. If you use --notice-ancestry, the ancestry of the paths in question will be taken into consideration when comparing revisions (that is, if you run svn diff on two files with identical contents but different ancestry you will see the entire contents of the file as having been removed and added again).

Alternate Names

di

Changes

Nothing

Accesses Repository

For obtaining differences against anything but BASE revision in your working copy

Switches

```
--revision (-r) REV
--old OLD-TARGET
--new NEW-TARGET
--extensions (-x) "ARGS"
--non-recursive (-N)
--diff-cmd CMD
--notice-ancestry
--username USER
--password PASS
--no-auth-cache
--non-interactive
--no-diff-deleted
--config-dir DIR
```

Examples

Compare BASE and your working copy (one of the most popular uses of svn diff):

```
$ svn diff COMMITTERS
Index: COMMITTERS
===================================================================
--- COMMITTERS       (revision 4404)
+++ COMMITTERS       (working copy)
```

See how your working copy's modifications compare against an older revision:

```
$ svn diff -r 3900 COMMITTERS
Index: COMMITTERS
===================================================================
--- COMMITTERS       (revision 3900)
+++ COMMITTERS       (working copy)
```

Compare revision 3000 to revision 3500 using @ syntax:

```
$ svn diff http://svn.collab.net/repos/svn/trunk/COMMITTERS@3000 http://svn.collab.
net/repos/svn/trunk/COMMITTERS@3500
Index: COMMITTERS
===================================================================
--- COMMITTERS       (revision 3000)
+++ COMMITTERS       (revision 3500)
...
```

Compare revision 3000 to revision 3500 using range notation (you only pass the one URL in this case):

```
$ svn diff -r 3000:3500 http://svn.collab.net/repos/svn/trunk/COMMITTERS
Index: COMMITTERS
================================================================
===
--- COMMITTERS          (revision 3000)
+++ COMMITTERS          (revision 3500)
```

Compare revision 3000 to revision 3500 of all files in *trunk* using range notation:

```
$ svn diff -r 3000:3500 http://svn.collab.net/repos/svn/trunk
```

Compare revision 3000 to revision 3500 of only three files in *trunk* using range notation:

```
$ svn diff -r 3000:3500 --old http://svn.collab.net/repos/svn/trunk COMMITTERS README
HACKING
```

If you have a working copy, you can obtain the differences without typing in the long URLs:

```
$ svn diff -r 3000:3500 COMMITTERS
Index: COMMITTERS
================================================================
===
--- COMMITTERS          (revision 3000)
+++ COMMITTERS          (revision 3500)
```

Use --diff-cmd *CMD* -x to pass arguments directly to the external diff program:

```
$ svn diff --diff-cmd /usr/bin/diff -x "-i -b" COMMITTERS
Index: COMMITTERS
================================================================
===
0a1,2
> This is a test
>
```

svn export

Exports a clean directory tree.

Synopsis

```
svn export [-r REV] URL [PATH]
svn export PATH1 PATH2
```

Description

The first form exports a clean directory tree from the repository specified by URL, at revision *REV* if it is given, otherwise at HEAD, into *PATH*. If *PATH* is omitted, the last component of the *URL* is used for the local directory name.

The second form exports a clean directory tree from the working copy specified by *PATH1* into *PATH2*. All local changes will be preserved, but files not under version control will not be copied.

Alternate Names

None

Changes

Local disk

Accesses Repository

Only if exporting from a URL

Switches

```
--revision (-r) REV
--quiet (-q)
--force
--username USER
--password PASS
--no-auth-cache
--non-interactive
--config-dir DIR
```

Examples

Export from your working copy (doesn't print every file and directory):

```
$ svn export a-wc my-export
Export complete.
```

Export directly from the repository (prints every file and directory):

```
$ svn export file:///tmp/repos my-export
A  my-export/test
A  my-export/quiz
...
Exported revision 15.
```

---

svn help   Provides Help!

Synopsis

```
svn help [SUBCOMMAND...]
```

Description

Displays Help documentation. This is your best friend when you're using Subversion and this book isn't within reach!

Alternate Names

?, h

Changes

Nothing

Accesses Repository

No

Switches

```
--version
--quiet (-q)
```

---

svn import

Synopsis

```
svn import [PATH] URL
```

Description

Recursively commits a copy of *PATH* to *URL*. If *PATH* is omitted . is assumed. Parent directories are created in the repository as necessary.

Alternate Names

None

Changes

Repository

Accesses Repository

Yes

Switches

```
--message (-m) TEXT
--file (-F) FILE
--quiet (-q)
--non-recursive (-N)
--username USER
--password PASS
--no-auth-cache
--non-interactive
--force-log
--editor-cmd EDITOR
--encoding ENC
--config-dir DIR
--auto-props
--no-auto-props
```

Examples

This imports the local directory *myproj* into the root of your repository:

```
$ svn import -m "New import" myproj http://svn.red-bean.com/repos/test
Adding         myproj/sample.txt
...
```

```
Transmitting file data ........
Committed revision 16.
```

This imports the local directory *myproj* into *trunk/vendors* in your repository. The directory *trunk/vendors* need not exist before you import into it—svn import will recursively create directories for you:

```
$ svn import -m "New import" myproj \
    http://svn.red-bean.com/repos/test/trunk/vendors/myproj
Adding         myproj/sample.txt
...
Transmitting file data ........
Committed revision 19.
```

---

svn info

Prints information about PATHs.

Synopsis

```
svn info [PATH...]
```

Description

Prints information about paths in your working copy, including:

- Path
- Name
- URL
- Revision
- Node kind
- Last changed author
- Last changed revision
- Last changed date
- Text last updated
- Properties last updated
- Checksum

Alternate Names

None

Changes

Nothing

Accesses Repository

No

Switches

```
--targets FILENAME
--recursive (-R)
--config-dir DIR
```

Examples

svn info shows you all the useful information that it has for items in your working copy. It shows information for files:

```
$ svn info foo.c
Path: foo.c
Name: foo.c
URL: http://svn.red-bean.com/repos/test/foo.c
Revision: 4417
Node Kind: file
Schedule: normal
Last Changed Author: sally
Last Changed Rev: 20
Last Changed Date: 2003-01-13 16:43:13 -0600 (Mon, 13 Jan 2003)
Text Last Updated: 2003-01-16 21:18:16 -0600 (Thu, 16 Jan 2003)
Properties Last Updated: 2003-01-13 21:50:19 -0600 (Mon, 13 Jan 2003)
Checksum: /3L38YwzhT93BWvgpdF6Zw==
```

It will also show information for directories:

```
$ svn info vendors
Path: trunk
URL: http://svn.red-bean.com/repos/test/vendors
Revision: 19
Node Kind: directory
Schedule: normal
Last Changed Author: harry
Last Changed Rev: 19
Last Changed Date: 2003-01-16 23:21:19 -0600 (Thu, 16 Jan 2003)
```

svn list
Lists directory entries in the repository.

Synopsis

```
svn list [TARGET...]
```

Description

Lists each *TARGET* file and the contents of each *TARGET* directory as they exist in the repository. If *TARGET* is a working copy path, the corresponding repository URL will be used.

The default *TARGET* is ., meaning the repository URL of the current working copy directory.

With --verbose, the following fields show the status of the item:

- Revision number of the last commit
- Author of the last commit
- Size (in bytes)
- Date and time of the last commit

Alternate Names

ls

Changes

Nothing

Accesses Repository

Yes

Switches

```
--revision (-r) REV
--verbose (-v)
--recursive (-R)
--username USER
--password PASS
--no-auth-cache
--non-interactive
--config-dir DIR
```

Examples

svn list is most useful if you want to see what files a repository has without downloading a working copy:

```
$ svn list http://svn.red-bean.com/repos/test/support
README.txt
INSTALL
examples/
...
```

Like Unix ls, you can also pass the --verbose switch for additional information:

```
$ svn list --verbose file:///tmp/repos
    16 sally        28361 Jan 16 23:18 README.txt
    27 sally            0 Jan 18 15:27 INSTALL
    24 harry              Jan 18 11:27 examples/
```

For further details, see "svn list.

---

svn log   Displays commit log messages.

Synopsis

```
svn log [PATH]
svn log URL [PATH...]
```

Description

The default target is the path of your current directory. If no arguments are supplied, svn log shows the log messages for all files and directories inside of (and including) the current working directory of your working copy. You can refine the results by specifying a path, one or more revisions, or any combination of the two. The default revision range for a local path is BASE:1.

If you specify a URL alone, then it prints log messages for everything that the URL contains. If you add paths past the URL, only messages for those paths under that URL will be printed. The default revision range for a URL is HEAD:1.

With --verbose, svn log will also print all affected paths with each log message. With --quiet, svn log will not print the log message body itself (this is compatible with --verbose).

Each log message is printed just once, even if more than one of the affected paths for that revision were explicitly requested. Logs follow copy history by default. Use --stop-on-copy to disable this behavior, which can be useful for determining branch points.

Alternate Names

None

Changes

Nothing

Accesses Repository

Yes

Switches

```
--revision (-r) REV
--quiet (-q)
--verbose (-v)
--targets FILENAME
--stop-on-copy
--incremental
--xml
--username USER
--password PASS
--no-auth-cache
--non-interactive
--config-dir DIR
```

Examples

You can see the log messages for all the paths that changed in your working copy by running svn log from the top:

```
$ svn log
------------------------------------------------------------------------
r20 | harry | 2003-01-17 22:56:19 -0600 (Fri, 17 Jan 2003) | 1 line
Tweak.
------------------------------------------------------------------------
r17 | sally | 2003-01-16 23:21:19 -0600 (Thu, 16 Jan 2003) | 2 lines
...
```

Examine all log messages for a particular file in your working copy:

```
$ svn log foo.c
------------------------------------------------------------------------
r32 | sally | 2003-01-13 16:43:13 -0600 (Mon, 13 Jan 2003) | 1 line
Added defines.
```

```
-----------------------------------------------------------------------
r28 | sally | 2003-01-07 21:48:33 -0600 (Tue, 07 Jan 2003) | 3 lines
...
```

If you don't have a working copy handy, you can log a URL:

```
$ svn log http://svn.red-bean.com/repos/test/foo.c
-----------------------------------------------------------------------
r32 | sally | 2003-01-13 16:43:13 -0600 (Mon, 13 Jan 2003) | 1 line
Added defines.
-----------------------------------------------------------------------
r28 | sally | 2003-01-07 21:48:33 -0600 (Tue, 07 Jan 2003) | 3 lines
...
```

If you want several distinct paths underneath the same URL, you can use the URL [PATH...] syntax.

```
$ svn log http://svn.red-bean.com/repos/test/ foo.c bar.c
-----------------------------------------------------------------------
r32 | sally | 2003-01-13 16:43:13 -0600 (Mon, 13 Jan 2003) | 1 line
Added defines.
-----------------------------------------------------------------------
r31 | harry | 2003-01-10 12:25:08 -0600 (Fri, 10 Jan 2003) | 1 line
Added new file bar.c
-----------------------------------------------------------------------
r28 | sally | 2003-01-07 21:48:33 -0600 (Tue, 07 Jan 2003) | 3 lines
...
```

That is the same as explicitly placing both URLs on the command line:

```
$ svn log http://svn.red-bean.com/repos/test/foo.c \
          http://svn.red-bean.com/repos/test/bar.c
...
```

When you're concatenating the results of multiple calls to the log command, you may want to use the --incremental switch. svn log normally prints out a dashed line at the beginning of a log message, after each subsequent log message, and following the final log message. If you ran svn log on a range of two revisions, you would get the following:

```
$ svn log -r 14:15
-----------------------------------------------------------------------
r14 | ...
-----------------------------------------------------------------------
r15 | ...
-----------------------------------------------------------------------
```

However, if you wanted to gather two nonsequential log messages into a file, you might do something such as this:

```
$ svn log -r 14 > mylog
$ svn log -r 19 >> mylog
$ svn log -r 27 >> mylog
$ cat mylog
-----------------------------------------------------------------------
r14 | ...
-----------------------------------------------------------------------
-----------------------------------------------------------------------
r19 | ...
-----------------------------------------------------------------------
```

```
-----------------------------------------------------------------------
r27 | ...
-----------------------------------------------------------------------
```

You can avoid the clutter of the double-dashed lines in your output by using the incremental switch:

```
$ svn log --incremental -r 14 > mylog
$ svn log --incremental -r 19 >> mylog
$ svn log --incremental -r 27 >> mylog
$ cat mylog
-----------------------------------------------------------------------
r14 | ...
-----------------------------------------------------------------------
r19 | ...
-----------------------------------------------------------------------
r27 | ...
```

The --incremental switch provides similar output control when using the --xml switch.

> If you run svn log on a specific path and provide a specific revision and get no output at all:
>
> ```
> $ svn log -r 20 http://svn.red-bean.com/untouched.txt
> ------------------------------------------------------------
> -----------
> ```
>
> That just means that the path was not modified in that revision. If you log from the top of the repository, or know the file that changed in that revision, you can specify it explicitly:
>
> ```
> $ svn log -r 20 touched.txt
> ------------------------------------------------------------
> -----------
> r20 | sally | 2003-01-17 22:56:19 -0600 (Fri, 17 Jan 2003) |
> 1 line
>
> Made a change.
> ------------------------------------------------------------
> -----------
> ```

---

svn merge

Applies the differences between two sources to a working copy path.

Synopsis

```
svn merge sourceURL1[@N] sourceURL2[@M] [WCPATH]
svn merge -r N:M SOURCE [PATH]
```

Description

In the first form, the source URLs are specified at revisions N and M. These are the two sources to be compared. The revisions default to HEAD if omitted.

In the second form, *SOURCE* can be a URL or working copy item, in which case the corresponding URL is used. This URL, at revisions *N* and *M*, defines the two sources to be compared.

WCPATH is the working copy path that will receive the changes. If *WCPATH* is omitted, a default value of . is assumed, unless the sources have identical basenames that match a file within, in which case the differences will be applied to that file.

Unlike `svn diff`, the merge command takes the ancestry of a file into consideration when performing a merge operation. This is very important when you're merging changes from one branch into another and you've renamed a file on one branch but not the other.

Alternate Names

None

Changes

Working copy

Accesses Repository

Only if working with URLs

Switches

```
--revision (-r) REV
--non-recursive (-N)
--quiet (-q)
--force
--dry-run
--diff3-cmd CMD
--ignore-ancestry
--username USER
--password PASS
--no-auth-cache
--non-interactive
--config-dir DIR
```

Examples

Merge a branch back into the trunk (assuming that you have a working copy of the trunk, and that the branch was created in revision 250):

```
$ svn merge -r 250:HEAD http://svn.red-bean.com/repos/branches/my-branch
U    myproj/tiny.txt
U    myproj/thhgttg.txt
U    myproj/win.txt
U    myproj/flo.txt
```

If you branched at revision 23, and you want to merge changes on trunk into your branch, you could do this from inside the working copy of your branch:

```
$ svn merge -r 23:30 file:///tmp/repos/trunk/vendors
U    myproj/thhgttg.txt
...
```

To merge changes to a single file:

```
$ cd myproj
$ svn merge -r 30:31 thhgttg.txt
U  thhgttg.txt
```

---

svn mkdir

Synopsis

```
svn mkdir PATH...
svn mkdir URL...
```

Description

Creates a directory with a name given by the final component of the *PATH* or URL. A directory specified by a working copy *PATH* is scheduled for addition in the working copy. A directory specified by a URL is created in the repository via an immediate commit. Multiple directory URLs are committed atomically. In both cases all the intermediate directories must already exist.

Alternate Names

None

Changes

Working copy, repository if operating on a URL

Accesses Repository

Only if operating on a URL

Switches

```
--message (-m) TEXT
--file (-F) FILE
--quiet (-q)
--username USER
--password PASS
--no-auth-cache
--non-interactive
--editor-cmd EDITOR
--encoding ENC
--force-log
--config-dir DIR
```

Examples

Create a directory in your working copy:

```
$ svn mkdir newdir
A         newdir
```

Create one in the repository (instant commit, so a log message is required):

```
$ svn mkdir -m "Making a new dir." http://svn.red-bean.com/repos/newdir
Committed revision 26.
```

svn move

Moves a file or directory.

Synopsis

```
svn move SRC DST
```

Description

This command moves a file or directory in your working copy or in the repository.

This command is equivalent to an svn copy followed by svn delete.

Subversion does not support moving between working copies and URLs. In addition, you can only move files within a single repository—Subversion does not support cross-repository moving:

WC -> WC
> Move and schedule a file or directory for addition (with history).

URL -> URL
> Complete server-side rename.

Alternate Names

mv, rename, ren

Changes

Working copy, repository if operating on a URL

Accesses Repository

Only if operating on a URL

Switches

```
--message (-m) TEXT
--file (-F) FILE
--revision (-r) REV
--quiet (-q)
--force
--username USER
--password PASS
--no-auth-cache
--non-interactive
--editor-cmd EDITOR
--encoding ENC
--force-log
--config-dir DIR
```

Examples

Move a file in your working copy:

```
$ svn move foo.c bar.c
A         bar.c
D         foo.c
```

Move a file in the repository (an immediate commit, so it requires a commit message):

```
$ svn move -m "Move a file" http://svn.red-bean.com/repos/foo.c \
                            http://svn.red-bean.com/repos/bar.c

Committed revision 27.
```

---

svn propdel   Removes a property from an item.

Synopsis

```
svn propdel PROPNAME [PATH...]
svn propdel PROPNAME --revprop -r REV [URL]
```

Description

Removes properties from files, directories, or revisions. The first form removes versioned properties in working copy, while the second removes unversioned remote properties on a repository revision.

Alternate Names

pdel, pd

Changes

Working copy, repository only if operating on a URL

Accesses Repository

Only if operating on a URL

Switches

```
--quiet (-q)
--recursive (-R)
--revision (-r) REV
--revprop
--username USER
--password PASS
--no-auth-cache
--non-interactive
--config-dir DIR
```

Examples

Delete a property from a file in your working copy:

```
$ svn propdel svn:mime-type  some-script
property 'svn:mime-type' deleted from 'some-script'.
```

Delete a revision property:

```
$ svn propdel --revprop -r 26 release-date
property 'release-date' deleted from repository revision '26'
```

svn propedit

Edits the property of one or more items under version control.

Synopsis

```
svn propedit PROPNAME PATH...
svn propedit PROPNAME --revprop -r REV [URL]
```

Description

Edits one or more properties using your favorite editor. The first form edits versioned properties in your working copy, while the second edits unversioned remote properties on a repository revision.

Alternate Names

pedit, pe

Changes

Working copy, repository only if operating on a URL

Accesses Repository

Only if operating on a URL

Switches

```
--revision (-r) REV
--revprop
--username USER
--password PASS
--no-auth-cache
--non-interactive
--encoding ENC
--editor-cmd EDITOR
--config-dir DIR
```

Examples

svn propedit makes it easy to modify properties that have multiple values:

```
$ svn propedit svn:keywords  foo.c
    <svn will launch your favorite editor here, with a buffer open
    containing the current contents of the svn:keywords property.  You
    can add multiple values to a property easily here by entering one
    value per line.>
Set new value for property 'svn:keywords' on 'foo.c'
```

svn propget

Synopsis

```
svn propget PROPNAME [PATH...]
svn propget PROPNAME --revprop -r REV [URL]
```

Description

Prints the value of a property on files, directories, or revisions. The first form prints the versioned property of an item or items in your working copy, while the second prints unversioned remote property on a repository revision. See "Properties" in Chapter 7 for more information on properties.

Alternate Names

pget, pg

Changes

Working copy, repository only if operating on a URL

Accesses Repository

Only if operating on a URL

Switches

```
--recursive (-R)
--revision (-r) REV
--revprop
--strict
--username USER
--password PASS
--no-auth-cache
--non-interactive
--config-dir DIR
```

Examples

Examine a property of a file in your working copy:

```
$ svn propget svn:keywords foo.c
Author
Date
Rev
```

The same goes for a revision property:

```
$ svn propget svn:log --revprop -r 20
Began journal.
```

svn proplist

Synopsis

```
svn proplist [PATH...]
svn proplist --revprop -r REV [URL]
```

Description

Lists all properties on files, directories, or revisions. The first form lists versioned properties in working copy, while the second lists unversioned remote properties on a repository
revision.

Alternate Names

plist, pl

Changes

Working copy, repository only if operating on a URL

Accesses Repository

Only if operating on a URL

Switches

```
--verbose (-v)
--recursive (-R)
--revision (-r) REV
--quiet (-q)
--revprop
--username USER
--password PASS
--no-auth-cache
--non-interactive
--config-dir DIR
```

Examples

You can use proplist to see the properties on an item in your working copy:

```
$ svn proplist foo.c
Properties on 'foo.c':
  svn:mime-type
  svn:keywords
  owner
```

But with the --verbose flag, svn proplist is extremely handy as it also shows you the
values for the properties:

```
$ svn proplist --verbose foo.c
Properties on 'foo.c':
  svn:mime-type : text/plain
  svn:keywords : Author Date Rev
  owner : sally
```

svn propset

Synopsis

```
svn propset PROPNAME [PROPVAL | -F VALFILE] PATH...
svn propset PROPNAME --revprop -r REV [PROPVAL | -F VALFILE] [URL]
```

Description

Sets *PROPNAME* to *PROPVAL* on files, directories, or revisions. The first example creates a versioned, local property change in the working copy, and the second creates an unversioned, remote property change on a repository revision.

 Subversion has a number of special properties that affect its behavior. See "Special Properties" in Chapter 7 for more on these properties.

Alternate Names

pset, ps

Changes

Working copy, repository only if operating on a URL

Accesses Repository

Only if operating on a URL

Switches

```
--file (-F) FILE
--quiet (-q)
--revision (-r) REV
--targets FILENAME
--recursive (-R)
--revprop
--username USER
--password PASS
--no-auth-cache
--non-interactive
--encoding ENC
--force
--config-dir DIR
```

Examples

Set the mimetype on a file:

```
$ svn propset svn:mime-type image/jpeg foo.jpg
property 'svn:mime-type' set on 'foo.jpg'
```

On a Unix system, if you want a file to have the executable permission set:

```
$ svn propset svn:executable ON somescript
property 'svn:executable' set on 'somescript'
```

Perhaps you have an internal policy to set certain properties for the benefit of your coworkers:

```
$ svn propset owner sally foo.c
property 'owner' set on 'foo.c'
```

If you made a mistake in a log message for a particular revision and want to change it, use --revprop and set svn:log to the new log message:

```
$ svn propset --revprop -r 25 svn:log "Journaled about trip to New York."
property 'svn:log' set on repository revision '25'
```

Or, if you don't have a working copy, you can provide a URL.

```
$ svn propset --revprop -r 26 svn:log "Document nap." http://svn.red-bean.com/repos
property 'svn:log' set on repository revision '25'
```

Lastly, you can tell propset to take its input from a file. You could even use this to set the contents of a property to something binary:

```
$ svn propset owner-pic -F sally.jpg moo.c
property 'owner-pic' set on 'moo.c'
```

 By default, you cannot modify revision properties in a Subversion repository. Your repository administrator must explicitly enable revision property modifications by creating a hook named pre-revprop-change. See "Hook Scripts" in Chapter 5 for more information on hook scripts.

svn resolved

Removes conflicted state on working copy files or directories.

Synopsis

```
svn resolved PATH...
```

Description

Removes conflicted state on working copy files or directories. This routine does not semantically resolve conflict markers; it merely removes conflict-related artifact files and allows PATH to be committed again; that is, it tells Subversion that the conflicts have been resolved. See "Resolve Conflicts (Merging Others' Changes)" for an in-depth look at resolving conflicts.

Alternate Names

None

Changes

Working copy

Accesses Repository

No

Switches

```
--targets FILENAME
--recursive (-R)
--quiet (-q)
--config-dir DIR
```

Examples

If you get a conflict on an update, your working copy sprouts three new files:

```
$ svn update
C  foo.c
Updated to revision 31.
$ ls
foo.c
foo.c.mine
foo.c.r30
foo.c.r31
```

Once you've resolved the conflict and *foo.c* is ready to be committed, run svn resolved to let your working copy know you've taken care of everything.

You *can* just remove the conflict files and commit, but svn resolved fixes up some bookkeeping data in the working copy administrative area in addition to removing the conflict files, so we recommend that you use this command.

---

svn revert

Undoes all local edits.

Synopsis

```
svn revert PATH...
```

Description

Reverts any local changes to a file or directory and resolves any conflicted states. svn revert will not only revert the contents of an item in your working copy, but also any property changes. Finally, you can use it to undo any scheduling operations that you may have done (e.g., files scheduled for addition or deletion can be unscheduled).

Alternate Names

None

Changes

Working copy

Accesses Repository

No

Switches

```
--targets FILENAME
--recursive (-R)
--quiet (-q)
--config-dir DIR
```

Examples

Discard changes to a file:

```
$ svn revert foo.c
Reverted foo.c
```

If you want to revert a whole directory of files, use the --recursive flag:

```
$ svn revert --recursive .
Reverted newdir/afile
Reverted foo.c
Reverted bar.txt
```

Lastly, you can undo any scheduling operations:

```
$ svn add mistake.txt whoops
A         mistake.txt
A         whoops
A         whoops/oopsie.c
$ svn revert mistake.txt whoops
Reverted mistake.txt
Reverted whoops
$ svn status
?         mistake.txt
?         whoops
```

 If you provide no targets to svn revert, it will do nothing—to protect you from accidentally losing changes in your working copy, svn revert requires you to provide at least one target.

---

svn status
Prints the status of working copy files and directories.

Synopsis

```
svn status [PATH...]
```

Description

Prints the status of working copy files and directories. With no arguments, it prints only locally modified items (no repository access). With --show-updates, add working revision and server out-of-date information. With --verbose, print full revision information on every item.

The first five columns in the output are each one character wide, and each column gives you information about different aspects of each working copy item.

The first column indicates that an item was added, deleted, or otherwise changed.

' ' (blank)

No modifications.

A

Item is scheduled for Addition.

D

Item is scheduled for Deletion.

M

Item has been modified.

C

Item is in conflict with updates received from the repository.

I

Item is being ignored (e.g., with the `svn:ignore` property)

?

Item is not under version control.

!

Item is missing (e.g., you moved or deleted it without using svn). This also indicates that a directory is incomplete (a checkout or update was interrupted).

~

Item is versioned as a directory, but has been replaced by a file, or vice versa

The second column tells the status of a file's or directory's properties.

' ' (blank)

No modifications.

M

Properties for this item have been modified.

C

Properties for this item are in conflict with property updates received from the repository.

The third column is populated only if the working copy directory is locked.

' ' (blank)

Item is not locked.

L

Item is locked.

The fourth column is populated only if the item is scheduled for addition-with-history.

' ' (blank)

No history scheduled with commit.

+

History scheduled with commit.

The fifth column is populated only if the item is switched relative to its parent (see "Switching a Working Copy" in Chapter 4).

' ' (blank)

Item is child of its parent directory.

S

    Item is switched.

The out-of-date information appears in the eighth column (only if you pass the `--show-updates` switch).

' ' (blank)

    The item in your working copy is up-to-date.

*

    A newer revision of the item exists on the server.

The remaining fields are variable width and delimited by spaces. The working revision is the next field if the `--show-updates` or `--verbose` switches are passed.

If the `--verbose` switch is passed, the last committed revision and last committed author are displayed next.

The working copy path is always the final field, so it can include spaces.

Alternate Names

stat, st

Changes

Nothing

Accesses Repository

Only if using `--show-updates`

Switches

```
--show-updates (-u)
--verbose (-v)
--non-recursive (-N)
--quiet (-q)
--no-ignore
--username USER
--password PASS
--no-auth-cache
--non-interactive
--config-dir
```

Examples

This is the easiest way to find out what changes you have made to your working copy:

```
$ svn status wc
 M      wc/bar.c
 A  +   wc/qax.c
```

If you want to find out what files in your working copy are out-of-date, pass the `--show-updates` switch (this will *not* make any changes to your working copy). Here you can see that *wc/foo.c* has changed in the repository since we last updated our working copy:

```
$ svn status --show-updates wc
 M           965   wc/bar.c
```

```
      *    965    wc/foo.c
A  +       965    wc/qax.c
Status against revision:    981
```

 --show-updates *only* places an asterisk next to items that are out of date (that is, items that will be updated from the repository if you run svn update). --show-updates does *not* cause the status listing to reflect the repository's version of the item.

And finally, the most information you can get out of the status subcommand:

```
$ svn status --show-updates --verbose wc
  M        965      938 sally      wc/bar.c
     *     965      922 harry      wc/foo.c
A  +       965      687 harry      wc/qax.c
           965      687 harry      wc/zig.c
Head revision:   981
```

For many more examples of svn status, see "svn status" in Chapter 3.

svn switch

Updates working copy to a different URL.

Synopsis

```
svn switch URL [PATH]
```

Description

This subcommand updates your working copy to mirror a new URL—usually a URL which shares a common ancestor with your working copy, although not necessarily. This is the Subversion way to move a working copy to a new branch. See "Switching a Working Copy" in Chapter 4 for an in-depth look at switching.

Alternate Names

sw

Changes

Working copy

Accesses Repository

Yes

Switches

```
--revision (-r) REV
--non-recursive (-N)
--quiet (-q)
--diff3-cmd CMD
--relocate
--username USER
```

```
--password PASS
--no-auth-cache
--non-interactive
--config-dir DIR
```

Examples

If you're currently inside the directory *vendors* which was branched to *vendors-with-fix* and you'd like to switch your working copy to that branch:

```
$ svn switch http://svn.red-bean.com/repos/branches/vendors-with-fix .
U  myproj/foo.txt
U  myproj/bar.txt
U  myproj/baz.c
U  myproj/qux.c
Updated to revision 31.
```

And to switch back, just provide the URL to the location in the repository from which you originally checked out your working copy:

```
$ svn switch http://svn.red-bean.com/repos/trunk/vendors .
U  myproj/foo.txt
U  myproj/bar.txt
U  myproj/baz.c
U  myproj/qux.c
Updated to revision 31.
```

 You can just switch part of your working copy to a branch if you don't want to switch your entire working copy.

If the location of your repository changes and you have an existing working copy that you'd like to continue to use, you can use svn switch --relocate to change your working copy from one URL to another:

```
$ svn checkout file:///tmp/repos test
A  test/a
A  test/b
...
$ mv repos newlocation
$ cd test/
$ svn update
svn: Unable to open an ra_local session to URL
svn: Unable to open repository 'file:///tmp/repos'
$ svn switch --relocate file:///tmp/repos file:///tmp/newlocation .
$ svn update
At revision 3.
```

svn update

Updates your working copy.

Synopsis

```
svn update [PATH...]
```

Description

svn update brings changes from the repository into your working copy. If no revision given, it brings your working copy up-to-date with the HEAD revision. Otherwise, it synchronizes the working copy to the revision given by the --revision switch.

For each updated item a line will start with a character reporting the action taken. These characters have the following meaning:

A

> Added

D

> Deleted

U

> Updated

C

> Conflict

G

> Merged

A character in the first column signifies an update to the actual file, while updates to the file's properties are shown in the second column.

Alternate Names

up

Changes

Working copy

Accesses Repository

Yes

Switches

```
--revision (-r) REV
--non-recursive (-N)
--quiet (-q)
--diff3-cmd CMD
--username USER
--password PASS
--no-auth-cache
--non-interactive
--config-dir DIR
```

Examples

Pick up repository changes that have happened since your last update:

```
$ svn update
A  newdir/toggle.c
A  newdir/disclose.c
A  newdir/launch.c
```

```
D  newdir/README
Updated to revision 32.
```

You can also update your working copy to an older revision (Subversion doesn't have the concept of sticky files like CVS does; see Appendix A):

```
$ svn update -r30
A  newdir/README
D  newdir/toggle.c
D  newdir/disclose.c
D  newdir/launch.c
U  foo.c
Updated to revision 30.
```

If you want to examine an older revision of a single file, you may want to use svn cat.

svnadmin

svnadmin is the administrative tool for monitoring and repairing your Subversion repository. For detailed information, see "svnadmin" in Chapter 5.

Since svnadmin works via direct repository access (and thus can only be used on the machine that holds the repository), it refers to the repository with a path, not a URL.

svnadmin Switches

--bdb-log-keep
    (Berkeley DB specific) Disable automatic log removal of database log files.

--bdb-txn-nosync
    (Berkeley DB specific) Disables fsync when committing database transactions.

--bypass-hooks
    Bypass the repository hook system.

--clean-logs
    Removes unused Berkeley DB logs.

--force-uuid
    By default, when loading data into repository that already contains revisions, svnadmin will ignore the UUID from the dump stream. This switch will cause the repository's UUID to be set to the UUID from the stream.

--ignore-uuid
    By default, when loading an empty repository, svnadmin will use the UUID from the dump stream. This switch will cause that UUID to be ignored.

--incremental
    Dump a revision only as a diff against the previous revision, instead of the usual fulltext.

--parent-dir DIR
    When loading a dumpfile, root paths at DIR instead of /.

--revision (-r) *ARG*
>   Specify a particular revision to operate on.

--quiet
>   Do not show normal progress—show only errors.

svnadmin Subcommands

svnadmin create
Creates a new empty repository at REPOS_PATH.

Synopsis

```
svnadmin create REPOS_PATH
```

Description

Creates a new empty repository at the path provided. If the provided directory does not exist, it will be created for you (svnadmin works only with local paths, not URLs).

Switches

```
--bdb-txn-nosync
--bdb-log-keep
```

Examples

Creating a new repository is just this easy:

```
$ svnadmin create /usr/local/svn/repos
```

svnadmin deltify
Deltify changed paths in a revision range.

Synopsis

```
svnadmin deltify [-r LOWER[:UPPER]]
REPOS_PATH
```

Description

svnadmin deltify only exists in 1.0.x due to historical reasons. This command is deprecated and no longer needed.

It dates from a time when Subversion offered administrators greater control over compression strategies in the repository. This turned out to be a lot of complexity for *very* little gain, and this feature was deprecated.

Switches

```
--revision (-r)
--quiet
```

svnadmin dump

Synopsis

```
svnadmin dump REPOS_PATH [-r LOWER[:UPPER]] [--incremental]
```

Description

Dumps the contents of filesystem to stdout in a dumpfile portable format, sending feedback to stderr. Dump revisions *LOWER* rev through *UPPER* rev. If no revisions are given, dump all revision trees. If only *LOWER* is given, dump that one revision tree. See "Migrating a Repository" in Chapter 5 for a practical use.

Switches

```
--revision (-r)
--incremental
--quiet
```

Examples

Dump your whole repository:

```
$ svnadmin dump /usr/local/svn/repos
SVN-fs-dump-format-version: 1
Revision-number: 0
* Dumped revision 0.
Prop-content-length: 56
Content-length: 56

...
```

Incrementally dump a single transaction from your repository:

```
$ svnadmin dump /usr/local/svn/repos -r 21 --incremental
* Dumped revision 21.
SVN-fs-dump-format-version: 1
Revision-number: 21
Prop-content-length: 101
Content-length: 101

...
```

svnadmin help

Synopsis

```
svnadmin help [SUBCOMMAND...]
```

Description

This subcommand is useful when you're trapped on a desert island with neither a net connection nor a copy of this book.

Alternate Names

?, h

---

svnadmin hotcopy
Makes a hot copy of a repository.

Synopsis

```
svnadmin hotcopy OLD_REPOS_PATH NEW_REPOS_PATH
```

Description

This subcommand makes a full hot backup of your repository, including all hooks, configuration files, and, of course, database files. If you pass the --clean-logs switch, svnadmin will perform a hotcopy of your repository, and then remove unused Berkeley DB logs from the original repository.

Switches

```
--clean-logs
```

---

svnadmin list-dblogs
Asks Berkeley DB which log files exist for a given svn repository.

Synopsis

```
svnadmin list-dblogs REPOS_PATH
```

Description

Berkeley DB creates logs of all changes to the repository, which allow it to recover in the face of catastrophe. Unless you enable DB_LOGS_AUTOREMOVE, the log files accumulate, although most are no longer used and can be deleted to reclaim disk space. See "Managing Disk Space" for more information.

---

svnadmin list-unused-dblogs
Asks Berkeley DB which log files can be safely deleted.

Synopsis

```
svnadmin list-unused-dblogs REPOS_PATH
```

Description

Berkeley DB creates logs of all changes to the repository, which allow it to recover in the face of catastrophe. Unless you enable DB_LOGS_AUTOREMOVE, the log files accumulate, although most are no longer used and can be deleted to reclaim disk space. See "Managing Disk Space" in Chapter 5 for more information.

Examples

Remove all unused log files from a repository:

```
$ svnadmin list-unused-dblogs /path/to/repos
/path/to/repos/log.0000000031
/path/to/repos/log.0000000032
/path/to/repos/log.0000000033
$ svnadmin list-unused-dblogs /path/to/repos | xargs rm
## disk space reclaimed!
```

svnadmin load
Reads a dumpfile-formatted stream from stdin.

Synopsis

```
svnadmin load REPOS_PATH
```

Description

Reads a dumpfile-formatted stream from stdin, committing new revisions into the repository's filesystem. Send progress feedback to stdout.

Switches

```
--quiet (-q)
--ignore-uuid
--force-uuid
--parent-dir
```

Example

This shows the beginning of loading a repository from a backup file (made, of course, with svn dump):

```
$ svnadmin load /usr/local/svn/restored < repos-backup
<<< Started new txn, based on original revision 1
     * adding path : test ... done.
     * adding path : test/a ... done.
...
```

Or if you want to load into a subdirectory:

```
$ svnadmin load --parent-dir new/subdir/for/project /usr/local/svn/restored < repos-backup
<<< Started new txn, based on original revision 1
     * adding path : test ... done.
     * adding path : test/a ... done.
...
```

svnadmin lstxns
Prints the names of all uncommitted transactions.

Synopsis

```
svnadmin lstxns REPOS_PATH
```

Description

Prints the names of all uncommitted transactions. See "Repository Cleanup" in Chapter 5 for information on how uncommitted transactions are created and what you should do with them.

Examples

List all outstanding transactions in a repository:

```
$ svnadmin lstxns /usr/local/svn/repos/
1w
1x
```

svnadmin recover

Recovers any lost state in a repository.

Synopsis

```
svnadmin recover REPOS_PATH
```

Description

Run this command if you get an error indicating that your repository needs to be recovered.

Examples

Recover a hung repository:

```
$ svnadmin recover /usr/local/svn/repos/
Acquiring exclusive lock on repository db.
Recovery is running, please stand by...
Recovery completed.
The latest repos revision is 34.
```

svnadmin rmtxns

Deletes transactions from a repository.

Synopsis

```
svnadmin rmtxns REPOS_PATH TXN_NAME...
```

Description

Deletes outstanding transactions from a repository. This is covered in detail in "Repository Cleanup" in Chapter 5.

Switches

```
--quiet (-q)
```

Examples

Remove named transactions:

```
$ svnadmin rmtxns /usr/local/svn/repos/ 1w 1x
```

Fortunately, the output of svn lstxns works great as the input for rmtxns:

```
$ svnadmin rmtxns /usr/local/svn/repos/ `svnadmin lstxns /usr/local/svn/repos/`
```

This will remove all uncommitted transactions from your repository.

---

svnadmin setlog
Sets the log message on a revision.

Synopsis

```
svnadmin setlog REPOS_PATH -r REVISION FILE
```

Description

Sets the log message on revision REVISION to the contents of FILE.

Similar to using svn propset --revprop to set the svn:log property on a revision, except that you can also use the option --bypass-hooks to avoid running any pre- or post-commit hooks, which is useful if the modification of revision properties has not been enabled in the pre-revprop-change hook.

 Revision properties are not under version control, so this command will permanently overwrite the previous log message.

Switches

```
--revision (-r) ARG
--bypass-hooks
```

Examples

Set the log message for revision 19 to the contents of the file *msg*:

```
$ svnadmin setlog /usr/local/svn/repos/ -r 19 msg
```

---

svnadmin verify
Verifies the data stored in the repository.

Synopsis

```
svnadmin verify REPOS_PATH
```

Description

Run this command if you wish to verify the integrity of your repository. This basically iterates through all revisions in the repository by internally dumping all revisions and discarding the output.

Examples

Verify a hung repository:

```
$ svnadmin verify /usr/local/svn/repos/
```

```
* Verified revision 1729.
```

svnlook

svnlook is a command-line utility for examining different aspects of a Subversion repository. It does not make any changes to the repository—it's just used for peeking. svnlook is typically used by the repository hooks, but a repository administrator might find it useful for diagnostic purposes.

Since svnlook works via direct repository access (and thus can only be used on the machine that holds the repository), it refers to the repository with a path, not a URL.

If no revision or transaction is specified, svnlook defaults to the youngest (most recent) revision of the repository.

svnlook Switches

Switches in svnlook are global, just like in svn and svnadmin; however, most switches only apply to one subcommand since the functionality of svnlook is (intentionally) limited in scope.

`--no-diff-deleted`
> Prevents svnlook from printing differences for deleted files. The default behavior when a file is deleted in a transaction/revision is to print the same differences that you would see if you had left the file but removed all the content.

`--revision (-r)`
> Specify a particular revision number that you wish to examine.

`--transaction (-t)`
> Specify a particular transaction id that you wish to examine.

`--show-ids`
> Show the filesystem node revision IDs for each path in the filesystem tree.

svnlook Subcommands

svnlook author   Prints the author.

Synopsis

```
svnlook author REPOS_PATH
```

Description

Prints the author of a revision or transaction in the repository.

Switches

```
--revision (-r)
--transaction (-t)
```

Examples

svnlook author is handy, but not very exciting:

```
$ svnlook author -r 40 /usr/local/svn/repos
sally
```

---

svnlook cat

Prints the contents of a file.

Synopsis

```
svnlook cat REPOS_PATH PATH_IN_REPOS
```

Description

Prints the contents of a file.

Switches

```
--revision (-r)
--transaction (-t)
```

Examples

This shows the contents of a file in transaction ax8, located at */trunk/README*:

```
$ svnlook cat -t ax8 /usr/local/svn/repos /trunk/README
            Subversion, a version control system.

            ======================================
$LastChangedDate: 2003-07-17 10:45:25 -0500 (Thu, 17 Jul 2003) $
Contents:
     I. A FEW POINTERS
    II. DOCUMENTATION
   III. PARTICIPATING IN THE SUBVERSION COMMUNITY
...
```

---

svnlook changed

Prints the paths that were changed.

Synopsis

```
svnlook changed REPOS_PATH
```

Description

Prints the paths that were changed in a particular revision or transaction, as well as an svn update–style status letter in the first column: A for added, D for deleted, and U for updated (modified).

Switches

```
--revision (-r)
--transaction (-t)
```

Examples

This shows a list of all the changed files in revision 39 of a test repository:

```
$ svnlook changed -r 39 /usr/local/svn/repos
A   trunk/vendors/deli/
A   trunk/vendors/deli/chips.txt
A   trunk/vendors/deli/sandwich.txt
A   trunk/vendors/deli/pickle.txt
```

svnlook date   Prints the datestamp.

Synopsis

```
svnlook date REPOS_PATH
```

Description

Prints the datestamp of a revision or transaction in a repository.

Switches

```
--revision (-r)
--transaction (-t)
```

Examples

This shows the date of revision 40 of a test repository:

```
$ svnlook date -r 40 /tmp/repos/
2003-02-22 17:44:49 -0600 (Sat, 22 Feb 2003)
```

svnlook diff   Prints differences of changed files and properties.

Synopsis

```
svnlook diff REPOS_PATH
```

Description

Prints GNU-style differences of changed files and properties in a repository.

Switches

```
--revision (-r)
--transaction (-t)
--no-diff-deleted
```

Examples

This shows a newly added (empty) file, a deleted file, and a copied file:

```
$ svnlook diff -r 40 /usr/local/svn/repos/
Copied: egg.txt (from rev 39, trunk/vendors/deli/pickle.txt)
Added: trunk/vendors/deli/soda.txt
================================================================
==============
Modified: trunk/vendors/deli/sandwich.txt
================================================================
==============
--- trunk/vendors/deli/sandwich.txt      (original)
+++ trunk/vendors/deli/sandwich.txt      2003-02-22 17:45:04.000000000 -0600
@@ -0,0 +1 @@
+Don't forget the mayo!
Deleted: trunk/vendors/deli/chips.txt
================================================================
==============
Deleted: trunk/vendors/deli/pickle.txt
================================================================
==============
```

svnlook dirs-changed

Prints the directories that were themselves changed.

Synopsis

```
svnlook dirs-changed REPOS_PATH
```

Description

Prints the directories that were themselves changed (property edits) or whose file children were changed.

Switches

```
--revision (-r)
--transaction (-t)
```

Examples

This shows the directories that changed in revision 40 in our sample repository:

```
$ svnlook dirs-changed -r 40 /usr/local/svn/repos
trunk/vendors/deli/
```

svnlook help

Displays the help message for svnlook.

Synopsis

```
Also svnlook -h and svnlook -?.
```

Description

Displays the help message for svnlook. This command, like its brother `svn help`, is also your friend, even though you never call it anymore and forgot to invite it to your last party.

Alternate Names

?, h

---

svnlook history

Prints information about the history of a path in the repository (or the root directory if no path is supplied).

Synopsis

```
svnlook history REPOS_PATH
            [PATH_IN_REPOS]
```

Description

Prints information about the history of a path in the repository (or the root directory, if no path is supplied).

Switches

```
--revision (-r)
--show-ids
```

Examples

This shows the history output for the path */tags/1.0* as of revision 20 in our sample repository:

```
$ svnlook history -r 20 /usr/local/svn/repos /tags/1.0 --show-ids
REVISION   PATH <ID>
--------   ---------
      19   /tags/1.0 <1.2.12>
      17   /branches/1.0-rc2 <1.1.10>
      16   /branches/1.0-rc2 <1.1.x>
      14   /trunk <1.0.q>
      13   /trunk <1.0.o>
      11   /trunk <1.0.k>
       9   /trunk <1.0.g>
       8   /trunk <1.0.e>
       7   /trunk <1.0.b>
       6   /trunk <1.0.9>
       5   /trunk <1.0.7>
       4   /trunk <1.0.6>
       2   /trunk <1.0.3>
       1   /trunk <1.0.2>
```

svnlook info

Prints the author, datestamp, log message size, and log message.

Synopsis

```
svnlook info REPOS_PATH
```

Description

Prints the author, datestamp, log message size, and log message.

Switches

```
--revision (-r)
--transaction (-t)
```

Examples

This shows the info output for revision 40 in our sample repository:

```
$ svnlook info -r 40 /usr/local/svn/repos
sally
2003-02-22 17:44:49 -0600 (Sat, 22 Feb 2003)
15
Rearrange lunch.
```

svnlook log

Prints the log message.

Synopsis

```
svnlook log REPOS_PATH
```

Description

Prints the log message.

Switches

```
--revision (-r)
--transaction (-t)
```

Examples

This shows the log output for revision 40 in our sample repository:

```
$ svnlook log /tmp/repos/
Rearrange lunch.
```

svnlook propget

Prints the raw value of a property on a path in the repository.

Synopsis

```
svnlook propget REPOS_PATH PROPNAME PATH_IN_REPOS
```

Description

Lists the value of a property on a path in the repository.

Alternate Names

pg, pget

Switches

```
--revision (-r)
--transaction (-t)
```

Examples

This shows the value of the file */trunk/sandwich* in the HEAD revision:

```
$ svnlook pg /usr/local/svn/repos seasonings /trunk/sandwich
mustard
```

---

svnlook proplist

Prints the names and values of versioned file and directory properties.

Synopsis

```
svnlook proplist REPOS_PATH PATH_IN_REPOS
```

Description

Lists the properties of a path in the repository. With --verbose, show the property values too.

Alternate Names

pl, plist

Switches

```
--revision (-r)
--transaction (-t)
--verbose (-v)
```

Examples

This shows the names of properties set on the file */trunk/README* in the HEAD revision:

```
$ svnlook proplist /usr/local/svn/repos /trunk/README
  original-author
  svn:mime-type
```

This is the same command as in the previous example, but this time showing the property values as well:

```
$ svnlook proplist /usr/local/svn/repos /trunk/README
  original-author : fitz
  svn:mime-type : text/plain
```

svnlook tree

Synopsis

```
svnlook tree REPOS_PATH [PATH_IN_REPOS]
```

Description

Prints the tree, starting at *PATH_IN_REPOS* (if supplied; at the root of the tree otherwise), optionally showing node revision ids.

Switches

```
--revision (-r)
--transaction (-t)
--show-ids
```

Examples

This shows the tree output (with node IDs) for revision 40 in our sample repository:

```
$ svnlook tree -r 40 /usr/local/svn/repos --show-ids
/ <0.0.2j>
 trunk/ <p.0.2j>
  vendors/ <q.0.2j>
   deli/ <1g.0.2j>
    egg.txt <1i.e.2j>
    soda.txt <1k.0.2j>
    sandwich.txt <1j.0.2j>
```


svnlook uuid

Prints the repository's UUID.

Synopsis

```
svnlook uuid REPOS_PATH
```

Description

Prints the UUID for the repository. the UUID is the repository's Universal Unique IDentifier. The Subversion client uses this identifier to differentiate between one repository and another.

Examples

This shows the UUID for the repository at *usr/local/svn/repos*:

```
$ svnlook uuid /usr/local/svn/repos
e7fe1b91-8cd5-0310-98dd-2f12e793c5e8
```

svnlook youngest
Prints the youngest revision number.

Synopsis

```
svnlook youngest REPOS_PATH
```

Description

Prints the youngest revision number of a repository.

Examples

This shows the youngest revision of our sample repository:

```
$ svnlook youngest /tmp/repos/
42
```

svnserve

svnserve lets you access Subversion repositories using the svn network protocol. You can run svnserve either as a standalone server process, or you can have another process, such as inetd, xinetd or sshd, launch it for you.

Once the client has selected a repository by transmitting its URL, svnserve reads a file named *conf/svnserve.conf* in the repository directory to determine repository-specific settings such as what authentication database to use and what authorization policies to apply. See "svnserve; A Custom Server" in Chapter 6 for details of the *svnserve.conf* file.

svnserve Switches

Unlike the previous commands we've described, svnserve has no subcommands— svnserve is controlled exclusively by switches.

--daemon *(-d)*

> Causes svnserve to run in daemon mode. svnserve backgrounds itself and accepts and serves TCP/IP connections on the svn port (3690, by default).

--listen-port=*PORT*

> Causes svnserve to listen on *PORT* when run in daemon mode.

--listen-host=*HOST*

> Causes svnserve to listen on the interface specified by *HOST*, which may be either a hostname or an IP address.

--foreground

> When used together with -d, this switch causes svnserve to stay in the foreground. This switch is mainly useful for debugging.

`--inetd` *(-i)*

    Causes svnserve to use the stdin/stdout file descriptors, as is appropriate for a daemon running out of `inetd`.

`--help` *(-h)*

    Displays a usage summary and exits.

`--root=ROOT` *(-r=ROOT)*

    Sets the virtual root for repositories served by svnserve. The pathname in URLs provided by the client is interpreted relative to this root, and is not allowed to escape this root.

`--tunnel` *(-t)*

    Causes svnserve to run in tunnel mode, which is just like the `inetd` mode of operation (serve one connection over stdin/stdout) except that the connection is considered to be pre-authenticated with the username of the current uid. This flag is selected by the client when running over a tunnel agent such as `ssh`.

`--threads` *(-T)*

    When running in daemon mode, causes svnserve to spawn a thread instead of a process for each connection. The svnserve process still backgrounds itself at startup time.

`--listen-once` *(-X)*

    Causes svnserve to accept one connection on the svn port, serve it, and exit. This option is mainly useful for debugging.

Subversion for CVS Users

This appendix is a guide for CVS users new to Subversion. It's essentially a list of differences between the two systems as viewed from 10,000 feet. For each section, we provide backreferences to relevant chapters, when possible.

Although the goal of Subversion is to take over the current and future CVS user base, some new features and design changes were required to fix certain broken behaviors that CVS had. This means that, as a CVS user, you may need to break habits—ones that you forgot were odd to begin with.

Revision Numbers Are Different Now

In CVS, revision numbers are per file. This is because CVS uses RCS as a backend; each file has a corresponding RCS file in the repository, and the repository is roughly laid out according to the structure of your project tree.

In Subversion, the repository looks like a single filesystem. Each commit results in an entirely new filesystem tree; in essence, the repository is an array of trees. Each of these trees is labeled with a single revision number. When someone talks about revision 54, they're talking about a particular tree (and, indirectly, the way the filesystem looked after the 54th commit).

Technically, it's not valid to talk about revision 5 of *foo.c*. Instead, one would say *foo.c* as it appears in revision 5. Also, be careful when making assumptions about the evolution of a file. In CVS, revisions 5 and 6 of *foo.c* are always different. In Subversion, it's most likely that *foo.c* did *not* change between revisions 5 and 6.

For more details on this topic, see "Revisions" in Chapter 2.

Directory Versions

Subversion tracks tree structures, not just file contents. It's one of the main reasons Subversion was written to replace CVS.

Here's what this means to you, as a former CVS user:

- The `svn add` and `svn delete` commands work on directories now, just as they work on files. So do `svn copy` and `svn move`. However, these commands do *not* cause any kind of immediate change in the repository. Instead, the working items are simply scheduled for addition or deletion. No repository changes happen until you run `svn commit`.

- Directories aren't dumb containers anymore; they have revision numbers like files. (Or more properly, it's correct to talk about directory *foo/* in revision 5.)

Let's talk more about that last point. Directory versioning is a hard problem; because we want to allow mixed-revision working copies, there are some limitations on how far we can abuse this model.

From a theoretical point of view, we define revision 5 of directory *foo* to mean a specific collection of directory entries and properties. Now suppose we start adding and removing files from *foo*, and then commit. It would be a lie to say that we still have revision 5 of *foo*. However, if we bumped *foo*'s revision number after the commit, that would be a lie too; there may be other changes to *foo* we haven't yet received, because we haven't updated yet.

Subversion deals with this problem by quietly tracking committed adds and deletes in the *.svn* area. When you eventually run `svn update`, all accounts are settled with the repository, and the directory's new revision number is set correctly. *Therefore, only after an update is it truly safe to say that you have a perfect revision of a directory*. Most of the time, your working copy will contain imperfect directory revisions.

Similarly, a problem arises if you attempt to commit property changes on a directory. Normally, the commit would bump the working directory's local revision number. But again, that would be a lie, because there may be adds or deletes that the directory doesn't yet have, because no update has happened. *Therefore, you are not allowed to commit property changes on a directory unless the directory is up-to-date*.

For more discussion about the limitations of directory versioning, see "The Limitations of Mixed Revisions" in Chapter 2.

More Disconnected Operations

In recent years, disk space has become outrageously cheap and abundant, but network bandwidth has not. Therefore, the Subversion working copy has been optimized around the scarcer resource.

The *.svn* administrative directory serves the same purpose as the *CVS* directory, except that it also stores read-only, pristine copies of your files. This allows you to do many things off-line:

svn status
>   Shows you any local changes you've made (see "svn status" in Chapter 3)

```
svn diff
```
Shows you the details of your changes (see "svn diff" in Chapter 3)

```
svn revert
```
Removes your local changes (see "svn revert" in Chapter 3)

Also, the cached pristine files allow the Subversion client to send differences when committing, which CVS cannot do.

The last subcommand in the list is new; it will not only remove local mods, but it will unschedule operations such as adds and deletes. It's the preferred way to revert a file: running `rm file`; `svn update` will still work, but it blurs the purpose of updating. And, while we're on this subject...

Distinction Between Status and Update

In Subversion, we've tried to erase a lot of the confusion between the `cvs status` and `cvs update` commands.

The `cvs status` command has two purposes: first, to show the user any local modifications in the working copy, and second, to show the user which files are out-of-date. Unfortunately, because of CVS's hard-to-read status output, many CVS users don't take advantage of this command at all. Instead, they've developed a habit of running `cvs up` or `cvs up -n` to quickly see their mods. If users forget to use the -n option, this has the side effect of merging repository changes that you may not be ready to deal with!

With Subversion, we've tried to remove this muddle by making the output of `svn status` easy to read for both humans and parsers. Also, `svn update` only prints information about files that are updated, *not* local modifications.

`svn status` prints all files that have local modifications. By default, the repository is not contacted. While this subcommand accepts a fair number of options, the following are the most commonly used ones:

-u

Contact the repository to determine, and then display, out-of-dateness information.

-v

Show *all* entries under version control.

-N

Run non-recursively (do not descend into subdirectories).

The status command has two output formats. In the default short format, local modifications look like this:

```
% svn status
M      ./foo.c
M      ./bar/baz.c
```

If you specify the --show-updates (-u) switch, a longer output format is used:

```
% svn status -u
M               1047    ./foo.c
        *       1045    ./faces.html
        *       -       ./bloo.png
M               1050    ./bar/baz.c
Status against revision:    1066
```

In this case, two new columns appear. The second column contains an asterisk if the file or directory is out-of-date. The third column shows the working copy's revision number of the item. In the previous example, the asterisk indicates that *faces.html* would be patched if we updated, and that *bloo.png* is a newly added file in the repository. (The - next to bloo.png means that it doesn't yet exist in the working copy.)

Lastly, here's a summary of the most common status codes that you may see:

```
A    Resource is scheduled for Addition
D    Resource is scheduled for Deletion
M    Resource has local modifications
C    Resource has conflicts (changes have not been completely merged
        between the repository and working copy version)
X    Resource is external to this working copy (comes from another
        repository.  See XREF linkend="svn-ch-7-sect-2.3.6")
?    Resource is not under version control
!    Resource is missing or incomplete (removed by another tool than
        Subversion)
```

Subversion has combined the CVS P and U codes into just U. When a merge or conflict occurs, Subversion simply prints G or C, rather than a whole sentence about it.

For a more detailed discussion of svn status, see "svn status" in Chapter 3.

Branches and Tags

Subversion doesn't distinguish between filesystem space and branch space; branches and tags are ordinary directories within the filesystem. This is probably the single largest mental hurdle a CVS user will need to climb. Read all about it in Chapter 4.

 Since Subversion treats branches and tags as ordinary directories, always remember to check out the trunk (http://svn.example.com/repos/calc/trunk/) of your project, and not the project itself (http://svn.example.com/repos/calc/). If you make the mistake of checking out the project itself, you'll wind up with a working copy that contains a copy of your project for every branch and tag you have.[*]

---

[*] That is, providing you don't run out of disk space before your checkout finishes.

Metadata Properties

A new feature of Subversion is that you can attach arbitrary metadata (or properties) to files and directories. Properties are arbitrary name/value pairs associated with files and directories in your working copy.

To set or get a property name, use the svn propset and svn propget subcommands. To list all properties on an object, use svn proplist.

For more information, see "Properties" in Chapter 7.

Conflict Resolution

CVS marks conflicts with in-line conflict markers, and prints a C during an update. Historically, this has caused problems, because CVS isn't doing enough. Many users forget about (or don't see) the C after it whizzes by on their terminal. They often forget that the conflict markers are even present, and then accidentally commit files containing conflict markers.

Subversion solves this problem by making conflicts more tangible. It remembers that a file is in a state of conflict, and won't allow you to commit your changes until you run svn resolved. See "Resolve Conflicts (Merging Others' Changes)" in Chapter 3 for more details.

Binary Files and Translation

In the most general sense, Subversion handles binary files more gracefully than CVS does. Because CVS uses RCS, it can only store successive full copies of a changing binary file. But internally, Subversion expresses differences between files using a binary-differencing algorithm, regardless of whether they contain textual or binary data. That means that all files are stored differentially (compressed) in the repository, and small differences are always sent over the network.

CVS users have to mark binary files with -kb flags, to prevent data from being garbled (due to keyword expansion and line-ending translations). They sometimes forget to do this.

Subversion takes the more paranoid route: first, it never performs any kind of keyword or line-ending translation unless you explicitly ask it do so (see "svn:keywords" and "svn:eol-style" in Chapter 7 for more details). By default, Subversion treats all file data as literal byte strings, and files are always stored in the repository in an untranslated state.

Second, Subversion maintains an internal notion of whether a file is text or binary data, but this notion is *only* extant in the working copy. During an svn update, Subversion will perform contextual merges on locally modified text files, but will not attempt to do so for binary files.

To determine whether a contextual merge is possible, Subversion examines the svn: mime-type property. If the file has no svn:mime-type property, or has a mime-type that is textual (e.g. text/*), Subversion assumes it is text. Otherwise, Subversion assumes the file is binary. Subversion also helps users by running a binary-detection algorithm in the svn import and svn add commands. These commands will make a good guess and then (possibly) set a binary svn:mime-type property on the file being added. (If Subversion guesses wrong, the user can always remove or hand-edit the property.)

Versioned Modules

Unlike CVS, a Subversion working copy is aware that it has checked out a module. That means that if somebody changes the definition of a module, then a call to svn update will update the working copy appropriately.

Subversion defines modules as a list of directories within a directory property: see "Externals Definitions" in Chapter 7.

Authentication

With CVS's pserver, you are required to login to the server before any read or write operation—you even have to login for anonymous operations. With a Subversion repository using Apache HTTPD as the server, you don't provide any authentication credentials at the outset—if an operation that you perform requires authentication, the server will challenge you for your credentials (whether those credentials are username and password, a client certificate, or even both). So, if your repository is world-readable, you will not be required to authenticate at all for read operations.

As with CVS, Subversion still caches your credentials on disk (in your *~/.subversion/ auth/* directory), unless you tell it not to by using the --no-auth-cache switch.

Converting a Repository from CVS to Subversion

Perhaps the most important way to familiarize CVS users with Subversion is to let them continue to work on their projects using the new system. And while that can be somewhat accomplished using a flat import into a Subversion repository of an exported CVS repository, the more thorough solution involves transferring not only the latest snapshot of their data, but all the history behind it as well, from one system to another. This is an extremely difficult problem to solve that involves deducing changesets in the absence of atomicity, and translating between the systems' completely orthogonal branching policies, among other complications. Still, there are a handful of tools claiming to at least partially support the ability to convert existing CVS repositories into Subversion ones.

One such tool is cvs2svn (*http://cvs2svn.tigris.org/*), a Python script originally created by members of Subversion's own development community. Others include Chialiang Kao's Subversion converter plugin to the VCP tool (*http://svn.clkao.org/revml/ branches/svn-perl/*) and Lev Serebryakov's RefineCVS (*http://lev.serebryakov.spb.ru/ refinecvs/*). These tools have various levels of completeness, and may make entirely different decisions about how to handle your CVS repository history. Whichever tool you decide to use, be sure to perform as much verification as you can stand on the conversion results—after all, you've worked hard to build that history!

For an updated collection of links to known converter tools, visit the Links page of the Subversion website (*http://subversion.tigris.org/project_links.html*).

Troubleshooting

Common Problems

There are a number of problems you may run into in the course of installing and using Subversion. Some of these will be resolved once you get a better idea of how Subversion does things, while others are caused because you're used to the way that other version control systems work. Still other problems might be unsolvable due to bugs in some of the operating systems that Subversion runs on (considering the wide array of operating systems that Subversion runs on, it's amazing that we don't encounter many more of these).

The following list has been compiled over the course of years of Subversion usage. If you can't find the problem you're having here, look at the most up-to-date version of the FAQ on Subversion's main website. If you're still stuck, then send email to *users@subversion.tigris.org* with a detailed description of the problem you're having.[*]

Problems Using Subversion

Here are some of the most popular questions from Subversion's FAQ.

Every time I try to access my repository, my Subversion client just hangs.

Your repository is not corrupt, nor is your data lost. If your process accesses the repository directly (mod_dav_svn, svnlook, svnadmin, or if you access a file:// URL), then it's using Berkeley DB to access your data. Berkeley DB is journaling system, meaning that it logs everything it is about to do before it does so. If your process is interrupted (kill signal or segfault), then a lockfile is left behind, along with a logfile describing unfinished business. Any other process that attempts to

---

[*] Remember that the amount of detail you provide about your setup and your problem is directly proportional to the likelihood of getting an answer from the mailing list. You're encouraged to include everything short of what you had for breakfast and your mother's maiden name.

access the database will just hang, waiting for the lockfile to disappear. To awaken your repository, you need to ask Berkeley DB to either finish the work, or rewind the database to a previous state that is known to be consistent.

Make sure you run this command as the user that owns and manages the database, and not as root, else it will leave root-owned files in the db directory which cannot be opened by the non-root user that manages the database, which is typically either you or your Apache process. Also, be sure to have the correct umask set when you run recover, since failing to do so locks out users that are in the group allowed to access the repository.

Simply run:

```
$ svnadmin recover /path/to/repos
```

Once the command has completed, check the permissions in the *db/* directory of the repository.

Every time I try to run svn, it says my working copy is locked.

Subversion's working copy, just like Berkeley DB, uses a journaling mechanism to perform all actions. That is, it logs everything it is about to do before it does so. If svn is interrupted while performing an action, then one or more lockfiles are left behind, along with log files describing then unfinished actions. (svn status will show an L next to locked directories.)

Any other process that attempts to access the working copy fails when it sees the locks. To awaken your working copy, you need to tell the client to finish the work. To fix this, run this command from the top of your working copy:

```
$ svn cleanup working-copy
```

I'm getting errors finding or opening a repository, but I know my repository URL is correct.

See "Every time I try to access my repository, my Subversion client just hangs."

You might also have a permissions problem opening the repository. See "Supporting Multiple Repository Access Methods."

How can I specify a Windows drive letter in a file:// URL?

See Chapter 2.

I'm having trouble doing write operations to a Subversion repository over a network.

If import works fine over local access:

```
$ mkdir test
$ touch test/testfile
```

```
$ svn import test file:///var/svn/test -m "Initial import"
Adding         test/testfile
Transmitting file data .
Committed revision 1.
```

But not from a remote host:

```
$ svn import test http://svn.red-bean.com/test -m "Initial import"
harry's password: xxxxxxx

svn_error: ... The specified activity does not exist.
```

We've seen this when the *REPOS/dav/* directory is not writable by the httpd process. Check the permissions to ensure that Apache httpd can write to the *dav/* directory (and to the corresponding *db/* directory, of course).

Under Windows XP, the Subversion server sometimes seems to send out corrupted data.

You need to install Window XP Service Pack 1 to fix a TCP/IP stack bug in the operating system. You can get all sorts of information about that Service Pack at *http://support.microsoft.com/default.aspx?scid=kb;EN-US;q317949.*

What is the best method of doing a network trace of the conversation between a Subversion client and Apache server?

Use Ethereal to eavesdrop on the conversation:

 The following instructions are specific to the graphical version of Ethereal, and may not apply to the command line version (whose binary is usually named tethereal).

1. Pull down the Capture menu, and choose Start.

2. Type port 80 for Filter, and turn off promiscuous mode.

3. Run your Subversion client.

4. Hit Stop. Now you have a capture. It looks like a huge list of lines.

5. Click on the Protocol column to sort.

6. Click on the first relevant TCP line to select it.

7. Right-click, and choose Follow TCP Stream. You'll be presented with the request/response pairs of the Subversion client's HTTP conversion.

Alternatively, you may set a parameter in your client's *servers* runtime configuration file to cause neon's debugging output to appear. The numeric value of neon-debug is a combination of the NE_DBG_* values in the header file *ne_utils.h*. Setting the neon-debug-mask variable to 130 (i.e. NE_DBG_HTTP + NE_DBG_HTTPBODY) will cause the HTTP data to be shown.

You may well want to disable compression when doing a network trace by tweaking the http-compression parameter in the same file.

I just built the distribution binary, and when I try to check out Subversion, I get an error about an "Unrecognized URL scheme."

Subversion uses a plugin system to allow access to repositories. Currently there are three of these plugins: ra_local allows access to a local repository, ra_dav allows access to a repository via WebDAV, and ra_svn allows local or remote access via the svnserve server. When you attempt to perform an operation in subversion, the program tries to dynamically load a plugin based on the URL scheme. A file:// URL will try to load ra_local, and an http:// URL will try to load ra_dav.

The error you are seeing means that the dynamic linker/loader can't find the plugins to load. This normally happens when you build subversion with shared libraries, then attempt to run it without first running make install. Another possible cause is that you ran make install, but the libraries were installed in a location that the dynamic linker/loader doesn't recognize. Under Linux, you can allow the linker/loader to find the libraries by adding the library directory to */etc/ld.so.conf* and running ldconfig. If you don't wish to do this, or you don't have root access, you can also specify the library directory in the LD_LIBRARY_PATH environment variable.

Why does the svn revert command require an explicit target? Why is it not recursive by default? This behavior differs from almost all the other subcommands.

The short answer: it's for your own good.

Subversion places a very high priority on protecting your data, and not just your versioned data. Modifications that you make to already-versioned files, and new files scheduled for addition to the version control system, must be treated with care.

Making the svn revert command require an explicit target—even if that target is just '.'—is one way of accomplishing that. This requirement (as well as requiring you to supply the --recursive flag if you want that behavior) is intended to make you really think about what you're doing, because once your files are reverted, your local modifications are gone forever.

When I start Apache, mod_dav_svn complains about a "bad database version," that it found db-3.X, rather than db-4.X.

Your apr-util linked against DB-3, and svn linked against DB-4. Unfortunately, the DB symbols aren't different. When mod_dav_svn is loaded into Apache's process-space, it ends up resolving the symbol names against apr-util's DB-3 library.

The solution is to make sure apr-util compiles against DB-4. You can do this by passing specific switches to either Apr-util's or Apache's configure: `--with-dbm=db4 --with-berkeley-db=/the/db/prefix`.

I'm getting "Function not implemented" errors on RedHat 9, and nothing works. How do I fix this?

This is not really a problem with Subversion, but it often affects Subversion users.

RedHat 9 and Fedora ship with a Berkeley DB library that relies on the kernel support for NPTL (the Native Posix Threads Library). The kernels that RedHat provides have this support built in, but if you compile your own kernel, then you may not have the NPTL support. If that is the case, then you will see errors such as this:

```
svn: Berkeley DB error
svn: Berkeley DB error while creating environment for filesystem tester/db:
Function not implemented
```

This can be fixed in one of several ways:

- Rebuild db4 for the kernel you're using.
- Use a RedHat 9 kernel.
- Apply the NPTL patches to the kernel you're using.
- Use a recent (2.5.x) kernel with the NPTL support included.
- Check if environment variable `LD_ASSUME_KERNEL` is set to 2.2.5, and if so, unset it before starting Subversion (Apache). (You usually would set this variable to run Wine or Winex on RedHat 9.)

Why does log say "(no author)" for files committed or imported via Apache (ra_dav)?

If you allow anonymous write access to the repository via Apache, the Apache server never challenges the client for a username, and instead permits the write operation without authentication. Since Subversion has no idea who did the operation, this results in a log like this:

```
$ svn log
------------------------------------------------------------------------
rev 24:  (no author) | 2003-07-29 19:28:35 +0200 (Tue, 29 Jul 2003)
...
```

Read about adding authentication in Chapter 6.

I'm getting occasional "Access Denied" errors on Windows. They seem to happen at random.

These appear to be due to the various Windows services that monitor the filesystem for changes (anti-virus software, indexing services, the COM+ Event Notification Service). This is not really a bug in Subversion, which makes it difficult to fix. A summary of the current state of the investigation is available at *http://www.contactor.se/*

~dast/svn/archive-2003-10/0136.shtml. A workaround that should reduce the incidence rate for most people was implemented in revision 7598.

On FreeBSD, certain operations (especially svnadmin create) sometimes hang.

This is usually due to a lack of available entropy on the system. Subversion asks APR to generate random numbers to create UUIDs from time to time, and certain operating systems will block for high-quality randomness. You probably need to configure the system to gather entropy from sources such as hard-disk and network interrupts. Consult your system manpages, specifically random(4) and rndcontrol(8) on how to effect this change. Another workaround is to compile APR against */dev/urandom* instead of */dev/random*.

I can see my repository in a web browser, but svn checkout gives me an error about "301 Moved Permanently".

It means your *httpd.conf* is misconfigured. Usually this error happens when you've defined the Subversion virtual "location" to exist within two different scopes at the same time.

For example, if you've exported a repository as <Location /www/foo>, but you've also set your DocumentRoot to be */www*, then you're in trouble. When the request comes in for */www/foo/bar*, Apache doesn't know whether to find a *real* file named */foo/bar* within your DocumentRoot, or whether to ask mod_dav_svn to fetch a file */bar* from the */www/foo* repository. Usually the former case wins, and hence the "Moved Permanently" error.

The solution is to make sure your repository <Location> does not overlap or live within any areas already exported as normal web shares.

I'm trying to look at an old version of my file, but svn says something about "path not found."

A nice feature of Subversion is that the repository understands copies and renames, and preserves the historical connections. For example, if you copy */trunk* to */branches/mybranch*, the repository then understands that every file in the branch has a "predecessor" in the trunk. Running svn log --verbose shows you the historical copy, so you can see the rename:

```
r7932 | joe | 2003-12-03 17:54:02 -0600 (Wed, 03 Dec 2003) | 1 line
Changed paths:
   A /branches/mybranch (from /trunk:7931)
```

Unfortunately, while the repository is aware of copies and renames, almost all the svn client subcommands in version 1.0 are *not* aware. Commands like svn diff, svn merge, and svn cat ought to understand and follow renames, but don't yet do this. It's scheduled as a post-1.0 feature. For example, if you ask svn diff to compare two earlier versions of *branches/mybranch/foo.c*, the command will not automatically understand that the task actually requires comparing two versions of *trunk/foo.c*, due to the rename. Instead, you'll see an error about how the branch-path doesn't exist in the earlier revisions.

The workaround for all problems of this sort is to do the legwork yourself. That is: *you* need to be aware of any renamed paths, discover them yourself using svn log -v, and then provide them explicitly to the svn client. For example, instead of running

```
$ svn diff -r 1000:2000 http://host/repos/branches/mybranch/foo.c
svn: Filesystem has no item
svn: '/branches/mybranch/foo.c' not found in the repository at revision 1000
```

...you would instead run

```
$ svn diff -r1000:2000 http://host/repos/trunk/foo.c
...
```

WebDAV and Autoversioning

WebDAV is an extension to HTTP, and is growing more and more popular as a standard for file-sharing. Today's operating systems are becoming extremely Web-aware, and many have now built-in support for mounting shares exported by WebDAV servers.

If you use Apache/mod_dav_svn as your Subversion network server, then to some extent, you are also running a WebDAV server. This appendix gives some background on the nature of this protocol, how Subversion uses it, and how well Subversion interoperates with other software that is WebDAV-aware.

Basic WebDAV Concepts

This section provides a very brief, very general overview of the ideas behind WebDAV. It should lay the foundation for understanding WebDAV compatibility issues between clients and servers.

Just Plain WebDAV

RFC 2518 defines a set of concepts and accompanying extension methods to HTTP 1.1 that make the Web into a more universal read/write medium. The basic idea is that a WebDAV-compliant web server can act like a generic file server; clients can mount WebDAV shares that behave much like NFS or SMB shares.

However, it's important to note that RFC 2518 does *not* provide any sort of model for version control, despite the V in DAV. Basic WebDAV clients and servers assume only one version of each file or directory exists, and can be repeatedly overwritten.[*]

---

[*] For this reason, some people jokingly refer to generic WebDAV clients as WebDA clients!

Here are the new concepts and methods introduced in basic WebDAV:

New write methods
> Beyond the standard HTTP PUT method (which creates or overwrites a web resource), WebDAV defines new COPY and MOVE methods for duplicating or rearranging resources.

Collections
> This is simply the WebDAV term for a grouping of resources (URIs). In most cases, it is analogous to a directory. You can tell something is a collection if it ends with a trailing /. Whereas file resources can be written or created with a PUT method, collection resources are created with the new MKCOL method.

Properties
> This is same idea present in Subversion—metadata attached to files and collections. A client can list or retrieve properties attached to a resource with the new PROPFIND method, and can change them with the PROPPATCH method. Some properties are wholly created and controlled by users (e.g., a property called color), and others are wholly created and controlled by the WebDAV server (e.g., a property that contains the last modification time of a file). The former kind are called dead properties, and the latter kind are called live properties.

Locking
> A WebDAV server may decide to offer a locking feature to clients—this part of the specification is optional, although most WebDAV servers do offer the feature. If present, then clients can use the new LOCK and UNLOCK methods to mediate access to a resource. In most cases these methods are used to create exclusive write locks (as discussed in "The Lock-Modify-Unlock Solution" in Chapter 2), although shared write locks are also possible.

DeltaV Extensions

Because RFC 2518 left out versioning concepts, another capable group was left with the responsibility of writing RFC 3253, which adds versioning to WebDAV. WebDAV/DeltaV clients and servers are often called just DeltaV clients and servers, since DeltaV implies the existence of basic WebDAV.

DeltaV introduces a whole slew of new acronyms, but don't be intimidated. The ideas are fairly straightforward. Here are the new concepts and methods introduced in DeltaV:

Per-resource versioning
> Like CVS and other version-control systems, DeltaV assumes that each resource has a potentially infinite number of states. A client begins by placing a resource under version control using the new VERSION-CONTROL method. This creates a new Version Controlled Resource (VCR). Every time you change the VCR (via PUT, PROPPATCH, etc.), a new state of the resource is created, called a Version Resource

(VR). VCRs and VRs are still ordinary web resources, defined by URLs. Specific VRs can have human-friendly names as well.

Server-side working-copy model

Some DeltaV servers support the ability to create a virtual workspace on the server, where all of your work is performed. Clients use the MKWORKSPACE method to create a private area, then indicate they want to change specific VCRs by checking them out into the workspace, editing them, and checking them in again. In HTTP terms, the sequence of methods would be CHECKOUT, PUT, CHECKIN. After each CHECKIN, a new VR is created, and edited VCR's contents now point to the latest VR. Each VCR has also has a history resource which tracks and orders its various VR states.

Client-side working-copy model

Some DeltaV servers also support the idea that the client may have a private working copy full of specific VRs. (This is how CVS and Subversion work.) When the client wants to commit changes to the server, it begins by creating a temporary server transaction (called an activity) with the MKACTIVITY method. The client then performs a CHECKOUT on each VR it wishes to change, which creates a number of temporary working resources in the activity, that can be modified using PUT and PROPPATCH methods. Finally, the client performs a CHECKIN on each working resource, which creates a new VR within each VCR, and the entire activity is deleted.

Configurations

DeltaV allows you define flexible collections of VCRs called configurations, which don't necessarily respond to particular directories. Each VCR's contents can be made to point to a specific VR using the UPDATE method. Once the configuration is perfect, the client can create a snapshot of the whole configuration, called a baseline. Clients use the CHECKOUT and CHECKIN methods to capture specific states of configurations, much like they use these methods to create specific VR states of VCRs.

Extensibility

DeltaV defines a new method, REPORT, which allows the client and server to perform customized data exchanges. The client sends a REPORT request with a properly-labeled XML body full of custom data; assuming the server understands the specific report-type, it responds with an equally custom XML body. This technique is very similar to XML-RPC.

Autoversioning

For many, this is the killer feature of DeltaV. If the DeltaV server supports this feature, then basic WebDAV clients (i.e., those unaware of versioning) can still write to the server, and the server will silently perform versioning anyway. In the simplest example, an ignorant PUT from a basic WebDAV client might be translated by the server as a CHECKOUT, PUT, CHECKIN.

Subversion and DeltaV

So, how compatible is Subversion with other DeltaV software? In two words: not very. At least, not in Subversion 1.0.

While libsvn_ra_dav sends DeltaV requests to the server, the Subversion client is *not* a general-purpose DeltaV client. In fact, it expects some custom features from the server (especially through custom REPORT requests). Further, mod_dav_svn is *not* a general-purpose DeltaV server. It only implements a strict subset of the DeltaV specification. A more general WebDAV or DeltaV client may very well be able to interoperate against it, but only if that client operates within the narrow confines of those features that the server has implemented. The Subversion development team plans to address general WebDAV interoperability in a future release of Subversion.

Mapping Subversion to DeltaV

Here is a very high-level description of how various Subversion client operations use DeltaV. In many cases, these explanations are gross oversimplifications. They should *not* be taken as a substitute for reading Subversion's source code or talking with its developers.

svn checkout/list
> Perform a PROPFIND of depth 1 on the collection to get a list of immediate children. Perform a GET (and possibly a PROPFIND) on each child. Recurse into collections and repeat.

svn commit
> Create an activity with MKACTIVITY, and do a CHECKOUT of each changed item, followed by a PUT of new data. Finally, a MERGE request causes an implicit CHECKIN of all working resources.

svn update/switch/status/merge/diff
> Send a custom REPORT request that describes the mixed-revision (and mixed-URL) state of the working copy. The server sends a custom response that describes which items need updating. The client loops over the response, performing GET and PROPFIND requests as needed. For updates and switches, install the new data in the working copy. For diff and merge commands, compare the data to the working copy, possibly applying changes as local modifications.

Autoversioning Support

At the time of writing, the truth is that there are very few DeltaV clients in the world; RFC 3253 is still relatively new. However users do have access to generic clients, because almost every modern operating system now has an integrated basic WebDAV client. With this in mind, Subversion developers realized that if Subversion 1.0

was to have *any* interoperability features, support for DeltaV autoversioning would be the best approach.

To activate autoversioning in mod_dav_svn, use the SVNAutoversioning directive within the *httpd.conf* Location block, like so:

```
<Location /repos>
  DAV svn
  SVNPath /absolute/path/to/repository
  SVNAutoversioning on
</Location>
```

Normally, if a generic WebDAV client attempted a PUT to a path within your repository location, mod_dav_svn would outright reject the request. (It normally only allows such operations on working resources within DeltaV activities.) With SVNAutoversioning turned on, however, the server interprets the PUT request as an internal MKACTIVITY, CHECKOUT, PUT, and CHECKIN. A generic log message is auto-generated, and a new filesystem revision is created.

Because so many operating systems already have integrated WebDAV abilities, the use-case for this feature borders on fantastical: imagine an office of ordinary users running Microsoft Windows or Mac OS. Each computer mounts the Subversion repository, which appears to be an ordinary network share. They use the server as they always do: open files from the server, edit them, and save them back to the server. But in this fantasy, the server is automatically versioning everything. Later on, a sysadmin can use a Subversion client to search and retrieve all older versions.

Is this fantasy real? Not quite. The main snag is that Subversion 1.0 has no support whatsoever for the WebDAV LOCK or UNLOCK methods. Most operating system DAV clients attempt to LOCK a resource opened directly from a DAV-mounted network share. For now, users may have to copy a file from the DAV share to local disk, edit the file, then copy it back again. Not ideal autoversioning, but still doable.

The mod_dav_lock Alternative

The mod_dav Apache module is a complex beast: it understands and parses all of the WebDAV and DeltaV methods, yet it depends on a back-end provider to access the resources themselves.

In its simplest incarnation, a user can use mod_dav_fs as a provider for mod_dav. mod_dav_fs uses the ordinary filesystem to store files and directories, and only understands vanilla WebDAV methods, not DeltaV.

Subversion, on the other hand, uses mod_dav_svn as a provider for mod_dav. mod_dav_svn understands all WebDAV methods except LOCK, and understands a sizable subset of DeltaV methods. It accesses data in the Subversion repository, rather than in the real filesystem. Subversion 1.0 doesn't support locking, because it would actually be quite difficult to implement, since Subversion uses the copy-modify-merge model.[*]

In Apache httpd-2.0, mod_dav supports the LOCK method by tracking locks in a private database, assuming that the provider is willing to accept them. In Apache httpd-2.1 or later, however, this locking support has been broken into an independent module, mod_dav_lock. It allows any mod_dav provider to take advantage of the lock database, including mod_dav_svn, even though mod_dav_svn doesn't actually understand locking.

Confused yet?

In a nutshell, you can use mod_dav_lock in Apache httpd-2.1 (or later) to create the *illusion* that mod_dav_svn is honoring LOCK requests. Make sure mod_dav_lock is either compiled into httpd, or being loaded in your *httpd.conf*. Then simply add the DAVGenericLockDB directive to your Location like so:

```
<Location /repos>
  DAV svn
  SVNPath /absolute/path/to/repository
  SVNAutoversioning on
  DavGenericLockDB /path/to/store/locks
</Location>
```

This technique is a risky business; in some sense, the mod_dav_svn is now lying to the WebDAV client. It claims to accept the LOCK request, but in reality the lock isn't being enforced at all levels. If a second WebDAV client attempts to LOCK the same resource, then mod_dav_lock will notice and correctly deny the request. But there's absolutely nothing preventing an ordinary Subversion client from changing the file via a normal svn commit! If you use this technique, you're giving users the opportunity to stomp on each others' changes. In particular, a WebDAV client might accidentally overwrite a change committed by regular svn client.

On the other hand, if you set up your environment very carefully, you may mitigate the risk. For example, if *all* of your users are working though basic WebDAV clients (rather than svn clients), then things should be fine.

Autoversioning Interoperability

In this section, we'll describe the most common generic WebDAV clients (at the time of writing), and how well they operate against a mod_dav_svn server using the SVNAutoversioning directive. RFC 2518 is a bit large, and perhaps a bit too flexible. Every WebDAV client behaves slightly differently, and creates slightly different problems.

---

[*] Subversion may someday develop a reserved-checkout locking model that can live peaceably with copy-modify-merge, but it probably won't happen soon.

Win32 WebFolders

Windows 98, 2000, and XP have an integrated WebDAV client known as WebFolders. On Windows 98, the feature might need to be explicitly installed; if present, a WebFolders directory appears directly within My Computer. On Windows 2000 and XP, simply open My Network Places, and run the Add Network Place icon. When prompted, enter the WebDAV URL. The shared folder will appear within My Network Places.

Most write operations work fine against an autoversioning mod_dav_svn server, but there are few problems:

- If the computer is a member of an NT Domain, then it seems to be unable to connect to the WebDAV share. It repeatedly asks for a name and password, even when the Apache server isn't issuing an authentication challenge! Some have speculated that this might happen because WebFolders is specifically designed to operate against Microsoft's SharePoint DAV server. If the machine isn't part of an NT Domain, then the share is mounted without a problem. This mystery is not yet solved.

- A file can't be opened for direct editing from the share; it always comes up read-only. The mod_dav_lock technique doesn't help, because WebFolders doesn't use the LOCK method at all. The previously mentioned copy, edit, re-copy method does work, however. The file on the share can be successfully overwritten by a locally edited copy.

Mac OS X

Apple's OS X operating system has an integrated WebDAV client. From the Finder, select the Connect to Server item from the Go menu. Enter a WebDAV URL, and it appears as a disk on the desktop, just like any file server.*

Unfortunately, this client refuses to work against an autoversioning mod_dav_svn because of its lack of LOCK support. Mac OS X discovers the missing LOCK ability during the initial HTTP OPTIONS feature exchange, and thus decides to mount the Subversion repository as a read-only share. After that, no write operations are possible at all. In order to mount the repository as a read-write share, you *must* use the mod_dav_lock trick discussed previously. Once locking seems to work, the share behaves very nicely: files can be opened directly in read/write mode, although each save operation will cause the client to do a PUT to a temporary location, a DELETE of original file, and a MOVE of the temporary resource to the original filename. That's three new Subversion revisions per save!

---

* Unix users can also run mount -t webdav URL /mountpoint.

One more word of warning: OS X's WebDAV client can be overly sensitive to HTTP redirects. If you're unable to mount the repository at all, you may need to enable the BrowserMatch directive in your *httpd.conf*:

```
BrowserMatch "^WebDAVFS/1.[012]" redirect-carefully
```

Unix: Nautilus 2

Nautilus is the official file manager/browser for the GNOME desktop. Its main home page is at *http://www.gnome.org/projects/nautilus/*. By simply typing a WebDAV URL into the Nautilus window, the DAV share appears like a local filesystem.

In general, Nautilus 2 works reasonably well against an autoversioning mod_dav_svn, with the following caveats:

- Any files opened directly from the share are treated as read-only. Even the mod_dav_lock trick seems to have no effect. It seems that Nautilus never issues the LOCK method at all. The copy locally, edit, copy back trick does work, however. Unfortunately, Nautilus overwrites the old file by issuing a DELETE first, which creates an extra revision.

- When overwriting or creating a file , Nautilus first does a PUT of an empty file, then overwrites it with a second PUT. This creates two Subversion filesystem revisions, rather than one.

- When deleting a collection, it issues an HTTP DELETE on each individual child instead of on the collection itself. This creates a whole bunch of new revisions.

Linux davfs2

Linux davfs2 is a filesystem module for the Linux kernel, whose development is located at *http://dav.sourceforge.net/*. Once installed, a WebDAV network share can be mounted with the usual Linux mount command.

The word on the street is that this DAV client doesn't work at all with mod_dav_svn's autoversioning. Every single attempt to write to the server is preceded by a LOCK request, which mod_dav_svn doesn't support. At this time, there is no data indicating whether the use of mod_dav_lock resolves this problem.

Third-Party Tools

Subversion's modular design (covered in "Layered Library Design" in Chapter 8) and the availability of language bindings (as described in "Using Languages Other than C and C++" in Chapter 8) make it a likely candidate for use as an extension or back-end to other pieces of software. In this appendix, we'll briefly introduce you to some of the many third-party tools that are using Subversion functionality under the hood.

For a more recently updated version of this information, check out the Links page on the Subversion website (*http://subversion.tigris.org/project_links.html*).

Clients and Plugins

AnkhSVN (http://ankhsvn.tigris.org/)
  Subversion add-in for Microsoft Visual Studio .NET

JSVN (http://jsvn.alternatecomputing.com/)
  Java Subversion Client, including a plugin for IDEA

psvn.el (http://xsteve.nit.at/prg/vc_svn/)
  Subversion interface for emacs

RapidSVN (http://rapidsvn.tigris.org/)
  Cross-platform Subversion GUI, based on the WxPython libraries

Subclipse (http://subclipse.tigris.org/)
  Subversion plugin for the Eclipse environment

Subway (http://nidaros.homedns.org/subway/)
  Microsoft SCC provider for Subversion

sourcecross.org (http://www.sourcecross.org/)
  Microsoft SCC provider for Subversion

Supervision (http://supervision.tigris.org/)
  Java/Swing visual client for Subversion

Sven (http://www.nikwest.de/Software/#SvenOverview)
Native GUI for Subversion using the Mac OS X Cocoa framework

Svn4Eclipse (http://svn4eclipse.tigris.org/)
Subversion plugin for the Eclipse IDE

Svn-Up (http://svnup.tigris.org/)
Java-based GUI for Subversion and plugin for the IDEA IDE

TortoiseSVN (http://tortoisesvn.tigris.org/)
Subversion client, implemented as a Microsoft Windows shell extension

WorkBench (http://pysvn.tigris.org/)
Cross-platform Python-based software development GUI built on Subversion

Language Bindings

PySVN (http://pysvn.tigris.org/)
Object-oriented Python bindings for the Subversion client API

Subversion (http://subversion.tigris.org/)
Python, Perl, and Java bindings to Subversion API, mirroring the core C API

SVNCPP (http://rapidsvn.tigris.org/)
C++ object-oriented bindings for the Subversion client API

Repository Converters

cvs2svn (http://cvs2svn.tigris.org/)
CVS-to-Subversion conversion

Subversion VCP Plugin (http://svn.clkao.org/revml/branches/svn-perl/)
VCP plugin for CVS-to-Subversion

Higher-Level Tools

Kwiki (http://www.kwiki.org/)
Wiki with a Subversion backup backend

Subissue (http://subissue.tigris.org/)
Track issues directly in your Subversion repository

Subwiki (http://subwiki.tigris.org/)
Wiki that uses Subversion for its data repository

svk (http://svk.elixus.org/)
Decentralized version control system based on Subversion

submaster (http://www.rocklinux.org/submaster.html)
System for distributed software development, based on Subversion

Repository Browsing Tools

SVN::Web (http://svn.elixus.org/repos/member/clkao/)
 Perl-based Subversion repository Web interface

ViewCVS (http://viewcvs.sourceforge.net/)
 Python-based CGI script for browsing CVS and Subversion repositories

WebSVN (http://websvn.tigris.org/)
 PHP-based Subversion repository browser

Trac (http://projects.edgewall.com/trac/)
 Minimalist web-based software project management and bug/issue tracking system with version control interfaces and integrated Wiki support

Creative Commons Attribution License

This work is licensed under the Creative Commons Attribution License. A summary of the license is given below, followed by the full legal text.

You are free:

- to copy, distribute, display, and perform the work
- to make derivative works
- to make commercial use of the work

Under the following conditions:

Attribution. You must give the original author credit.

- For any reuse or distribution, you must make clear to others the license terms of this work.
- Any of these conditions can be waived if you get permission from the author.

Your fair use and other rights are in no way affected by the above.

Creative Commons Legal Code

Attribution 2.0

CREATIVE COMMONS CORPORATION IS NOT A LAW FIRM AND DOES NOT PROVIDE LEGAL SERVICES. DISTRIBUTION OF THIS LICENSE DOES NOT CREATE AN ATTORNEY-CLIENT RELATIONSHIP. CREATIVE COMMONS PROVIDES THIS INFORMATION ON AN "AS-IS" BASIS. CREATIVE COMMONS MAKES NO WARRANTIES REGARDING THE INFORMATION PROVIDED, AND DISCLAIMS LIABILITY FOR DAMAGES RESULTING FROM ITS USE.

License

THE WORK (AS DEFINED BELOW) IS PROVIDED UNDER THE TERMS OF THIS CREATIVE COMMONS PUBLIC LICENSE ("CCPL" OR "LICENSE"). THE WORK IS PROTECTED BY COPYRIGHT AND/OR OTHER APPLICABLE LAW. ANY USE OF THE WORK OTHER THAN AS AUTHORIZED UNDER THIS LICENSE OR COPYRIGHT LAW IS PROHIBITED.

BY EXERCISING ANY RIGHTS TO THE WORK PROVIDED HERE, YOU ACCEPT AND AGREE TO BE BOUND BY THE TERMS OF THIS LICENSE. THE LICENSOR GRANTS YOU THE RIGHTS CONTAINED HERE IN CONSIDERATION OF YOUR ACCEPTANCE OF SUCH TERMS AND CONDITIONS.

1. 1. **Definitions**

a. "Collective Work" means a work, such as a periodical issue, anthology or encyclopedia, in which the Work in its entirety in unmodified form, along with a number of other contributions, constituting separate and independent works in themselves, are assembled into a collective whole. A work that constitutes a Collective Work will not be considered a Derivative Work (as defined below) for the purposes of this License.

b. "Derivative Work" means a work based upon the Work or upon the Work and other pre-existing works, such as a translation, musical arrangement, dramatization, fictionalization, motion picture version, sound recording, art reproduction, abridgment, condensation, or any other form in which the Work may be recast, transformed, or adapted, except that a work that constitutes a Collective Work will not be considered a Derivative Work for the purpose of this License. For the avoidance of doubt, where the Work is a musical composition or sound recording, the synchronization of the Work in timed-relation with a moving image ("synching") will be considered a Derivative Work for the purpose of this License.

c. "Licensor" means the individual or entity that offers the Work under the terms of this License.

d. "Original Author" means the individual or entity who created the Work.

e. "Work" means the copyrightable work of authorship offered under the terms of this License.

f. "You" means an individual or entity exercising rights under this License who has not previously violated the terms of this License with respect to the Work, or who has received express permission from the Licensor to exercise rights under this License despite a previous violation.

2. **Fair Use Rights.** Nothing in this license is intended to reduce, limit, or restrict any rights arising from fair use, first sale or other limitations on the exclusive rights of the copyright owner under copyright law or other applicable laws.

3. **License Grant.** Subject to the terms and conditions of this License, Licensor hereby grants You a worldwide, royalty-free, non-exclusive, perpetual (for the duration of the applicable copyright) license to exercise the rights in the Work as stated below:

   a. to reproduce the Work, to incorporate the Work into one or more Collective Works, and to reproduce the Work as incorporated in the Collective Works;

   b. to create and reproduce Derivative Works;

   c. to distribute copies or phonorecords of, display publicly, perform publicly, and perform publicly by means of a digital audio transmission the Work including as incorporated in Collective Works;

   d. to distribute copies or phonorecords of, display publicly, perform publicly, and perform publicly by means of a digital audio transmission Derivative Works.

   e. For the avoidance of doubt, where the work is a musical composition:

      i. Performance Royalties Under Blanket Licenses. Licensor waives the exclusive right to collect, whether individually or via a performance rights society (e.g. ASCAP, BMI, SESAC), royalties for the public performance or public digital performance (e.g. webcast) of the Work.

      ii. Mechanical Rights and Statutory Royalties. Licensor waives the exclusive right to collect, whether individually or via a music rights agency or designated agent (e.g., Harry Fox Agency), royalties for any phonorecord You create from the Work ("cover version") and distribute, subject to the compulsory license created by 17 USC Section 115 of the US Copyright Act (or the equivalent in other jurisdictions).

   f. Webcasting Rights and Statutory Royalties. For the avoidance of doubt, where the Work is a sound recording, Licensor waives the exclusive right to collect, whether individually or via a performance-rights society (e.g. SoundExchange), royalties for the public digital performance (e.g. webcast) of the Work, subject to the compulsory license created by 17 USC Section 114 of the US Copyright Act (or the equivalent in other jurisdictions).

The above rights may be exercised in all media and formats whether now known or hereafter devised. The above rights include the right to make such modifications as are technically necessary to exercise the rights in other media and formats. All rights not expressly granted by Licensor are hereby reserved.

4. **Restrictions.** The license granted in Section 3 above is expressly made subject to and limited by the following restrictions:

a. You may distribute, publicly display, publicly perform, or publicly digitally perform the Work only under the terms of this License, and You must include a copy of, or the Uniform Resource Identifier for, this License with every copy or phonorecord of the Work You distribute, publicly display, publicly perform, or publicly digitally perform. You may not offer or impose any terms on the Work that alter or restrict the terms of this License or the recipients' exercise of the rights granted hereunder. You may not sublicense the Work. You must keep intact all notices that refer to this License and to the disclaimer of warranties. You may not distribute, publicly display, publicly perform, or publicly digitally perform the Work with any technological measures that control access or use of the Work in a manner inconsistent with the terms of this License Agreement. The above applies to the Work as incorporated in a Collective Work, but this does not require the Collective Work apart from the Work itself to be made subject to the terms of this License. If You create a Collective Work, upon notice from any Licensor You must, to the extent practicable, remove from the Collective Work any reference to such Licensor or the Original Author, as requested. If You create a Derivative Work, upon notice from any Licensor You must, to the extent practicable, remove from the Derivative Work any reference to such Licensor or the Original Author, as requested.

b. If you distribute, publicly display, publicly perform, or publicly digitally perform the Work or any Derivative Works or Collective Works, You must keep intact all copyright notices for the Work and give the Original Author credit reasonable to the medium or means You are utilizing by conveying the name (or pseudonym if applicable) of the Original Author if supplied; the title of the Work if supplied; to the extent reasonably practicable, the Uniform Resource Identifier, if any, that Licensor specifies to be associated with the Work, unless such URI does not refer to the copyright notice or licensing information for the Work; and in the case of a Derivative Work, a credit identifying the use of the Work in the Derivative Work (e.g., "French translation of the Work by Original Author," or "Screenplay based on original Work by Original Author"). Such credit may be implemented in any reasonable manner; provided, however, that in the case of a Derivative Work or Collective Work, at a minimum such credit will appear where any other comparable authorship credit appears and in a manner at least as prominent as such other comparable authorship credit.

5. **Representations, Warranties and Disclaimer.** UNLESS OTHERWISE MUTUALLY AGREED TO BY THE PARTIES IN WRITING, LICENSOR OFFERS THE WORK AS-IS AND MAKES NO REPRESENTATIONS OR WARRANTIES OF ANY KIND CONCERNING THE WORK, EXPRESS, IMPLIED, STATUTORY OR OTHERWISE, INCLUDING, WITHOUT LIMITATION, WARRANTIES OF TITLE, MERCHANTIBILITY, FITNESS FOR A PARTICULAR PURPOSE, NONINFRINGEMENT, OR THE ABSENCE OF LATENT OR OTHER DEFECTS, ACCURACY, OR THE PRESENCE OF ABSENCE OF

ERRORS, WHETHER OR NOT DISCOVERABLE. SOME JURISDICTIONS DO NOT ALLOW THE EXCLUSION OF IMPLIED WARRANTIES, SO SUCH EXCLUSION MAY NOT APPLY TO YOU.

6. **Limitation on Liability.** EXCEPT TO THE EXTENT REQUIRED BY APPLICABLE LAW, IN NO EVENT WILL LICENSOR BE LIABLE TO YOU ON ANY LEGAL THEORY FOR ANY SPECIAL, INCIDENTAL, CONSEQUENTIAL, PUNITIVE OR EXEMPLARY DAMAGES ARISING OUT OF THIS LICENSE OR THE USE OF THE WORK, EVEN IF LICENSOR HAS BEEN ADVISED OF THE POSSIBILITY OF SUCH DAMAGES.

7. **Termination.**

a. This License and the rights granted hereunder will terminate automatically upon any breach by You of the terms of this License. Individuals or entities who have received Derivative Works or Collective Works from You under this License, however, will not have their licenses terminated provided such individuals or entities remain in full compliance with those licenses. Sections 1, 2, 5, 6, 7, and 8 will survive any termination of this License.

b. Subject to the above terms and conditions, the license granted here is perpetual (for the duration of the applicable copyright in the Work). Notwithstanding the above, Licensor reserves the right to release the Work under different license terms or to stop distributing the Work at any time; provided, however that any such election will not serve to withdraw this License (or any other license that has been, or is required to be, granted under the terms of this License), and this License will continue in full force and effect unless terminated as stated above.

8. **Miscellaneous.**

a. Each time You distribute or publicly digitally perform the Work or a Collective Work, the Licensor offers to the recipient a license to the Work on the same terms and conditions as the license granted to You under this License.

b. Each time You distribute or publicly digitally perform a Derivative Work, Licensor offers to the recipient a license to the original Work on the same terms and conditions as the license granted to You under this License.

c. If any provision of this License is invalid or unenforceable under applicable law, it shall not affect the validity or enforceability of the remainder of the terms of this License, and without further action by the parties to this agreement, such provision shall be reformed to the minimum extent necessary to make such provision valid and enforceable.

d. No term or provision of this License shall be deemed waived and no breach consented to unless such waiver or consent shall be in writing and signed by the party to be charged with such waiver or consent.

e. This License constitutes the entire agreement between the parties with respect to the Work licensed here. There are no understandings, agreements or representations with respect to the Work not specified here. Licensor shall not be bound by any additional provisions that may appear in any communication from You. This License may not be modified without the mutual written agreement of the Licensor and You.

Creative Commons is not a party to this License, and makes no warranty whatsoever in connection with the Work. Creative Commons will not be liable to You or any party on any legal theory for any damages whatsoever, including without limitation any general, special, incidental or consequential damages arising in connection to this license. Notwithstanding the foregoing two (2) sentences, if Creative Commons has expressly identified itself as the Licensor hereunder, it shall have all rights and obligations of Licensor.

Except for the limited purpose of indicating to the public that the Work is licensed under the CCPL, neither party will use the trademark "Creative Commons" or any related trademark or logo of Creative Commons without the prior written consent of Creative Commons. Any permitted use will be in compliance with Creative Commons' then-current trademark usage guidelines, as may be published on its web site or otherwise made available upon request from time to time.

Creative Commons may be contacted at *http://creativecommons.org/*.

Index

About the Authors

Ben Collins-Sussman is one of the original designers and authors of Subversion. He currently works for CollabNet as a Subversion developer and community leader. He has a degree in mathematics from the University of Chicago, and his home page can be found at *http://www.red-bean.com/sussman*. When away from his computer, he moonlights as a musical theater composer at theaters around Chicago. He lives with his lovely wife and three cats and can be found practicing his banjo on sunny afternoons.

Brian W. Fitzpatrick has been involved with open source software for over seven years and is a member of the Apache Software Foundation. A volunteer Subversion developer since 2000, he is now employed full-time by CollabNet to work on Subversion and related version control tools. He spends his spare time relaxing with family and friends, reading, traveling, and eating. Especially eating—his wife Marie is a wonderful cook. Originally from New Orleans, Brian moved to Chicago to attend Loyola University, where he received a degree in Latin and Greek. After a three-year stint in Rome, Italy, he moved back to Chicago, where he currently resides with his wife.

C. Michael Pilato (Mike) is a leader in the Subversion community and a core developer of both Subversion and ViewCVS. He is currently employed by CollabNet, where he spends his days (and many nights) improving Subversion and other tools with which it integrates. When he's not programming, Mike enjoys composing and performing music, freelance graphic design work, hiking, and spending quality time with his wife and son. Mike holds a degree in computer science and mathematics from the University of North Carolina at Charlotte. He maintains a personal web site at *http://cmichaelpilato.com/*.

Colophon

Our look is the result of reader comments, our own experimentation, and feedback from distribution channels. Distinctive covers complement our distinctive approach to technical topics, breathing personality and life into potentially dry subjects.

The animals on the cover of *Version Control with Subversion* are hawksbill sea turtles (*Eretmochelys imbricatta*) or Honu 'Ea, as they are known in Hawaii. The hawksbill is a medium-sized turtle weighing up to 270 pounds, with a shell of about 3 feet in length. This sea turtle can be found around tropical reef areas in the Atlantic, Pacific, and Indian oceans. The hawksbill gets its name from its distinctive sharp beak-like mouth and is also known for its beautiful shell coloring, referred to as "tortoise shell," which was exploited by the fashion industry for many years. Hawksbill sea turtles are listed as an endangered species in Hawaii, and are protected under the state law, as well as many other endangered species laws.

At birth, a hatchling is so small it can fit into the palm of your hand. The incubation period ranges from 50 to 70 days. Hatchlings usually emerge in groups at night, when the sand temperature is cool and when there is a lesser threat of predators. Hatching may take place over several evenings, and the sea turtles immediately head toward the sea, guided by the light of the moon and the stars' reflection off the oceans. The mortality rate is high, due to the physical challenges that face their tiny bodies. Those that safely reach the water disappear into the ocean and will reappear when they are older. Male sea turtles are easily distinguished from females by their longer and thicker tails, which extend beyond the posterior part of their shell.

Nesting also occurs at night, mostly between the months of May and October. Females will go ashore to choose the site for laying their eggs. They look for small isolated beaches. When they find their site, which is usually beyond the tideline and underneath vegetation, they dig a body pit with their fore and hind flippers, excavating the egg chamber. Once the last egg has been laid, they refill the chamber with sand and return to the sea. Females only nest every two to three years, but can lay up to six groups of eggs within one breeding season. A nesting can contain from a few eggs to 230 small eggs, with an average of 130. Females that are re-nesting often return to the same beach, sometimes very close to the previous spot.

Reg Aubry was the production editor and copyeditor for *Version Control with Subversion*. Leanne Soylemez was the proofreader. Leanne Soylemez, Darren Kelly, and Claire Cloutier provided quality control. Jamie Peppard provided production assistance. Lucie Haskins wrote the index.

Ellie Volckhausen designed the cover of this book, based on a series design by Edie Freedman. The cover image is a 19th-century engraving from *Cuvier's Animals*. Emma Colby produced the cover layout with QuarkXPress 4.1 using Adobe's ITC Garamond font.

Melanie Wang designed the interior layout, based on a series design by David Futato. Joe Wizda converted the files from XML to FrameMaker 5.5.6 using tools created by Mike Sierra. The text font is Linotype Birka; the heading font is Adobe Myriad Condensed; and the code font is LucasFont's TheSans Mono Condensed. The illustrations that appear in the book were produced by Robert Romano and Jessamyn Read using Macromedia FreeHand 9 and Adobe Photoshop 6. The tip and warning icons were drawn by Christopher Bing. This colophon was written by Janet Santackas.